The *Phaedo:* A Platonic Labyrinth

The *Phaedo:* A Platonic Labyrinth

RONNA BURGER

Yale University Press
New Haven and London

Designed by James J. Johnson
and set in Trump Mediaeval Roman.
Printed in the United States of America by
BookCrafters, Chelsea, Michigan.

Library of Congress Cataloging in Publication Data

Burger, Ronna, 1947–
    The Phaedo : a Platonic labyrinth.

    Bibliography: p.
    Includes index.
    1. Plato. Phaedo.   2. Immortality (Philosophy)—
History.   I. Title.
B379.B87   1984   184   84–40191
ISBN 0–300–03163–7

The paper in this book meets the guidelines
for permanence and durability of the Committee
on Production Guidelines for Book Longevity
of the Council on Library Resources.

10 9 8 7 6 5 4 3 2 1

Das Sein—wir haben keine andere Vorstellung davon als Leben—
Wie kann also etwas Totes 'sein'?

(Nietzsche, from the *Nachlass der Achtzigerjahre*)

Contents

Acknowledgments

The opportunity to write the original draft of this book was provided by a fellowship in 1979–80 at Tübingen University, for which I express appreciation to the Alexander von Humboldt Foundation, and in particular to Professor H. J. Krämer. Maureen MacGrogan of Yale University Press offered valuable suggestions and encouragement in seeing the manuscript through the early stages of preparation for publication; at later stages the manuscript benefited from the editorial comments of Jean van Altena. Many improvements in the final product are due to the thoughtful recommendations of Michael Davis. I am grateful to Robert Berman for innumerable discussions inspired by the *Phaedo* but ranging far beyond it.

This project began with Seth Benardete, with whom I read and studied the *Phaedo* in 1978–79, and has been sustained since then by our correspondence and conversation. Having shared in this turn to the *logos*, I find it difficult to determine the limits of what this work owes him.

Introduction

The doctrines of "Platonism," as typically understood throughout the Western philosophical tradition, do not always seem to be substantiated by, and often seem to conflict with, the evidence of the Platonic dialogues. The various strategies pursued in the attempt to account for this discrepancy are distinguished by the different consequences they draw from a common recognition of the peculiar character of the dialogue as a literary form.[1] The admittedly elusive and perplexing character of the dialogue, however, has not often put into doubt the presumably clear and obvious character of the doctrines assumed to be Platonic. This lack of skepticism would indeed be inexplicable were there no evidence at all in the dialogues for these purported teachings: those dialogues, or passages therefrom, that most readily appear to provide such evidence have long enjoyed, for just that reason, a privileged status. This is illustrated, perhaps more explicitly than in any other case, by the reception, interpretation, and evaluation of Plato's *Phaedo*.

Agreement on the status of the *Phaedo* as a *locus classicus* of the Platonic teaching has been shared by contemporary scholars no less than by ancient commentators, beginning with Aristotle. And despite centuries of debate about the success or failure of its execution, there has been little dispute about the intention of the dialogue: the *Phaedo* is meant to be an exposition and defense of "the twin pillars" of Platonic philosophy, the theory of ideas and the immortality of the soul.[2] On the basis of this double theme, the *Phaedo* has been accorded the distinction—sometimes thought to be a dubious honor—of having inaugurated Western metaphysics, in its double form of *Metaphysica generalis* and *Metaphysica specialis*.[3] Even when these metaphysical themes are not taken to be the primary objective of the dialogue, they are not disclaimed but are only considered to be subordinate, for example, to the Socratic teaching concerning the supreme importance of man's "tendance of his soul."[4] That the *Phaedo* is Plato's "tribute of admiration to his beloved friend and master" may be hard to deny,[5] although there has been much controversy over the issue of the accuracy of its representation of the historical Socrates.[6] This controversy, however, concerns only the extent to which Socrates is portrayed as the originator of the doctrines assumed to be Platonic—namely, the theory of ideas, and the immortality of the soul.

It is, more precisely, the mutual interdependence of these two doctrines that is thought to constitute the theme of the *Phaedo*. The immutable and eternal ideas, which exist apart from the sphere of ever changing phenomena, furnish the objects of pure reason when it operates unhampered by perception and bodily desire. To apprehend and thus realize its kinship with the ideas, the soul must be freed from reliance on the senses and attachment to the passions, released from its corporeal prison. Since death is nothing but this separation of the soul from the body, it is to be sought after and welcomed by the lover of wisdom: the result of the philosopher's success in "the practice of dying and being dead" is fulfillment of the desire for communion of the pure soul with the pure beings. Such "pure intellectualism divorced from life" would indeed seem to have as its aim "the eternal preservation of the soul in the cold storage of eternally frozen absolute Forms."[7]

This account of the "Platonism" of the *Phaedo* is surely not conjured up out of thin air: it is more or less the understanding of the speeches of Socrates displayed by his interlocutors. But should one assume that Plato, in fabricating this image of Socratic conversation, intends to present to his readers no more, and no less, than Socrates appears to address to his interlocutors? To make this assumption would be to ignore the very character of the dialogue as a dialogue, which more often than not displays the intellectual limitations of the characters it represents. If Socrates is indeed the Platonic spokesman, it is only to the extent that he speaks over the heads of his interlocutors, whose very partial understanding of his speeches affects the direction in which the conversation develops. Plato's address to his readers cannot be assumed to be identical, then, with Socrates' address to his interlocutors. Since Plato speaks nowhere in his own name, no particular position presented in the dialogue can be directly identified as *the* Platonic teaching.[8]

The distance between the Platonic dialogue as an imitation and the Socratic conversation it imitates is signified in the following way: everything contingent in spontaneous speech is transformed, by the written work, into a necessity. Certainly, if the dialogue is to have the appearance of a live conversation, it must represent the arbitrary and superfluous factors that characterize any particular encounter; but what appears accidental—if we forget we are reading—belongs in the representation only if it has some significance which is not arbitrary or superfluous. Whatever role chance plays in the object of imitation, teleology reigns supreme in the work as imitation. This issue is made thematic by the Platonic dialogue in which Socrates criticizes the dangers of the written word—and thus indicates, of course, the obstacles that Platonic writing seeks to overcome.[9] In that context, Socrates offers this criterion of a properly constructed written work: it must be organized like a living animal, with every joint and member designed to serve a particular purpose in the whole. It must be governed by "logographic necessity."[10]

To the extent that the Platonic dialogue fulfills this criterion—and it is hard to imagine any written work that does so more adequately—no argument can be immediately isolated from its context; its significance, particularly if it is or appears to be unsound, can be grasped only by taking into account its function in the whole. The discovery of the definitive purpose

served in the dialogue by an unsound argument or an undefended position suggests its intentional status; but in that case,
the very charges typically directed against Plato—which make
him seem, at least on occasion, like a rather primitive or care-
less thinker—would be precisely the critical issues deliberately
raised by the dialogue itself. At the same time, what is of
genuine philosophical import in the dialogue, if it is indeed
governed by the principle of logographic necessity, is not immediately self-evident; or rather, if that principle is strictly
heeded, nothing that appears in the dialogue—including the
title, the setting, the explicit opinions and implicit interests of
the interlocutors, the images and examples together with the
arguments—is without philosophical import. It is the failure
to give sufficient consideration to this character of the dialogue
as a dialogue that is exemplified in the prevailing account of
the Platonism of the *Phaedo*, and it is the attempt to overcome
that failure that motivates the present study.

Such an attempt must be guided by the recognition that
every dialogue represents speeches in the context of deeds.[11] It
adjusts the argument, consequently, to the circumstances, and
that adjustment challenges, at the same time as it must direct,
our interpretation. Of course, the hermeneutic principle that
may be a necessary condition for reading the dialogue is not a
sufficient condition to guarantee the result of its application:[12]
to construe it as an automatic "method" for interpretation
would be self-contradictory. The dialogues do indeed furnish
explicit methodological analyses of the proper way to think
and speak; but since these speeches, like any others, are embedded in a drama, they cannot simply be extracted from the
various contexts in which they appear. In fact, the analysis in
one dialogue often seems not only to conflict with that in
another, but even to be put into question, rather than confirmed, by the very discussion in which it appears. It is precisely this tension, however, between the theoretical proposals
for procedure and the practice exemplified by the conversation
that serves as a clue to the intended limitations of each.

It is necessary to recognize the Platonic dialogue as a representation of *conversation* in order to avoid mistaking it for a

treatise. But it is necesary to recognize it as a *representation* of conversation in order to discover the carefully constructed plan in accordance with which it is organized. The structure of the dialogue, just for that reason, provides one, if not the, guide for interpretation. The so-called "digression," for example, that often appears in the very center of a dialogue, seems to be—and in a spontaneous conversation would be—an interruption of the subject under discussion; but in the Platonic repesentation, this deliberate "digression" typically uncovers what is conspicuously absent from the discussion, and hence reorients our understanding and evaluation of it. A spontaneous conversation, furthermore, may just happen to be conducted by particular individuals in a particular situation; but the Platonic representation connects by design a certain topic of discussion with certain types of individuals who conduct it. The opinions expressed in the discussion must be examined, consequently, in the light of the characters and motivations of those who express them. Only through this examination can the reader distance himself from the limited understanding that Socrates' interlocutors may have of his aims, and of his success or failure in fulfilling them. Those aims may be partly disclosed by his intermittent reflections on the status of the arguments, particularly his confessions of ignorance. Socrates' ability to speak in a way that conceals what he means from the person whom he is addressing arouses resentment in those who suspect they are its victims; but the audience that should benefit from this practice in the dialogue is Plato's reader.

This potential benefit, however, is not necessarily actualized by every reader; for the Platonic dialogue, being itself an imitation of Socratic irony, addresses different meanings to different audiences through the same words. Nor is this merely ornamental: the multiplicity of meaning that is the condition for Platonic irony is the very material out of which the dialogue is fabricated. The germ out of which each dialogue unfolds is a connection between some concrete phenomenon, or more than one, and an abstract notion. Such a connection—between, say, the experience of a mixture of pleasure and pain, the death of a living animal, and the analytic and synthetic processes of thought—looks necessary by the end of the dialogue but rather arbitrary at the beginning. It is forged by linking through some common ground, the ordinary understanding of a term with a philosophic reconstruction of it. This is exemplified in the *Phaedo* by the way in which Socrates appeals to the ordinary understanding of "death" or "immortality," while deriving, from reflection on the unrecognized presuppositions and implications of that ordinary understanding, his own philosophic reconstruction of it. These double meanings are linked, in turn, to a twofold determination of psychē.[13] Indeed, the latter is brought to our attention especially by death, or more precisely, by Plato's representation of Socrates dying. Our inability to comprehend how thought or awareness can be affected by the cessation of certain mechanistic processes in the body leads us to an understanding of psychē that affirms its independence from the body, precisely when we are compelled to confront just the opposite. The transition, inspired by this paradox, from one implicit sense of psychē to another explicit one determines the structure of the *Phaedo*. And that structure, as we shall see, governs the relation between the arguments of the dialogue and its dramatic action.

The inseparability of argument and action, which is displayed by every Platonic dialogue, would seem nowhere more unavoidable than on the occasion represented in the *Phaedo*, which portrays Socrates between dawn and sunset on the last day of his life.[14] No one, Socrates remarks, could accuse him now of idly chattering about matters of no immediate concern to him. Yet, as Socrates also warns his companions, it is in precisely this situation, with the powerful emotions it evokes, that it is especially necessary for them to judge the soundness of their reasoning by separating it from its particular context. Since the arguments, however, are indeed motivated by the immediate, perhaps distorting, interests of Socrates or his companions, it is only by taking those interests into account that Plato's reader can accomplish the required separation of the *logos*.[15] To pursue this task of interpretation is to engage in what Socrates calls "the practice of dying and being dead," which he describes as a kind of "purification."

The separation of argument from action, which becomes an explicit theme in the dialogue, is reflected at the same time in its form of presentation. For there is in fact no Platonic dramatization of the death of Socrates, but only of Phaedo's retelling of that event some time after and at some distance from Socrates' last hours in the Athenian prison. The conversation Socrates conducts on the day of his death is thus transformed from a deed into a speech conducted by Phaedo in a Pythagorean community and addressed to a man associated with the Pythagoreans. The Pythagoreans, Aristotle argues, differ from Plato only in denying any separation between the first principles—which they identify with numbers rather than "ideas"—and the things said to be their imitations;[16] the Pythagorean teaching on reincarnation, on the other hand, presupposes the separability of the psychē from the body.[17] The attempt to reinterpret the meaning of "separation," and in so doing to reverse the Pythagorean position, is, one might say, the fundamental intention of the *Phaedo*.

The clue to this intention is provided by the first word of the dialogue—*autos*. The very expression that will be used to designate the "idea," that which is "itself by itself," refers at the outset to the individual and identifies the self with the living being, without implying any separation of psychē from body: "Yourself, Phaedo, were you present with Socrates on that day when he drank the poison in prison or did you hear of it from another?" While Phaedo seeks to relive his own experience, having been present himself at the event of Socrates' death, Plato, he announces, was sick that day: the fabricator of the logos is not himself present at the conversation he represents. With Phaedo's attempt to recreate in his audience the emotions of pity and fear that he and the others suffered, the *Phaedo* would seem to be *the* Platonic tragedy. But if it is the separation of the logos from such emotions that is indicated by Plato's reported absence, the kind of "purification" identified with such separation would be accomplished by the dialogue itself.

It is not only the Pythagorean setting of Phaedo's report that explains the centrality of the theme of purification but, at the same time, the ceremony that provides the context for the conversation he narrates. It takes place in the interval between Socrates' trial and death brought about by an Athenian ritual of abstention from public execution. While the guilt from which the Athenian *dēmos* seeks purification, as this ritual suggests, is its condemnation of Socrates, Socrates himself begins the conversation by acknowledging the need to purify himself before dying. Throughout his life, Socrates explains, a dream repeatedly came to him, in different shapes but invariably conveying the same command, to "make music and work at it"— to practice, that is, the arts over which the Muses preside.[18] Having always interpreted the dream as encouragement to continue what he was already doing, practicing philosophy as "the greatest music," Socrates suspects now, after his trial and before his death, that he may be guilty of having neglected to produce "demotic music." He expresses concern about the insufficiency of his attempt to make himself understood by the nonphilosophers who have convicted him. Purification from this guilt would require a combination of demotic music with the greatest music. And this is precisely what is accomplished by Plato's *Phaedo:* the arguments that appear unsound insofar as they appeal to the ordinary understanding of "death" or "immortality" are open to a very different interpretation based on the philosophical reconstruction of those terms.

That the parallel guilt of Socrates and Athens should provide the context for the last of the Platonic dialogues centering on Socrates' trial and death is hardly accidental. At his public trial on the charges of injustice and impiety, Socrates insists on his unwillingness to run away from the practice of philosophy, the post where he has stationed himself or has been stationed by his commander;[19] at his self-imposed trial before the laws of Athens, which Socrates conducts in his private conversation with Crito, he insists on his unwillingness to run away from the prison to which he has been committed by the Athenian jury.[20] Socrates is compelled, consequently, to run away from life, and for this he is put on trial once more in this final conversation. Although his apparent eagerness for death would seem to be a violation of the divine prohibition against suicide, as Socrates himself admits, he absolves himself of this responsibility by interpreting his conviction as "some kind of necessity" imposed upon him by a god. The potential charge of impiety is replaced, therefore, by an accusation against the imprudence Socrates displays in wanting to run away from his good masters the gods and another accusation against the injustice he displays in wanting to run away from his present companions. Socrates' defense against these charges consists in an *apologia* for "the practice of dying and being dead," which he delivers as a description of, partly in the voice of, those whom he calls the genuine philosophers. In this speech, Socrates constructs the "idea" of the class of philosophers, which is as alien to himself as the philosophers' understanding of the "ideas" is to his own.

Like these genuine philosophers, the young men to whom Socrates addresses his defense understand the practice of dying to consist in the separation of the psychē from the body: they warn Socrates that his defense will be acceptable to them only if it can be shown that after death the psychē does indeed have "some kind of power and *phronēsis.*"[21] It is, presumably, the attempt to provide this justification of his defense that guides the first series of arguments in the dialogue. Socrates thus pursues the purification he sought to compensate for his neglect of demotic music; for his account of the fate of the psychē after death is, he admits at one point, an "incantation" designed to charm the child in us who is overcome with fright at the thought of death. Socrates thus tries, or seems to try, to satisfy the challenge issued by his interlocutors, whose understanding of the practice of dying is motivated by the fear of annihilation and the correlative hope for immortality. But precisely by calling attention to that motivation, Socrates transforms the meaning of the practice of dying; he brings to light his own understanding of it as a separation of logos from just that attachment to the self that the hope for immortality betrays.

The necessity of this transformation is exhibited at the very center of the dialogue, when Phaedo, after describing the failure of the first series of arguments to prove the immortality of the psychē, interrupts his account to report the exchange he shared with Socrates. Warning Phaedo not to cut off his hair on the morrow in mourning for Socrates, but to cut it immediately if they cannot revive the logos, Socrates establishes an alliance with Phaedo against the most threatening danger facing them, which is not the fear of death, but the loss of trust in argumentation altogether. This experience of "misology," which Socrates considers the greatest evil, is the inevitable result of a misconception of wisdom as direct contact of the pure psychē with the "beings themselves." For, Socrates explains, just as the eyes are blinded by the attempt to observe the sun directly in an eclipse, the psychē is blinded by the attempt to investigate the beings directly in the *pragmata*, the many, variously qualified things that come to be and pass away.[22] While Socrates' conduct may provide the most effective weapon against the fear of death, the only defense against misology that is capable of protecting the psychē from blinding itself is an art of argumentation. This *technē* of logos[23] Socrates identifies as a "second sailing": it abandons the attempt to investigate the beings themselves in order to investigate their truth through logoi and is illustrated by the turn from the first to the second half of the dialogue.

The division of the *Phaedo* into halves, separated by this central interlude, exhibits the tension between concern with the self and concern with the argument for its own sake, between the fear of death together with the hope for immortality and the fear of misology together with a technē of logos. This tension is reflected not only in the transformed understanding of what it is to think and to know, but at the same time in the transformed meanings of psychē, death, and immortality. The series of arguments in the first half of the dialogue assumes the identification of psychē with mind, medium of cognition; it defines death as the separation of pyschē from body and takes that separation to be the necessary condition for knowledge.

But this series of arguments turns out to be as incapable of accounting for life as it is of demonstrating the continued existence of the psychē after death. In the second half of the dialogue, consequently, the psychological analysis of knowledge is replaced—in part for psychological reasons—by a logical one. Not despite, therefore, but precisely because it illustrates the Socratic technē of logos, the final argument ignores the understanding of psychē as mind. It attempts, rather, to account for what the first half of the dialogue left inexplicable by identifying psychē as that which "brings forward life to the body it occupies" and defining death as the destruction of that vital principle. It establishes only that it would be a contradiction to speak of psychē, whenever it exists, as dead; but this conclusion appears to contradict the fundamental presupposition of the first series of arguments—that the psychē is most pure and in contact with the pure beings only when it is "dead," separated from the body.

The model for this structural and thematic division of the dialogue is provided by Socrates' seemingly arbitrary remarks at the outset of the conversation, just after being released from his fetters—the deed that is mirrored, according to the imagery of the dialogue, in the final deed of release from the chains binding Socrates to life. The pleasure Socrates experiences once the chains are removed from his leg only retrospectively uncovers the pain that must have preceeded it; Socrates, filled with wonder, offers a double account of this union of apparent opposites. According to his own explanation, neither pleasure nor pain "wishes" to be present in a man at the same time as the other, yet whenever a man pursues one he gets the other as well, as if the two were joined in one head. An Aesopian *mythos*, on the other hand, might claim that the god, seeing the two at war and wishing to reconcile them but unable to do so, fastened their two heads together so that one always follows upon the other. This double account is a model in miniature of both the form and the content of the dialogue as a whole: while it is derived from the tension between logos, or what Socrates considers the greatest music, and mythos, or demotic music, it

reflects at the same time the tension between the philosopher's desire for release of the psychē from the body and the
divine will responsible for imprisoning the psychē in the body.

Socrates' twofold account of the relation between pleasure
and pain—an original unit that human desire attempts to separate into two or an original dyad that divine will attempts to
put together—presents opposite causes of the same result; it
exhibits precisely that perplexity—the coming to be of two by
the addition of two ones or by the division of one into two—
that made Socrates, according to the intellectual autobiography he offers, recognize the danger of self-contradiction lurking behind all mechanistic explanation of how something
comes into being. He discovered a protection against that
danger by applying his technē of logos to the question of
cause—the cause, that is, of something being *what* it is. That
anything which is to be two, for example, must participate in
the dyad is the "safe but foolish" answer to the question of the
"cause" of the doubleness of pleasure and pain, and consequently of the twofold structure of the dialogue modeled on
that account.

Participation in the dyad, then, is the cause of the dialogue
being *what* it is; it does not inform us whether it comes into
being by the addition of two originally separate units or by the
division in two of an original unity. But the necessity of there
being two opposing parts is the same necessity that compels
Socrates to explain his second sailing only after showing the
deficiencies of a first sailing.[24] The way in which the second
half of the dialogue serves as a corrective for the first is manifest in the internal structure of each, for which Socrates' remarks on the relation of pleasure and pain furnish the model.
The opposites that are united in the first half of the dialogue,
when Socrates invites his interlocutors to "investigate and
mythologize" about his imminent journey abroad, are separated in the second half of the dialogue: the pure argument,
which considers the immortality of the psychē only as an illustration of the danger of self-contradiction, is followed by a pure
mythos, which illustrates the danger of neglecting "care for the

psychē" by describing the psychai of the dead, assigned to their proper dwelling places within the great body of the earth. The separability of the psychē from the body is established in the first half of the dialogue only through an inseparable mixture of logos and mythos; the inseparability of the psychē from the body is established in the second half of the dialogue only by the separation of logos from mythos.

The tension between the "mythological" interpretation of purification as the separation of the psychē from body and the "dialogic" interpretation as the separation of logos from the psychē united with the body is reflected in Socrates' last words, acknowledging his debt to Aesclepius, the god of healing, son of Apollo, the god of purification. At the moment when he seems to give thanks for his own release from the long disease of life, Socrates expresses gratitude for a concurrent recovery of a different sort: Plato, who has Phaedo tell us that he was sick on the day of Socrates' death, is in fact very much present—not indeed "himself," but in and through the dialogue "itself by itself." The practice of dying as Socrates understands it is accomplished by the logos as a written product, separated from the living Socrates whose image it represents. The desired purification, not of the psychē from the body but of the logos from the psychē united with the body, is produced not by the *pharmakon*—poison and remedy—that brings Socrates release from life, but by the pharmakon of the Platonic dialogue.[25]

CHAPTER ONE

Prologue

[57a1–58a5]   The title of the *Phaedo* does not inform us about the subject of the conversation it represents but indicates only the proper name of the narrator, who simply reports a discussion in which he was almost entirely an observer. Phaedo plays a role only in the dramatic prologue, the concluding statement, and a brief interlude in the exact center of the dialogue; yet he perhaps justifiably provides its title, for the long speech he delivers takes the place of a Platonic dramatization of the last day of Socrates' life.[1]

Although a substantial period of time must have elapsed between Socrates' death and Phaedo's report (cf. 57a–b), Phaedo promises to try to satisfy Echecrates' request to hear as precisely and clearly as possible everything that was said and done (cf. 58d). At only three points in the course of the report does Phaedo's narrative omniscience falter. That Plato was absent because of illness Phaedo believes but does not know for certain (59b). He expresses the same uncertainty in reporting the transition between Socrates' account of his own philosophic procedure and its application to the final argument on immortality.[2] Of this crucial transition, in which the interlocutors establish their agreement on the relation between the ideas and the things said to get their names from them (102a–b), Phaedo provides only a minimal summary, in indirect discourse, which stands out from the direct discourse through

14

which he claims to present an imitation of the original conversation in its entirety. When he returns to his narration after this moment of uncertainty, Phaedo relates the objection of the one person who recognizes the apparent contradiction between Socrates' first and last arguments; but the name of the speaker responsible for this observation—it turns out to be a fundamental problem of the entire discussion—Phaedo, unfortunately, cannot remember (103a).

While these lapses in Phaedo's memory might seem to reflect the accidental character of spontaneous speech, they prove to be a sign of the artfulness of the Platonic dialogue, for they point to the way in which this representation of Socrates' last conversation is determined by the perspective of its narrator. The clues to that perspective are provided not only in the opening prologue, which dramatizes Phaedo's exchange with Echecrates, but also in Phaedo's presentation of the brief exchange he shared with Socrates on that last day. In the course of this central interlude, Phaedo enters into an alliance with Socrates for the sake of preserving the logos, which is under attack. Their discussion seems to be a mere interruption of the attempt to demonstrate the immortality of the psychē, which Socrates' interlocutors take to be the goal of their conversation. But the subsequent return to that topic in the second half of the dialogue is influenced in important ways by the apparently digressive discussion devoted to the subject of logos itself that Socrates shares with Phaedo in the intervening interlude.

The relation between Phaedo's role as narrator and the theme of the conversation he reports is implicitly introduced by the first word of the dialogue. When asked if he "himself" (autos) was present at Socrates' death, or whether he only heard of it from another, Phaedo replies "myself" (autos). The dialogue, traditionally understood as the Platonic account of the separability of the psychē from the body, begins by referring to the self as an inseparable unity of psychē and body.[3] But Phaedo's claim to have been present "in the flesh" is almost immediately contrasted with his remark that Plato was not present. On this very rare occasion in the dialogues when Plato allows his own name to appear,[4] he does so only to mark his absence from Socrates' death. Whatever historical significance this may bear, its function as a dramatic element is to call attention to the narrative form of the dialogue, which creates a separation between the experience of being present at Socrates' death and the logos in which that event is represented. As a transformation of deed into speech, the narrative form is *the* exemplification of what Socrates will present as the crucial turn in his own philosophic development: insisting that speeches are no more images of the beings than deeds are, he will defend the necessity of turning away from the attempt to observe the beings themselves in order to invesigate their truth in logoi (99d–100a).

Such a turn would seem to be especially necessitated by the deeds of this particular occasion—the most emotional represented in the Platonic dialogues.[5] Everyone but Socrates— and he too was forced in the end to cover his face—is incapable of restraining himself from intermittent laughing and weeping. Apollodorus is only the most extreme,[6] but Phaedo admits that he himself was stirred up, as well as the others (cf. 117c–d). Yet the distance that could accompany the narration of a past event is just what Phaedo wants to overcome; he hopes to recreate the original experience as closely as possible and seems to succeed, for Echecrates is overcome by the same emotions, at the same moments as the participants present on the occasion. He does not take Phaedo's report as a special opportunity of attending to the logos separated from its emotional context, but only as a compromising alternative to the more desirable opportunity of being an eyewitness to the deed itself. One should not assume that the exchange between Phaedo and Echecrates is intended as a model to be imitated by the reader of the dialogue; it may be dramatized by Plato, rather, as a warning of what is to be overcome.

It is only at the conclusion of their preliminary conversation that Echecrates restricts his request to hear not about *how* Socrates died, but about the logoi that were spoken (59c). Yet he immediately indicates the importance of hearing Phaedo's logos, when he reveals what it would be like to know only the deed: since no stranger has come for a long time from Athens to Phlius,[7] the Phliasians know only that Socrates drank the poison and died. They have indeed been informed about the trial; yet Echecrates, like the interlocutors present with Socrates in the Athenian prison, shows no interest in discussing its implications but is curious only about the length of time intervening between Socrates' condemnation and death. In the explanation of this lapse of time that Phaedo offers,[8] however, he illuminates, without being aware of doing so, the connection between Socrates' death and its political context.

[58a6–59b2]   It just so happens, Phaedo explains, that Socrates' trial took place on the very day after the Athenians sent their sacred ship on its mission to Delos, and no public execution is allowed to occur until the ship returns. In this yearly ritual, the Athenians purify the city before Apollo, the god of purification, while acknowledging the heroism of the legendary founder of Athens. For it is the very ship in which Theseus once went to Crete, the Athenians claim, that the priest of Apollo crowns every year. The identity that the Athenians ascribe to the ship itself, however, seems to belong to nothing but the logos in which that ascription is made; for what else is it that remains the same over time as each plank of the ship is worn away and replaced by another? The ship of Theseus thus introduces what will prove to be a crucial question of the dialogue:[9] if the material components of the human body are constantly being worn away and replaced by others (cf. 87d–e), what is it that accounts for the identity of the individual over even one life span, let alone beyond that?

Through the logos that proclaims the identity of their sacred ship, the Athenians associate their yearly mission to Delos with the journey in which Theseus sailed to Crete with "those two times seven" companions and saved them as well as himself. He thus liberated the Athenians from the tribute imposed by King Minos of Crete, who demanded that every ninth year a mission of seven young men and seven young women be sacrificed to the Minotaur. It was on the third of these sacrificial voyages, according to legend, that Theseus determined to kill the Minotaur. He took with him five young women, seven young men, and two additional young men with girlish faces but manly spirits who were to dress and walk like women. He owed his success, however, not only to this clever ruse, but also to his good fortune in meeting Ariadne, the daughter of Minos; for, falling in love with Theseus, she gave him a ball of thread that allowed him, after killing the Minotaur, to find his way back through the twisted labyrinth in safety.

Because of the public ceremony recalling this legend, Phaedo repeats, Socrates passed a long time in prison between his trial and his death. But Echecrates does not ask about Socrates' response to this delay; he is eager to hear only about what took place at his death, and in particular whether the authorities allowed his friends to be present or compelled him to die alone. Since he is at leisure, Phaedo admits, he will attempt to relate the whole story; for he finds it the greatest of all pleasures to remember Socrates, in either speaking of him or listening. And when Echecrates affirms that Phaedo will have listeners who share that feeling, perhaps Plato's readers are meant, at least in this respect, to be included among them.

In contrast, however, with being reminded of Socrates, which produces the greatest of pleasures, being present at his death, Phaedo confesses, produced in him a strange and wondrous mixture of pleasure and pain. He did not feel the pity one might expect to feel at the death of a friend, he tells Echecrates, since Socrates seemed happy in his manner and speeches, dying fearlessly and nobly; nor, on the other hand, did he feel pleasure as he usually would when occupied with philosophic speeches. In construing philosophy as pure pleasure, Phaedo shows no awareness of the possiblity of a painful gap between its ambition and its achievement; in construing pity as pure pain, he is unaware of the possibility of pleasure in one's distance from the sufferer. If he could not pity Socrates because he seemed to be going into Hades "with some kind of divine lot," he might have felt envy at this selfish escape;[10] this is suggested in fact by his portrayal of the other participants in the conversation, who express pity only in combination with resentment of Socrates for abandoning them (cf. 63a–b). Phaedo unwittingly points to the necessity of a complicated mixture, in which neither pleasure nor pain is free from the presence of the other, despite his naive account of each as naturally separate, combined only on this unique occasion.

[59b3–59c7] Judging by the behavior Phaedo ascribes to them, the others who were present at Socrates' death experienced the same strange mixture of emotions. Prompted by Echecrates' question of who these men were, Phaedo offers a list: first three (Apollodorus, Critoboulos, and Critoboulos's father), then four (Hermogenes, Epigenes, Aeschines, and Antisthenes) native Athenians, two additional Athenians (Ctesippus and Menexenus), then three non-Athenians (Simmias and Cebes of Thebes and Phaedonides), and finally two others (Eucleides and Terpsion of Megara).[11] Phaedo lists five strangers, seven native Athenians, and two additional Athenians, young men of manly spirit.[12] The group present with Socrates on the day of his death, which takes place just after completion of the public ritual celebrating the mythical voyage of Theseus, matches the group of nine youths and five maidens present with Theseus on that voyage.[13] But while the Athenians present with Socrates might have been flattered by their identification with those nine youths, it is to the group of strangers identified with the maidens that the two active participants in the conversation belong. While explicitly mentioning the names of three others who were absent,[14] the non-Athenian Phaedo leaves his own name out of the list of those present at Socrates' death. Yet he points to his own role in the Platonic drama by reporting his exchange with Socrates at the center of the conversation: gathering Plaedo's long hair at the back of his neck, advising him to cut it not in mourning for Socrates' imminent death, but only in mourning for the logos if they cannot save it (89b), Socrates singles out Phaedo to play the role, it seems, of Ariadne, an ally necessary for the success of his mission. The Minotaur that they must together confront is the childish fear of death that threatens to overcome all manliness (cf. 77d–e).

The miraculous convergence of the historical celebration of a mythical event with the situation of the conversation he is about to relate, Phaedo judges to be "some kind of chance or fate" (*tuchē tis*). Phaedo is an unwitting vehicle for the Platonic logographic necessity[15] that represents Socrates' last conversation as a reenactment in logos of Theseus' victory over the Minotaur, dramatically embedded in the context of the Athenian reenactment of the same heroic myth. The sense of guilt from which the Athenians seek purification is revealed by the law that prohibits public execution during the period of the sailing of the sacred ship. The ritual pretense of the city that it has no involvment with killing is the purification of the pollution it experiences from just that involvement. The convergence of the mission to Delos and the trial of Socrates is hardly then a matter of chance, as Phaedo believes, but is rather the sign identifying the condemnation of Socrates as the immediate source of guilt that the Athenians feel compelled to expiate.

Nor is it accidental that, on the day when the sacred ship has returned and his sentence is to be carried out, Socrates begins the conversation with an account of his own act of purification. The suspected guilt for which Socrates seeks purification, as he will explain, is his lifelong neglect of producing "music for the *dēmos*" (cf. 60e–61b). Because of Socrates, Athens bears the weight of guilt for the possibly unjust execution of a citizen, indeed the citizen who may have been the god's gift to the city;[16] because of Athens, Socrates bears the weight of guilt for his exclusive concern with philosophy as "the greatest music," and consequent neglect of "demotic music." To purify itself, Athens delays the execution of Socrates long enough to send out the sacred mission; to purify himself, Socrates takes advantage of that delay to make up for what he may have neglected throughout his life. Yet precisely because of its ceremony of purification, Athens is able to carry out the act through which its guilt would have been incurred: having performed a mere ritual,[17] the Athenians hand over the cup of hemlock to Socrates, thus effecting the form of an "involuntary suicide."[18] Perhaps in the same way, the demotic music that Socrates will claim to have produced during his days in prison is no more than a mere ritual, which does not preclude his persistence, to his final hour, in the lifelong pursuit for which this purification was required.

The city's concealment of the execution under the guise of a self-inflicted death is appropriately reflected in the attitude of Socrates' companions, who accuse him of being eager to abandon both his friends and his good masters the gods (cf. 63a). Having refused the opportunity to escape from the Athenian prison, having conducted his trial as if he hoped to provoke the sentence of death, having allowed the case to come before the court in the first place,[19] Socrates must begin his final conversation with a defense of what seems to be an act of running away from life. But rather than defend himself by forcing responsibility back upon the city, he saves himself and Athens by seeing in his trial and conviction the sign of divine necessity (cf. 62c). He thus appears to imitate the Athenians, who seek divine sanction for a political act of execution. Only their mutual appeal to Apollo, the god of purification and music, provides the common ground for the reconciliation of Socratic philosophy and Athenian law; it is a reconciliation, of course, that takes place only on the level of ritual and thus seems to confirm, rather than resolve, the conflict it brings to light.

What Phaedo interprets as a mark of chance emerges— through the logographic necessity of the Platonic dialogue, at least—as an account of the "causes" of Socrates' death: the will of the gods coincides perfectly with the decision of the Athenian dēmos, and both coincide with Socrates' own desire, which he will defend by identifying philosophy as "the practice of dying and being dead." This practice will itself be described as a kind of purification: it entails liberation from the illusions that accompany submission to pleasure and pain. Since, however, the confrontation of philosophy and death produced in Phaedo, as he explained, only a strange and wondrous mixture of pleasure and pain, it is not at all evident what reasons motivate Socrates to choose Phaedo as his ally.

Socrates requires this alliance, as he suggests in his exchange with Phaedo, because he can overcome the Minotaur that consists in the fear of death only by discovering a safe thread leading through the twisted passages of the logos in which that monster hides. And that very effort is itself threatened by another danger: Socrates will have to overcome the many-headed monster of misology, which consists in distrust not just of the present argument for the immortality of the psychē, but of the power of logos in general (cf. 89c–d). The fear of death, which motivates the desire for a demonstration of the immortality of the psychē, can be subdued only by being transformed into the fear of misology, which would motivate the desire for an art of argumentation capable of defending its own trustworthiness. And while the analysis of this technē of logos may appear, to Socrates' companions, subordinate to the goal of demonstrating the immortality of the psychē, the overturning of that appearance is precisely the challenge presented by the dialogue to its reader.

[59c8–59d8] Phaedo began his exchange with Echecrates by referring to the conduct of Socrates' trial; he concludes by describing the days following the trial, when the young men met each day at dawn and made the same journey Socrates once made from the Athenian court to the prison. Despite this reminder of the political context, however, Phaedo and the others speak as though Socrates' death were entirely willful, or simply a natural phenomenon. Despite the one moment, moreover, when Socrates admits that the causes of his present situation are the judgment of the Athenian dēmos and his own acceptance of it (98e), he seems to adapt himself all too readily to the perspective of his interlocutors. In constructing a model of "the best city in speech," Socrates identifies the city, the domain of political authority and opinion, as the prison in which the philosopher is interned and from which he longs to escape;[20] in attempting to demonstrate the immortality of the psychē, he identifies that prison no longer with the city, but with the body (cf. 82d–83c).

In adopting a perspective that seems to conceal the political context of his death, Socrates acts as if he knew that this conversation would be transported beyond the Athenian prison in which it takes place. At his public trial, he argued that, if his only alternative were to give up philosophy, and thus lead a life not worth living, death would be preferable.[21] In his private conversation with Crito, he implied that philosophy could not be carried on in a lawless regime, or even in a regime totally governed by law:[22] for Socrates, philosophy—that is, political philosophy—requires Athens. To the nearby and well-governed cities like Thebes or Megara, Socrates says he could not escape, for he would be received as an enemy, bringing with him the reputation of philosophy as a destroyer of the laws, hence of thoughtless young men.[23] But if the historical Socrates could not make this journey,[24] the Socrates of the Platonic dialogues, in the days following his condemnation, shows how philosophy can be exported to safety outside Athens: in the *Theaetetus*, Socratic philosophy is carried to Megara,[25] and in the *Phaedo*, to Phlius, the Pythagorean community associated with Thebes.[26]

The dramatic prologue of the *Phaedo* sheds light not only on the themes of the dialogue but also on its structure, articulated by the opening and closing frame as well as by the central interlude in which Phaedo plays a part. The outermost frame of the dramatic prologue, alluding to Socrates' trial as the background of his death, encloses an internal frame, linking the Athenian mission to Delos, as a ritual enactment of the legend of Theseus, with the Socratic mission, as a philosophically reconstructed enactment of that legend. At the center of this double frame stands Phaedo's account of the strange mixture of pleasure and pain he experienced at Socrates' death; at the center of the converation he is about to narrate stands his exchange with Socrates on the necessity of achieving liberation from pleasure and pain by directing attention to the logos itself. The Platonic prologue representing the exchange between Phaedo and Echecrates is a mirror that seems to present an inverted image of the whole of which it is a part.

CHAPTER TWO

Logos and Mythos

[59d8–60a9]   Phaedo refers to the many conversations Socrates conducted in the Athenian prison prior to this last one, but the Platonic dialogues present only the one in which Socrates, speaking in the voice of the personified laws of Athens, rejects the entreaty of his old friend Crito to escape. Crito comes to the prison immediately upon receiving a report concerning the arrival of the ship from Delos, since this means that Socrates will have to drink the poison on the following day. But Socrates seems assured that his life will not come to an end on the morrow; for during the time that Crito has been watching him asleep and marveling at his apparent calmness in the face of death, Socrates has been dreaming of a beautiful woman in white, who informs him that "on the third day you would come to fertile Phthia." Socrates' dream conflates the words of Homer's Achilles, who refuses Odysseus' entreaty to return and fight for the common cause, with the figure of the goddess Thetis, who warns her son Achilles, unsuccessfully, against acting in a way that will result in his death;[1] it thus implies that Socrates' death is the fulfillment of his own wish, against the command of his superiors, to return to his homeland, and at the same time, the result of a decision to die nobly rather than go on living disgracefully.

But Socrates' interpretation of his dream, with its denial of the rumor reported by Crito, is not confirmed by the series of

24

Platonic dialogues in which it is presented. For Phaedo does not announce when it is that the young men receive the report of the arrival of the sacred ship; he explains only that, on the following morning, they gathered together as early as possible at the prison but were compelled to wait outside by the jailer—the same man, perhaps, who let Crito in before dawn after receiving a small favor from him.[2] The first direct speech that makes the past into the present is the jailer's announcement that "the eleven are releasing Socrates from his chains and giving directions on how he is to die";[3] it is the "servant of the eleven" who enters at sunset to announce the time to drink the poison, which should release Socrates from the chains binding him to life.

When his visitors enter, they find Socrates just released, with Xanthippe and their child sitting beside him.[4] Phaedo has promised to narrate all the deeds and speeches, but he cannot, of course, recognize the logographic necessity that binds them in the Platonic dialogue: he gives no interpretation of the fact that Socrates must at first have been lying down, although he remarks that as soon as Xanthippe left, Socrates sat up (60b), and that, finally, with the introduction of the issue of the philosopher's desire for death, Socrates put his feet on the ground (61c) and remained in that position until the end of the day, after drinking the poison.[5] Like Socrates' reclining position, Xanthippe's presence belongs to the dramatic action that frames the logos but remains apart from it: she departs before the conversation begins and presumably returns with the women of the family when it is ended. With what appears to be a selfless grief, Xanthippe laments the last occasion on which Socrates will be able to speak with his companions. But when she cries out[6]—according to Phaedo, the way women always do—Socrates looks up at Crito in the first of a series of increasingly intense glares. Just as Socrates will address a request to Crito in his last words, he addresses to Crito, in his first words, the request that Xanthippe be taken home. She departs wailing and beating her breast in her sorrow, while perhaps finding some relief in the very deed of expressing it:[7] she enacts her own version of the strange mixture of pleasure and pain that Phaedo first ascribed to himself and now reports as the theme of Socrates' first reflections.

[60b1–60c7]   Whereas Phaedo marveled at his experience of a unique combination, Socrates' wonder is aroused at the thought of an inseparable union by nature between what men call pleasant and what is thought to be its opposite, the painful.[8] The pain that must have been present when his leg was fettered, Socrates can recognize only in contrast with the pleasure he subsequently experiences once the chain is removed: his experience of pleasure is nothing but the absence of a pain that was determined by objective causes but did not appear in experience as such. In his interpretation, Socrates attempts to correct Phaedo's misunderstanding of pleasure and pain as autonomous and indifferent to each other: though neither "wishes" to come to be present in a man at the same time as the other, if someone pursues one and gets it, he is almost always compelled to take the other with it.[9] It is as if the so-called pleasant and the painful were joined together in "one head," so that neither term is independent, and each—or at least one of them—is nothing but the absence of the other.[10] Now if Aesop had thought about this experience, Socrates imagines, he would have put together the following mythos: the god, wishing to reconcile pleasure and pain, which were at war with each other, but finding himself unable to do so, instead fastened them together in "two heads," so that whenever one comes to be present, the other always follows it later.

In accordance with this Aesopian story, the chains that imprison the psychē in the body make life a present experience of pain, which will be followed by the release of the psychē at death as a subsequent experience of pleasure. In accordance with Socrates' original account, on the other hand, to construe the union of psychē with body as painful would require an inference made retrospectively if and when the psychē were released from the body, and the pleasure of that release, in turn, would be nothing but recognition of the absence of a prior union. While it seeks to explain why pleasure follows on the withdrawal of pain, the Aesopian mythos presupposes that each is nonproblematic in itself. The Socratic account, in contrast, which considers how strangely these apparent opposites are related by "nature," points to the problematic character of each in itself. The Aesopian mythos thus assumes what the Socratic account makes into a problem: What is the so-called pleasant or the painful? It is because it implicitly raises this question—at least once it is contrasted with the mythos—that Socrates' account can be labeled a logos. It nevertheless preserves a mythological element. For its description of pleasure and pain "wishing" not to come to be present together is, we would say, a personification: it is the projection onto the feelings themselves of the human will to separate them.

By supplementing his own description of the attempted divison of an original unit with an Aesopian mythos about the attempted unification of an original dyad, Socrates provides a double account of how pleasure and pain come to be two. If, on the other hand, the attempt to unify pleasure and pain were really successful, they would together become one, or if the attempt to separate them were really successful, each would become one with no relation to the other. Addition and division thus constitute not only opposite causes of how two comes to be, but the same opposite causes of how one comes to be. This was just the perplexity, Socrates later reports, that compelled him to abandon any claim to know the "refined cause" of how something comes to be and to replace it with a safe hypothesis: the cause of anything being two is its participation in the dyad, of anything being one its participation in the monad (cf. 96e–97b, 101c). Still, despite their problematic status, the operations of addition and division are informative in a way that cannot be replaced by the noncontradictory "cause" of *what* it is to be two or one. Despite its problematic status, therefore, the juxtaposition of a Socratic logos about pleasure and pain with an Aesopian mythos is informative: it identifies separation as an effort based on the desire of a man, unification as an effort based on the will of the god. The union of psychē with body, which will be identified with life (cf. 103c–d), must be explained, accordingly, through a mythos about divine will, while their separation, which will be identified with death (64c), must be explained through a logos about human desire. That these two models for the relation of opposites should be determined by the opposition of human desire and divine will is hardly accidental, for Socrates will soon be called upon to defend his apparent desire for death, when he himself admits that life is a god-given responsibility (cf. 61c–63c).

[60c8–61e9]   In the transition leading to this issue of the divine prohibition against suicide, Socrates justifies the necessity of his juxtaposition of logos and mythos. He does so in response to the first question raised by Cebes, who is surprised—he swears by Zeus—at how fittingly Socrates' mention of an Aesopian mythos reminds him of rumors he has heard about Socrates' recent poetic productions. He had been questioned by the poet Evenus about the meaning of Socrates' sudden turn to writing poetry, Cebes explains, only two days earlier—the very day, perhaps, on which Crito questioned Socrates about his apparently sudden appeal to the laws of Athens as the highest authority. But this possible coincidence is even more fitting than Cebes could realize. For his turn to poetry was motivated, Socrates acknowledges, by a suspicion of having neglected to fulfill the command of certain dreams—that is, of one dream that came to him throughout his life in various shapes but always saying the same thing. The identity of the Athenians' sacred ship, despite its constantly changing components, was nothing but the logos that declared it one and the same; the identity of Socrates' dream, despite its constantly changing appearances, is determined by one and the same logos it commands—to "make music and work at it."[11] Socrates felt compelled to test this dream in these last days, he explains to Cebes, just as he felt compelled, he explained to the Athenian jury, to test the oracle of Apollo that declared no man wiser than he was. As a result of that lifelong testing, Socrates discovered his unique significance: he arrived at his understanding that the greatest human wisdom is knowledge of ignorance.[12] On that basis, Socrates could interpret his recurrent dream simply as encouragement to continue his practice of philosophy, which he takes to be "the greatest music";[13] only his trial and the festival of the god that has delayed his death make him suspect his possible guilt in having neglected demotic music—poetry, that is, that would communicate with the dēmos.

Believing it safer, Socrates claims, to purify himself before departing, he has spent his days in prison composing a hymn to the god whose festival it is—the same who proclaimed him the wisest of men—and, since he considers himself no mythmaker—though he seems to have no trouble inventing a tale to conclude this conversation—Socrates claims to have taken over the mythoi of Aesop and set them to verse. Socrates suggests the double source of his possible guilt in describing this work of ritual purification, which combines a display of piety to the god with moral fables comprehensible to children. But even if the poetic work Socrates claims to have produced were not merely a fiction in the Platonic dialogue, it is questionable whether such demotic music would be capable of combination with "the greatest music"; perhaps, then, only Plato's *Phaedo*—in part a hymn to Apollo, the god of purification, in part an elaborate mythos about the human psychē—could sufficiently purify Socrates from his suspected guilt without abandoning the pursuit that causes it. That this issue should be raised by Socrates' mention of an Aesopian mythos is, in any case, no contingency, as Cebes believes, but one more instance of Platonic logographic necessity; for the tension between the philosopher's desire to practice the greatest music and the divine command to produce demotic music reflects precisely the tension between the human desire to pursue pleasure in separation from pain and the god's will to unite them, or the human desire to seek death as the separation of the psychē from the body and the god's will to unite them.

Socrates asks Cebes to bid farewell to Evenus, the poet and sophist,[14] bearing the message to follow after him, if he is indeed a philosopher, as quickly as possible; only in that way could he correct his commitment to demotic music, just as Socrates had to correct his commitment to philosophy. Evenus is advised to pursue what will soon be called "the practice of dying," but he is to do so, Socrates adds, without taking his own life, which is said to be forbidden.[15] The tension within this double message shows up in the split between the responses of Socrates' two interlocutors: while Simmias is surprised by Socrates' recommendation that Evenus follow after him, Cebes is puzzled by the claim that it is not lawful to take one's own life, though the philosopher wishes to follow after one who is dying. Socrates, in turn, claims to be surprised that Simmias and Cebes, who have heard the teachings of the Pythagorean Philolaus, nevertheless know nothing definite about the prohibition against suicide.[16] He himself is willing to say what he knows from hearsay, Socrates admits, since it seems fitting on this particular occasion to "investigate and mythologize" about his journey abroad: this double enterprise may be necessitated, Socrates implies, by the double content of his message to Evenus.

[62a1–62c5]   Socrates begins, understandably enough, by warning Cebes that he must strive eagerly if he is to grasp this paradoxical law:[17]

> Perhaps, however, it will appear wondrous to you, if this alone of all others is simple and, unlike other things, it never happens to man that for some and at some times it is better to be dead than alive; but for whom (or for what) it is better to be dead, it is perhaps wondrous to you if, for those men, it is not holy to benefit themselves but necessary to wait for some other benefactor.[18]

Socrates himself experienced wonder at the conjunction of pleasure and pain when the chain was removed from his leg; of the two models he presented for this relaton of opposites, one was based on the human desire for separation of an original unit, the other on the divine will to unify an original dyad. Socrates now expects his interlocutors to undergo a corresponding experience of wonder at the opposition between the divine command against suicide and the possible superiority of death to life. If the divine command were indeed the only law without exception, it might seem to entail the universal superiority of life over death[19]—if, at least, the gods know and support the good for man. Precisely because it is a prohibition, on the other hand, the law against suicide presupposes the possibility of the human desire for death. But this admission in itself is a puzzling one: there seems to be no standpoint from which one could make the judgment that it is better to be dead, since it is a judgment that can only be made by one who is alive, and it is for himself, presumably, that he determines what is preferable.[20] Socrates thus indicates a tension within the divine prohibition and within the human desire for death, as well as between them.

The two clauses through which Socrates describes this structure of opposition, however, are only apparently parallel. For while the first is entirely conditional—it will appear wondrous *if* the divine prohibition is universal and entails the universal superiority of life over death[21]—the second clause is introduced with an unconditional claim—since there is someone for whom or something for which death is better, it may appear wondrous *if* the pursuit of that benefit were forbidden. The asymmetry of the two clauses is indicated, moreover, by the distinction between future and present: the univeral goodness of life, construed as a consequence of the "simplicity" of the divine prohibition against suicide, *will* perhaps appear wondrous, and this prediction is fulfilled at the moment Socrates begins the second clause, with its admission of the possible superiority of death. But the one unconditional claim asserted by Socrates could be accepted, without contradicting that which precedes or follows, only if those for whom or that for which it is better to be dead is not a man: Socrates is about to argue that it may be better if one is a philosopher—not for the man himself, however, but only for his psychē.[22] The kind of "death" that is preferable, consequently, may not be the physiological phenomenon that constitutes the ordinary understanding of the word.[23]

Socrates' paradoxical formulation does indeed so arouse

Cebes' wonder that he utters an oath, slipping into his native dialect—"Let Zeus know!"—while smiling gently. That the prohibition that simultaneously implies and denies the possible superiority of death to life would fill even Zeus with wonder makes Cebes smile for the first time,[24] just as Simmias is about to smile for the first time in acknowledging that the many would make fun of the philosopher's desire for death (64b). A surprising alliance is thus implied between the gods and the many, with their natural desire for life, over against the philosopher, with his strange desire for death. But this conflict as a rule is confirmed by its one exception: Socrates' apparent readiness for death is to be satisfied only through the cooperation of the Athenian dēmos, who believe death to be the greatest evil, while their decision is in turn interpreted by Socrates as a sign of "some necessity sent by a god" (cf. 62c).

Since his statement, Socrates admits, must appear irrational (alogos), to consider what sense it may have, he must initiate his interlocutors into a secret logos, which describes both the desire for liberation from life and the source of restraint against it. It is as if we men are on some kind of guard duty or in some kind of prison and are not allowed to set ourselves free or run away. With this secret logos, Socrates tranforms the political significance of his discussion with Crito concerning his responsibility not to run away from the Athenian prison;[25] at the same time, he transforms the significance of his defense before the Athenian jury concerning his responsibility not to run away from the post where he believed the god stationed him, engaging in the activity of examination, any more than he ran away from the post in battle where his Athenian commanders stationed him.[26] But the "great secret" Socrates now divulges, which presents life itself as the true prison or the true guard duty, puts those prior claims into question: if the highest responsibility were the obligation not to run away from the prison of life, Socrates would have had to run away from the Athenian prison, as Crito entreated, or if it were the obligation not to run away from the guard duty of life, Socrates would have had to run away from the duty of philosophy, no less than from a post in battle, as he admitted to his Athenian judges.

The secret logos, which Socrates finds "weighty and not easy to see through," says either that life is an imprisonment, without revealing the guilt for which we are incarcerated, or that we are ourselves guardians, without revealing that for which we are responsible, nor why we are compelled to maintain this position.[27] The intentional exploitation of this ambiguity is indicated by its exemplification of the conflicting assumptions of the dialogue as a whole: while the sense of imprisonment suggests the desire of the psychē for contact with the beings themselves, which would require its separability from the body, the image of the guard post suggests the responsibility of the psychē for animating the body, which requires its inseparability. To clarify the secret logos, with its ambiguous assumptions concerning the relation between psychē and body, Socrates turns to the "well-spoken" claim that the gods are our guardians and we men their chattel.[28] That the gods, however, might not have the best human interests in mind in their support of human life is suggested by the illustration Socrates offers to Cebes: if one of your chattel should kill itself before you indicated that you wished it to die, you would be angry and would punish it, if you could.

[62c6–63d2]   Socrates absolves himself from this potential accusation simply by asserting his recognition of the divine necessity now sent upon him. He is saved from having to defend himself only because Cebes is troubled, not so much by the impiety of suicide, as by the foolishness—if the god is indeed our guardian and we his possession—of the desire for death. While a foolish man, Cebes argues, might thoughtlessly desire to run away from a good master, the most prudent (phronimos) man would never think he could take better care of himself when free but would wish to be always with one who is better than himself;[29] but in that case, it is the wise who ought to be troubled by dying and only the foolish who would rejoice.

Cebes' earnestness seemed to please Socrates, Phaedo believes, although he casts doubt on that interpretation when he reports that Socrates, for the second time, stared upward at his companions. Just because of the threat posed by Cebes' discovery of an apparent contradiction, Socrates praises him for his relentless pursuit of the logos and his unwillingness to be convinced by anyone apart from it. What Cebes points to, however, in his insistence on the prudence of submission to good masters, is the situation of himself and his friends, who every day since the trial, have come to be in the presence of Socrates. Indeed, Simmias immediately takes up the argument as a direct accusation against Socrates' willingness to abandon not only his good masters the gods, but his friends as well.

Socrates managed to avoid, in his public trial, any attempt to defend himself against the charge of not believing in the gods of the city,[30] although that very avoidance is of course suspicious. He manages now to avoid any attempt to defend himself against the apparently justifiable charge of impiety; for that charge, although it has been suggested by the conflict between the philosopher's desire for death and the divine prohibition against suicide, has been replaced by Cebes' attack on Socrates' foolishness and Simmias' attack on his injustice. Although Socrates immediately responds to Simmias' demand for a defense of his conduct, he directs his response to Cebes' accusation: by admitting that he would be wrong in not grieving at death only if he did not believe that he was going to other wise and good gods and to men better than those here, Socrates displays more concern with defending his prudence than his justice.

He seems, indeed, to go out of his way to insult his companions by declaring his hope of traveling to the company of better men, especially since, Socrates adds, he is not willing to insist on this claim, as he would about the gods—as much as he would insist on any such matters. He is confident that, in going to Hades, he goes to good and wise gods, for Hades is nothing but the name of the good and wise god (cf. 80d, 81a):[31] Socrates is willing to insist, as he later makes clear, only on a nonfalsifiable logos.[32] But the defense of this kind of confidence, which Socrates will provide through his analysis of a technē that guarantees the safety of logos, is not identical with the defense his interlocutors now demand, although Simmias believes it would be a benefit to all in common:[33] the benefit Socrates bestows by providing his companions with a defense he himself does not require itself constitutes the apologia of his prudence and his justice.

[63d3–63e7]   But the apologia that Socrates hopes to make more persuasive than the one he offered the Athenian jury is momentarily delayed. For Socrates is aware that Crito has been attempting to interrupt for quite a while and now gives him a chance to speak. Crito has been eager to issue the warning, on behalf of the man who is to administer the poison, that Socrates must converse (*dialegesthai*) as little as possible to avoid getting heated up, which would interfere with the effects of the hemlock. The war of opposites, which Socrates described in his account of the relation between pleasure and pain and will analyze in his final argument,[34] is reflected in the dramatic deeds of the dialogue: the activity of conversing, which brings forth heat and thus prolongs life, is engaged from the outset in a battle against the poison, which brings forth cold, and with it death. But conversing has in fact a double function: if, in its physiological effect, it chains the psychē to the body, it is at the same time the means of separating the logos from the psychē united with the body. Socrates allows Crito to interrupt only after he has committed himself to delivering a defense and is therefore compelled to continue: he demonstrates his allegiance to life and logos in the interval between announcing and carrying out his defense of philosophy as the practice of dying.

The series of leave-takings,[35] which ends when Socrates bids farewell (*chairein*) to the servant of the eleven who announces the time to drink the hemlock (116d), begins when Socrates now commands Crito to bid farewell to the man who warns him of the oppositiion between the effect of conversing

and that of the poison. Just as Socrates displayed his willingness, at his public trial, to obey every law of the city but not
the command to cease the practice of philosophy,[36] he refuses
now, on the day of his execution, to heed the warning to converse as little as possible. Let twice as much of the poison be
prepared, or even three times if necessary, Socrates boasts,
calling to mind the proverb, "Twice and even thrice the beautiful things!"[37]

CHAPTER THREE

The Practice of Dying

[63e8–64c9]   Prepared to defend his justice and prudence in not grieving at the approach of death, Socrates addresses Simmias and Cebes as his "judges." He refused to assign that name to the Athenians who condemned him of injustice and impiety, assigning it only to those who acquitted him.[1] Yet Socrates has just expressed his hope of offering a more persuasive speech now than the one he offered to the judges at his trial (63b). Was Socrates, then, unable to persuade those who acquitted him that death was, at this point, preferable? He wishes now, in any case, to give a logos explaining why it appears to him likely that a man who really spent his life in philosophy would be confident in dying and hopeful of finding the greatest goods "there" when he has died. Socrates is silent about the nature of these goods to be received after death, which seems to be a place as well as a time; nor does he confirm whether such hope for the future is identical with the philosopher's confidence in dying based on the life he has led.

That identity is implicitly put into question by the premise with which Socrates begins his defense. If it is true that those who happen to grasp philosophy correctly practice nothing but dying and being dead, it would surely be strange if they were troubled in the achievement of what they eagerly pursued throughout their lives. It is no wonder that, as Socrates claims, others are unaware of this. To die and to be dead would seem to be one thing that could never be a habitual practice. The formulation sounds as strange as does that of its practitioners, those who "correctly grasp philosophy," as if it were an object that could be possessed once and for all. It is clear, in any case, that Socrates intends to respond to the attack against his acceptance of death, understood simply as the termination of life, by reinterpreting death as the goal of a lifelong practice of dying. But whatever death turns out to mean, if this practice of dying is a progressive activity that ceases with death in the ordinary sense, its practitioners might well lament the moment that puts an end to their lifelong pursuit;[2] the man who "really spent his life in philosophy" might well regret its termination, which is not necessarily its fulfillment.

In spite of himself, Simmias is forced to laugh, for Socrates' assertion is actually in perfect accordance with the opinion of the many, who agree quite disdainfully that "the philosophizers" do desire death and indeed deserve it.[3] They would speak the truth, Socrates admits, but without realizing what they say, since they do not know what kind of death it is that the "true philosophers" desire and deserve. Socrates reproaches the ignorance of the many on the basis of the very ambiguity he himself exploits; for if the practice of being dead implies something other than the ordinary understanding of death as a physiological phenomenon, why would it necessarily exclude the fear based on that ordinary understanding? To clarify what kind of death it is that the philosophers desire, they must "bid farewell" to the many, Socrates recommends, and speak only among themselves; yet the account that follows betrays a harmony between the opinion of the many and that of the true philosophers, which Socrates indicates only by implying his own distance from both.[4]

It is striking, then, that Socrates calls them "the true philosophers," or a little later "the genuine philosophers." He gives them a name that reflects perfectly their own self-understanding. Each identifies himself with the pure psychē, which will reach its goal when it is released from the body at death and reunited with "the true" (66b). Given this interpretation of truth, "true lover of wisdom" looks like a contradicton in terms. Yet it is in accordance with this self-understanding that the true philosophers construct their understanding of the "pure beings" to which the pure psychē is thought to be akin. If the union of these assumed kindred were realized, the psychē of the philosopher would be indistinguishable from its object of knowledge. In fact, if each true philosopher actualized his nature as a pure psychē, none could be differentiated from any other: Socrates does not arbitrarily refer to them in the plural. The traditional reading of the *Phaedo* takes the following account to be a genuine formulation of the Socratic-Platonic view of the "ideas" and the way they are known; it naturally turns Socrates, therefore, into one more indistinguishable member of the class of genuine philosophers. But Socrates fails to breed true to this *genos*. If he shares with the genuine philosophers in the practice of dying and being dead, he will eventually disclose his own unique interpretation of it.

Socrates begins his account of this practice with a presumably self-evident question: "Do we believe that death (*to thanatos*) is something?" And Simmias enthusiastically affirms this before inquiring about what it is he affirms.[5] He does not consider the possibility of a distinction between death and dying, nor the association of death with nonbeing,[6] and he seems to have already forgotten Socrates' immediately preceding reference to the different kind of death desired by the philosopher. Socrates himself, however, now proceeds to offer three formulations of what death is:

> Is it anything other than the release of the psychē from the body? And is this 'being dead' (*to tethnanai*), on the one hand, the body itself by itself becoming separate, released from the psychē, on the other, the psychē itself by itself being separate, having been released from the body? Is death anything other than this? (64c4–9)

If "death," according to Simmias, is some one thing, "being dead," Socrates now suggests, is a state that represents two different results of the event of dying. While the body only becomes separate, the psychē is separate; from the perspective of the body, its union with the psychē is primary, whereas from the perspective of the psychē, its separation from the body is primary. There is, consequently, no single subject that undergoes death. Socrates suppresses the fact that it is a man who dies. At the moment that he defines death as a separation, he performs a separation. It is not a physiological change but the Socratic logos that divides the living animal into body and psychē.

In accomplishing this separation, Socrates at the same time points to the hidden union between the many and the true philosophers. Just as the philosophers seek the separation of the pure psychē from the body, the many—who want to "die of pleasure"[7]—seek the separation of pure body from psychē. The hedonist, who pursues nothing but pleasure, resenting the psychē as an impediment to the fulfillment of his desire, and the ascetic, who flees from pleasure, resenting the body as an impediment to the fulfillment of his desire, exhibit the same union of opposites that Socrates initially described in his account of pleasure and pain themselves. In disclosing this relation between hedonism and asceticism mistaken for philosophy, Socrates stands back from both at once.

[64d1–66a10]   He indicates this distance by beginning with a description of the effort of the "philosophic man" to flee from the body, without offering any explanation of the purpose of that attempt. Nor does Socrates need any argument to obtain Simmias' agreement that such a man "could not take seriously" the so-called pleasures such as eating and drinking and the *aphrodisia;* that he would not "honor" the other cares of the body "except as necessary;" that he "more than most men" would separate the psychē from communion with the body. However much Socrates adopts a perspective that is not his own, he speaks only the truth. His boldest claim is to assert that the philosopher, more than most men, does not assign the highest priority to the pleasures and adornments of the body.

Only after describing this attempted flight from the body does Socrates identify its goal—the acquisition of phronēsis. This goal, he implies, is derived from the desire for purification of the psychē, since phronēsis, as understood by the true phi-

losophers, is precisely the condition of the psychē in its separation from the body.[8] Only, they believe, when the psychē has
"bid farewell" to the body[9]—for the senses together with the
passions are identified as mere affections of the body—can it
"reach out and grasp the being."[10] The acquisition of phronēsis
is described as a matter of "grasping," "reaching out," "seiz-
ing," "possessing," or "hitting." This unacknowledged metaphoric language, in which the allegedly purest state of the
psychē is depicted in terms of the sense of touch,[11] betrays the
same union of opposites implicitly ascribed to asceticism and
hedonism. It expresses the understanding of phronēsis as nothing but a paradoxically noncorporeal contact with noncorporeal entities, whose necessary counterpart is the abstraction of
a pure psychē. For if one were to admit that perception and the
passions belong to the psychē itself, even its release from the
body could not serve as a sufficient condition for the acquisition of phronēsis. Motivated by this goal, the psychē of the
philosopher dishonors the body and flees from it to be alone by
itself; while presumably aiming at contact with "the beings,"
the psychē in fact desires to be only with itself as a separate
being.

Socrates draws attention to this implication by turning,
with an apparent abruptness, from considering psychē itself by
itself to ask Simmias, "Do we say that the just itself is something or nothing?" When Simmias shows no more hesitation
than he did in agreeing that we believe death is something,
Socrates supplements his question about the just with one
about the beautiful and good. He does not raise the question of
how, if each is "itself by itself," there could be any relation
between them, and if there is not, how it is possible to formu-
late *what* each is. Socrates first inquires whether such things
are ever seen with the eyes or grasped by any of the senses,
through the body, before he adds to his list size, health, and
strength,[12] which seem to be necessarily related to our perception of bodies as characterized by a particular size, state of
health, or degree of strenth. Socrates' apparently superfluous
reference to these characteristics tacitly invites us to step back
and reconsider the cases of the just, beautiful, and good. In fact,

Socrates observes, his account concerns "all the others, in a word (*heni logō*), the being (*ousia*), what each in fact is."[13] But the figure of speech he uses indicates, if read literally, that this being is "in logos," its unity "in one logos."

At the moment, however, Socrates avoids confronting the questions implicitly raised by his account. He can do so because he speaks here from the perspective of the true philosophers, who conceive of the pure beings simply in opposition to objects of perception, just as they conceive of the pure psychē simply in opposition to the body. The being, however, that the true philosophers understand as the object of a nonaesthetic vision by the passive psychē becomes, in Socrates' account of his own way of reasoning, the object of a hypothesis, laid down as the necessary foundation for investigating "the truth of the beings" through logoi (cf. 100b–d, 101c). Socrates presents this procedure, moreover, as an escape from the danger of the psychē blinding itself by attempting to investigate the beings directly in the pragmata—in the many, variously qualified things that come to be and pass away (cf. 99d–100a). But it is precisely that danger which is represented by the true philosophers' understanding of phronēsis as direct contact of the psychē with "the *pragmata* themselves" (cf. 66e).

Socrates seems to include himself for the first time when he refers to "whoever among us most precisely prepared himself to think about (*dianoēthenai*) what he investigates." *If* anyone were to "hit upon the being," Socrates acknowledges with qualification, "it would be accomplished most purely by one who approached each with thought (*dianoia*) alone, as much as possible," without introducing the senses into his calculation. In elaborating this account, Socrates preserves the true philosophers' insistence on the necessity of investigation independent of perception, but, at the same time, he replaces psychē as the agent of that activity by thought itself.[14] He admits, furthermore, the separation of thought from the senses only "as much ·as possible" and speaks not of automatically grasping the beings, but of a twice-removed striving—"trying to hunt the beings."[15] He expresses not resentment against the body as *the* insurmountable obstacle, but only recognition that it does not in itself lead to the goal, which is no longer identified as a condition of the separate psychē, but as phronēsis in conjunction with truth.

[66b1–67b6]   Socrates does not, however, explore his own interpretation of this somewhat cryptic account. Instead he offers to clarify the opinion of the "genuine philosohers" by imitating the speeches they might exchange—without explaining why they would have any desire for communication, given their understanding of phronēsis. As long as our psychē is mixed up with the evil of the body, the genuine philosophers complain,[16] we can never acquire sufficiently what we desire, namely "the true"; and "the true," as Socrates has them surmise at the end of their speech, is perhaps that, released from the body after death, being pure, "we shall through ourselves know all the pure."[17] Their claim to be led to this insight by some kind of "short-cut" may be a sign of their awareness of its inexplicability: apparently conversing while alive, "in the body," how could they justify the truth of the claim that the body prevents all possible access to the truth?

But it is the body, they are convinced, that produces loves, desires, fears, and illusions; it demands money for its needs and is *the* cause of wars and factions. The genuine philosophers seem to have misdirected their anger and resentment. They are eager to cast blame on the body not only for the distractions of the senses and the passions, but also for political opinions and economic conditions. They have mistaken all internal dissension within the psychē for dissension between the pure psychē and the alien body. Because it interrupts any rare moment of leisure, the genuine philosophers conclude, the body makes it almost impossible to think at all. Reducing every obstacle to a corporeal one, while identifying the self with the psychē, the genuine philosophers absolve themselves of all responsibility for their inability to obtain the phronēsis they desire. But this is precisely the condition for what Socrates will later attack as the greatest evil: to maintain a false standard of absolute wisdom, while refusing to acknowledge one's own deficiency, results in that resentment against logos through which one deprives oneself of the very possibility of seeking truth and knowledge of the beings (cf. 90c–d).

If phronēsis were indeed what the genuine philosophers believe, either it could not be acquired at all or it could be acquired only after death. The genuine philosophers can claim, therefore, only to be as close as possible to knowledge by keeping as purified as possible from the contamination of the body "until the god releases us." Yet the value of this preparation is unintelligible, for if death itself is a release of the psychē from the body, it must automatically lead to the goal consisting of union of "the pure with the pure." When Socrates concludes his imitation by attributing these opinions to all "correct lovers of learning,"[18] he ironically casts judgment on their position: between a lifetime of deception guaranteed by communion with the body and an afterlife of wisdom guaranteed by separation of the psychē, why should learning be necessary, and how could it be possible at all?

[67b7–68c4]   If there is any truth in this speech, Socrates reflects with restraint:

> there is much hope that one, arriving where I am traveling, there if anywhere, would sufficiently acquire that which has been the object of much concern for us in this life, so that the journey now imposed on me is begun with good hope, and for any other man who believes he has prepared his thought (dianoia) as if having been purified. (67b–c)

The genuine philosophers long to possess "there," that for the sake of which Socrates has lived "here"; but whether their hope for a purified psychē that could be in communion with the pure beings after death is identical with "preparation of dianoia" remains in question. Purification not of the psychē but of thought itself requires, as Socrates discloses in the course of the conversation, separation not from the body alone but from the self and its passions, including the fear of death and correlative hope for immortality.

Socrates believes that he has prepared his thought *as if* having been purified, and he referred previously to that knowledge of the beings that is "most purely" pursued by one who attempts to hunt each with thought alone (65e–66a); but he now claims that purification (*katharsis*) was "long ago in the *logos*" said to consist in the separation of the psychē from the body, "habituating itself to collect itself together from everywhere in the body."[19] Katharsis is an activity of "collection" and "division"; but the very terms that could describe the practice of "dialectics"[20]—which might indeed constitute the "preparation of *dianoia*"—are now applied to the psychē, in its attempt to release itself from the body "as from a prison," and to be alone by itself, both now and hereafter. Is this katharsis, Socrates asks, what we call "death"? Death, which was first defined as a separation of likes, of psychē from body as well as of body from psychē, is now redefined as a purification—that is, a separation of better from worse.[21] By emphasizing, however, that the question concerns what we *call* death, Socrates indicates his exploitation of its ambiguous meaning: the name that refers, on the one hand, to a physiological phenomenon, the destruction, namely, of the living being, has been applied, on the other hand, to the way of investigation practiced by the philosopher throughout his life.

Just that ambiguity underlies Socrates' repetition of the claim with which he began his defense: for the man who prepared himself by living as closely as possible to being dead, it would be laughable to fear death when it comes.[22] For if one's life were determined by the erōs of phronēsis, Socrates asks, would it not be irrational to fear what is acknowledged as the condition for its attainment? In order to explore this apparent absurdity, Socrates reminds his interlocutors of familiar stories: when "human loves"—boys or wives or sons—have died, many have willingly gone to Hades, led by the hope of seeing and being with the beloved there. But, given the ambiguous meaning of death defined as the separation of the psychē from the body, the lover's wish for communion in Hades—the invisible place[23]—would not arise simply with the termination of the life of his beloved, with whom he was once united but from whom he is now painfully separated; it points, rather, to the truth of erōs that always moved him—the unfulfilled longing for simultaneous contemplation and possession of the pure psychē of his beloved. The lover somehow recognizes the body as the obstacle to the fulfillment of his desire, without perhaps understanding what it would mean to see and be with a pure psychē. Socrates has discovered an illuminating model for the lover of phronēsis, who should not grieve when he dies, clinging to the hope that he will meet nowhere else but in Hades the object of his desire. Yet if he, like the human lover, construes erōs as a merely provisional route toward a goal, which could be overcome with the arrival at that goal, he would misunderstand its nature: the genuine philosophers misunderstood the nature of philosophy.

Now Socrates, of all men, might be thought the least susceptible to such a misunderstanding; yet his ability and willingness to defend philosophy as the practice of dying and being dead do seem to depend upon having lost or abandoned his lifelong "art of erotics."[24] But whereas the genuine philosophers' longing for death is based on a resentment of life that is unconditional, it is Socrates' awareness of his particular—political—circumstances that allows him to construe as a benefit his imminent release from the city, from the body, from life itself.[25] When Socrates concludes that a man who is troubled at the approach of death cannot be a lover of wisdom, he affirms the common ground he shares with the genuine philosophers. But he reveals its internal articulation when he adds that such a man must be a lover of the body, hence necessarily of money or honor or both;[26] for while Socrates would understand these desires as conflicting motives within the psychē,[27] the genuine philosophers deny the possibility of any internal dissension, just as they misunderstand the nature of erōs. They would want to oppose, then, to the lover of the body a "lover of psychē," but the latter is precisely the formula for one who clings to life at all costs.[28] It is, therefore, the appropriate, if paradoxical, label for those whose longing for death is motivated by hope for the survival of the separate psychē in contact with the beings themselves. That this hope is not the ground for Socrates' practice of dying and for his steadfast conduct in the face of death becomes the implicit argument of the final phase of his defense.

[68c5–69c3]   Simmias readily agrees—before any examination—that what is called courage is most characteristic of the philosopher, while superiority over the desires, which the many call moderation, is characteristic only of him. But since most men consider death to be the greatest of evils, Socrates reasons, those who face it bravely must do so through fear of even greater evils; they are courageous, although it is irrational (alogon), through fear and cowardice. And those among the many who are moderate refrain from present pleasures only because they fear being deprived of others: they are moderate, although it is said to be impossible, through incontinence. Socrates does not give a parallel account of courage resulting from fear and moderation resulting from desire but condemns both for coming into being through fear, either of greater pains or of deprivation of pleasures: demotic virtue, he suggests, is a flight from the reality of pain rather than a positive search for pleasure.[29] To bring out its irrationality, Socrates must juxtapose the speech of the many, which implies that the cause of any courageous action is courage itself, of any moderate action moderation itself, with the practice of the many, in which each purported virtue comes into being through its opposite. Demotic virtue, determined entirely by pleasure and pain,[30] furnishes one more model for the structure of opposition that Socrates first exemplified in describing the relation of pleasure and pain themselves; it exhibits precisely the perplexity that compelled Socrates, according to the report he will give of his own philosophic development, to abandon all investigation of the beings in order to preserve the safety of logos.[31]

As for his own conduct in the face of death, Socrates may display justice and prudence but apparently neither courage—since he claims not to count death among the greatest evils—

nor moderation—since he claims to have no desire for the pleasures he will be leaving behind.[32] The possible autonomy of
courage and moderation is indeed rendered problematic by
Socrates' concluding account of "true virtue together with
phronēsis."[33] He introduces this account through the metaphor
of monetary transaction: the correct exchange for acquiring
virtue cannot be that practiced by the many, in which pleasure
is exchanged against pleasure, pain against pain, and fear
against fear,[34] greater against less, as if they were coins; but the
only correct coin for which and with which all these are to be
bought and sold is phronēsis.[35] This image, which has understandably puzzled readers of the dialogue,[36] is in fact a most
appropriate form to mirror the content it expresses: the structure of monetary exchange is reflected, first in the structure of
metaphoric exchange, with money standing in the place of
phronēsis, while the latter is itself thereby described as belong-
ing to a context of exchange. The acquisition of money may be
the immediate end for which goods are sold, but its proper
function would be abused if taken to be solely an end in itself,
and not rather a medium for the exchange of goods. The proper
function of phronēsis, accordingly, is abused when construed—
as by the genuine philosophers—to be solely an end in itself,
separated from the exchange of the passions with one another.
For the latter, apart from phronēsis, is in reality, Socrates
maintains, a slavish sort of virtue, neither healthy nor true, a
kind of shadow-painting determined by the shifting appearances of pleasures, pains, and fears.[37]

From this illusion, Socrates concludes, the true virtue is
in reality some kind of purification (*katharsis tis*), as are
moderation and justice and courage, and phronēsis itself
some kind of purgation (*katharmos tis*). Socrates seems to
distinguish between the purified state constituted by true
virtue and the purgation by phronēsis through which that
state is achieved; he maintains his original obscurity about
the status of phronēsis, which was presented as both the
means by which virtue is to be acquired and a part of true
virtue—that which makes it possible to speak of virtue as a

whole.[38] He puts into question, in any case, the genuine philosophers' understanding of phronēsis as nothing but a goal to be awaited after death, when the pure psychē would be united with the pure beings. That goal could not be identified with the phronēsis Socrates now displays through his conduct in the face of death—the phronēsis that this entire speech is intended to defend.

[69c3–69e5]   Socrates began his defense by discovering, in the demotic opinion that the philosophers do indeed desire and deserve death, the truth of philosophy as the practice of dying. He concludes by uncovering the hidden meaning in the dark language of the mysteries, contrasting the uninitiated and unpurified who will lie in the mud in Hades with the initiated and purified who will dwell with the gods.[39] Appealing to the formula of initiation—"The thyrsus-bearers are many but the Bacchae are few"—Socrates surmises that the latter must be those who have correctly philosophized. He adopts the distinction within the mysteries between the many and the few only to imply a distinction between the philosophers, who are few, and the pious, who are many. That distinction is not made explicit until the myth Socrates addresses to Simmias at the end of the dialogue, to persuade him that "we must do our best to acquire virtue and phronēsis in life" (114c), which serves as a counterpart to the speech Socrates now addresses to Simmias in order to defend the phronēsis of his acceptance of death. Just as the first half of the dialogue consists in an inseparable mixture of "investigating and mythologizing," while the second half accomplishes their separation, Socrates' opening defense presents the philosopher through the mask of the pious ascetic, while the final myth explicitly separates them. For it contrasts the initiates who will dwell among the gods with those "sufficiently purified by philosophy" (114b–c). This sufficient purification consists, as Socrates will show, in the turn to a technē of logos that is designed to guarantee consistency in reasoning: it replaces the genuine philosophers' understanding of phronēsis as direct contact of the pure psychē with the pure beings.

To become one of those who have perfectly philosophized, Socrates admits at the end of his defense speech, he has striven throughout his life, though he may not have done so correctly. But it is only on this last day that he could acknowledge his eagerness "to have philosophized correctly"; to understand philosophy as a completed action seems to be a contradiction in terms. Socrates corrects it, however, at the moment he expresses it. For when he concludes that he may know shortly, if god is willing, whether or not he has striven correctly, what he confirms is his present knowledge of ignorance. In light of that admission, the belief he first expressed and now repeats—that he will find good masters "there no less than here"—must be intended less as a prediction of the unknown future than as a judgment of the present: "here" in the Athenian prison, Socrates' immediate master is the servant of the eleven, representative of the Athenian dēmos, and among the circle of his friends, Plato is absent. Socrates' speech is in fact a test of his judgment, for he completes it by repeating his hope that, in comparison with his public defense, this one will prove more persuasive—not necessarily more true. Socrates could hardly be more overt in acknowledging the status of his defense, without altogether defeating the rhetorical purpose he ascribes to it. That rhetorical purpose is necessitated by interlocutors who are moved by their own fear of death, together with pity at the imprudence, and anger at the injustice, of Socrates' acceptance of his own death. Precisely by representing these motivating grounds, the Platonic dialogue attempts to protect its reader from the persuasion Socrates claims to want to induce in his companions.

CHAPTER FOUR

Genesis

[69e6–70c3]   Socrates' defense apparently satisfies Simmias, who is silent at its conclusion, but Cebes immediately speaks up with an objection: however persuasively Socrates may have spoken of the philosopher's desire for the acquisition of phronēsis after death, he has simply presupposed the continued existence of the psychē. Yet men are filled with distrust, for they fear that, upon leaving the body, the psychē is no longer "anywhere" but is corrupted and destroyed when the man dies, dissipating like breath or smoke.[1] There would be good grounds for the great and beautiful hope Socrates expresses only if it could be shown that after death the psychē is gathered together "somewhere," itself by itself, freed from all the evils Socrates has just described. Cebes makes a reasonable criticism of the preceding speech; but he does not make the reasonable assumption that Socrates is equally aware of the problem and consequently, must have intentionally invited this distrust in the great and beautiful hope that his defense appears to offer.

Cebes has been preoccupied, perhaps, with the thought of what it will be like to look upon the corpse of Socrates, pure body itself, after the sudden disappearance of whatever made it alive. If psychē is anything more than the name for this quality of the body, then it too after death must be "somewhere," itself by itself. To be, Cebes assumes, means to be in some place;[2]

51

but that is the unique characteristic of a body, and the psychē, which is only a subtle form of body, like breath or smoke, must be especially subject to destruction. Cebes speaks as if the issue ought to be the object of a physicist's investigation. Yet he betrays the self-interest that motivates his question by limiting it to the fate of the human psychē. He earns Socrates' praise for speaking the truth when he guesses that no little encouragement or persuasion would be needed to show that the psychē of the dying man exists and has some power (dunamis) and phronēsis. Cebes does not specify what this power is that, in addition to phronēsis, remains after death. If he did, he would confront the contradiction that turns out to haunt the series of arguments that follows; for the power besides phronēsis that would ordinarily be thought to belong to psychē is its function as the cause of life.[3] It is no wonder that, despite his criticism of Socrates' defense speech, Cebes neglects as much as Socrates did to raise the question, "What is psychē?".[4]

Socrates responds to Cebes' challenge by asking what they should do. He inquires, more literally, "What shall we make?" and clarifies the question by asking if Cebes wishes to "mythologize" about what is likely.[5] He could not, now at any rate, Socrates insists, be accused even by a comic poet of chattering at leisure and making logoi that are of no concern to him. It was the accusation of a comic poet, according to Plato's *Apology of Socrates*, that inspired the long-standing prejudice against Socrates. The source of his condemnation by the Athenian dēmos was Aristophanes' portrayal of Socrates as an investigator of "things beneath the earth and above the heavens."[6] But this image, Socrates complains at his trial, makes him appear indistinguishable from Anaxagoras, and Socrates denies its truth, albeit with qualification: no one present ever heard him *speak* of such things.[7] He seems willing now, however, to confirm it; he will conclude the argument that follows, at least, with an allusion to the Anaxagorean cosmology.

That he was indeed attracted to the Anaxagorean project, Socrates will admit in the course of his intellectual autobiography. But he will disclose at the same time the disappointment that compelled him to find a replacement for Anaxagoras' teaching, and he now foreshadows that correction. For even if the forthcoming argument looks like an assimilation of Socratic to Anaxagorean philosophy, Socrates justifies it by the urgency of his concerns at the moment; and it is this very admission of his self-interest, Socrates indicates, that distinguishes him from Anaxagoras. It denies, at the same time, the Aristophanic charge against him as an "idle babbler,"[8] whose concern with things in the heavens and beneath the earth makes him blind to "the human things" right at his feet. Socrates' allusion to that Aristophanic charge brings to mind not only his public trial, but also his self-accusation this final day for his guilt in separating the greatest music from demotic music:[9] his reminder of Aristophanes does not by accident stand between his invitation to mythologize and his subsequent recommendation, that "it is necessary to investigate." Socrates introduces the first argument, which sets the pattern for the first half of the dialogue, as an inseperable mixture of mythos and logos, like pleasure and pain joined "in one head."

This opening argument is, perhaps, the most perplexing in the entire dialogue. In contrast with the subsequent arguments, which are more evidently determined by the unresolved problems preceding them, this first argument is the one Socrates seems to choose most freely. Yet it turns out to be surreptitiously determined by the beliefs of the genuine philosophers; and while Socrates is supposedly trying to defend those beliefs, he will in fact attempt to disclose their incoherence. That attempt, however, has no effect whatsoever on those to whom the argument is addressed. We are therefore deprived of the clues customarily provided by the responses of Socrates' interlocutors, since they do not say a word in response to this first argument, either immediately after its conclusion or as the conversation develops. There is, however, one individual—whom Phaedo cannot identify—who does not simply ignore the first argument: he objects that its fundamental assumption seems to be contradicted by that of the last argument, which brings the discussion full circle, back to its beginning. But it is not evident why Socrates is compelled to wait to provide the clarification he offers in response to that objection: he seems purposely to delay precisely the considerations that might have helped overcome the obscurities in the present speech.

This speech turns out to be an analysis of the logic of becoming, but it never specifies unambiguously what it is that undergoes *genesis*. While this first argument looks, at least to begin with, as if it is meant to be a Socratic "physics," it is paradoxically silent about body. This is especially surprising following immediately after the speech of the genuine philosophers, who never cease speaking of the body, even if only as the obstacle to the attainment of phronēsis. But in fact the first argument only carries out the radical consequences of the genuine philosophers' suppression of the body: it identifies the psychē with the living being, while inconsistently construing it as the neutral subject that can be alive or dead. Of course, with its silence about the body, the first argument must ignore the original definition of death as the separation of psychē from body. The change from being alive to being dead becomes, therefore, nothing but a change of place. Thus the suppressed body returns in the guise of psychē, whose only motion is locomotion.

Just because of the opposition that the anonymous interlocutor observes, the last argument brings to light what is conspicuously absent in the first. The genesis described in the last argument, accordingly, is the transformation of the living body into the corpse, the former distinguished from the latter by its "participation" in the *eidos* of life. The last argument thus reveals the silence of the first, not only about the body, but at the same time and with equally perplexing implications, about beings that are not subject to becoming: it is the one argument in the dialogue that never mentions the "ideas" in any form. It thus avoids simultaneously the question of how pyschē is related, on the one hand, to the body, on the other, to the objects of knowledge, although these two relations emerge together as the fundamental problem of the dialogue.

[70c4–70d9]   Socrates did warn Cebes before plunging into this argument that it would be some kind of "mythological investigation." That mixture is exemplified when Socrates re-

formulates Cebes' question as to whether the psychē is somewhere after death. Let us investigate it in this way, whether the
psychai of men who have died are in Hades or not. As a starting
point for this inquiry Socrates recalls "some kind of ancient
logos": they are there after arriving from here and then come
back here again, being born from the dead. Whatever kind of
logos it may be, this ancient tale describes a journey from this
world to another and back again, without mentioning what it
is that makes this journey—though it is presumably the
psychai[10]—and without explaining what "the dead" are from
which these travelers return to life again.

If this is true, Socrates ostensibly repeats, that the living
are born again from those who have died, then, he reasons,
"our psychai would be there."[11] Yet Socrates has transformed
the antecedent of the argument, replacing "the psychai born
from the dead" with "the living born again from those who
have died," as well as its consequent, replacing "the psychai of
men who have died" with "our psychai." Making use of this
transformation without explaining it, Socrates defends his reasoning: if our psychai did not continue to exist, they could not
be born again, so it would be "sufficient witness" that they
exist if it could really be made evident that the living come to
be from nothing but, and from nowhere else than, the dead;
otherwise, he admits, some other logos would be needed (cf.
76e, 106d). This generation of the living from the dead would
mean, in accordance with the original definition of death, the
coming to be united of separate psychē and body; but Socrates
conceals, as much as the ancient tale did, the role of the body,
hence the relation between the psychē born again and the living generated from the dead.

In presenting the strategy of the argument, Socrates anticipates its systematic confusion of two alternatives: either the
psychē is an enduring subject that undergoes a genesis from
one place to another, from Hades to the body and back again, or
there is a genesis of one thing, the living, into another, the
dead, and back again but with no enduring subject that persists
through the change. The dead, in any case—from nowhere else
but whence the living come to be—seem to be identified with

Hades itself, the invisible place (80d, 81a) appropriate for the separate psychē that is invisible but somewhere. Yet in sliding from the first consideration about the psychai of the dead to the subsequent one about our psychai, Socrates transforms the meaning of being "in Hades": it seems to be no longer the place of the psychē after death but rather a characterization of psychē as such, whenever it is, or perhaps, as Socrates suggested in the previous speech, whenever it is engaged in a particular mode of investigation.[12] Socrates may be interested only in demonstrating that our invisible psychai are; but in adjusting this aim to meet Cebes' challenge, he treats the being of the psychē simply as the condition for the possibility of coming back to life again.

The demonstration would be carried out most easily, Socrates advises, if considered with regard not only to men, but also to plants, animals, and everything that comes into being. Socrates does appear to display his Aristophanic image, conspicuously distant from the concern with "the human things" that might be considered his essential contribution to the philosophic tradition.[13] He seems to prepare his audience for the later account he will offer of his own philosophic development, beginning with the pre-Socratic investigation of nature and never turning to "the human things" in particular. Despite this initial appearance, however, the argument Socrates is about to conduct in fact examines not the nature of plants and animals, but the structure of any logos about becoming.

[70d9–71a11] Concerning everything that has genesis, Socrates begins, let us see if each necessarily comes into being from its opposite if, that is, there happens to be one. After offering as examples the beautiful and the ugly, or just and unjust, and "thousands of others"—opposites that do not seem to "have *genesis*" at all[14]—Socrates claims to repeat the original question. Only now, instead of asking whether everything that comes into being does so from its opposite, he asks whether everything that is an opposite necessarily comes to be from "nowhere else" than its own opposite.[15] Socrates does not insist, then, that all opposites do come into being, nor that everything that comes into being has an opposite, but only that any opposite that comes into being must do so from its opposite. Although he does not clarify the meaning of this "from," he preserves the general assumption of the argument by implying that one opposite is the place from whence the other emerges.

The restricted scope of the principle is confirmed, in any case, by Socrates' illustration of it on the model of comparatives: when something comes to be greater, it must first have been smaller, and if it later becomes smaller, it must first have been greater. Socrates does not argue that something that is small must necessarily become greater, or something great smaller, but only that something that does become greater or smaller must have previously been less so. The "now" in which something is said to have become greater is the same "now" that determines its having been smaller. To determine, as in Socrates' further examples, that something has become stronger, quicker, or better is simultaneously to determine that it must have been weaker, slower, or worse. A prior condition is not what it is until a posterior condition makes it so—like the painful revealed to be such only by comparison with the so-called pleasant that follows from it (cf. 60b).

The coming to be of a present "more" is by definition from a past "less," the coming to be of a present "less" by definition from a past "more": the principle is based on the necessity not of *phusis*, but of logos. Yet what is it exactly that does thereby come to be from its opposite? Socrates will attempt to clarify this principle only when it later emerges as an apparent contradiction of the final argument based on the principle of mutual exclusion of opposites. The generation of opposites from each other refers, Socrates will then explain, not to the opposite qualities themselves, which would lead to a violation of the law of noncontradiction, nor to the coming to be and passing away of a subject as such, which may not have an opposite, but rather, to the pragmata—like "Socrates greater" and "Socrates smaller"—each of which is the inseparably bonded union of a subject with one or two opposite qualities (cf. 102d–103b).[16] It is precisely this distinction between opposite pragmata and opposites themselves, however, that Socrates seems intentionally to suppress in the present argument. He has established the mutual generation of opposites, furthermore, only on the model of comparative states, without explaining whether or how this model can be applied to the generation of the living and the dead from each other, which is presumably the intention of the argument.

[71a12–71b11]   Socrates claims nevertheless to have established sufficiently that all things come to be in this way, opposite pragmata from their opposites. And since Cebes does not dispute it, Socrates proceeds to inquire whether there are between each member of a pair of opposites two geneseis, mediating processes from each to the other.[17] Before giving Cebes a chance to answer, Socrates offers the example of increase, the genesis from a smaller pragma to a greater, and decrease, the genesis from a greater pragma to a smaller. But since the standard in relation to which something becomes greater or smaller is not necessarily its own prior state, it could come to be one or the other of these opposites without either increasing or decreasing.[18] Simmias, Socrates later insists, comes to be greater when compared with Socrates who is smaller, smaller when compared to Phaedo who is greater (102b–e). The relational qualities Socrates chooses as examples thus put into question, rather than confirm, the necessary connection between opposite states and the geneseis mediating them. Perhaps dying, Socrates implies, cannot be connected with being dead, or being alive with having come to be so. Even to grant the connection, in any case, between one opposite state and the genesis leading to it does not entail a connection between that genesis and its opposite: even if something does become greater by increasing, it is not by definition true that it must have been previously decreasing, or conversely. It would be a mistake—which Socrates seems to have invited—to interpret his reference to two mediating geneseis as a claim about a continual cycle of alteration.

Whether or not we have names to designate these processes, Socrates inquires, is it not necessary in deed that there be "everywhere" a genesis from one opposite to the other? Cebes is certain of this, without asking Socrates to clarify what the subject is of these geneseis. But while increase and decrease, Socrates' first example, or cooling and heating, his last example, refer by definition to the becoming greater or smaller, cooler or hotter, of one subject, Socrates' central example, the geneseis of separation and combination, does not seem to fit this pattern. For, strictly speaking, at least two units would be required for combination, while one unit would be the subject of separation (cf. 96e, 97b): if dying is a separation, it is the living being as a whole that undergoes that genesis, and if coming to life is, by analogy, a combination, two separate entities would undergo that genesis. This central example thus points to the unspecified alternative at stake in the argument from the outset. For combination and separation seem to be the geneseis through which the living and the dead would come to be from each other, with no identical subject enduring through the cycle, rather than geneseis mediating between the states of being alive and being dead, which would characterize the psychē as one enduring subject.[19]

[71c1–71e3]   Socrates has spoken only of cases in which the coming to be of one opposite is by definition the passing away of the other. Since, however, the scope of this model may be too restricted for its intended application,[20] Socrates begins his attempt to supplement it by proposing an analogy. Is there something, he asks, that is the opposite of being alive, just as being asleep is the opposite of being awake? Cebes responds, "Being dead," as quickly as Simmias responded to Socrates' original question, whether we believe that death is something (64c). He does not stop to consider the possibility that there may be no opposite state applicable to a thing characterized as "being alive"; whether life has an opposite is still an open question, apparently, in the final argument (105d). Nor does Cebes consider the possibility that the only opposite of "living" is simply the negation, "not-living."[21] Of course in that case, the claim that one comes to be from the other might appear to be a claim that something comes into being from nothing, and it is the intention of this argument to preclude just such a possibility.

If being alive and being dead are opposites, Socrates reasons—without confirming this condition—they must come to be from each other and have two geneseis mediating between them. But while dying appears to be a genesis from one opposite state to another, Socrates has not shown that there is an existing subject that is dead after having come to be so. Being born, on the other hand, is not by definition the genesis from one opposite state to another, and Socrates has not identified a subject that exists before coming to be alive. He could have done so, one might think, by emphasizing the difference between conception and birth. Such a proposal calls attention, of course, to what the entire argument seeks to avoid, namely the origin of a living animal through sexual reproduction. It points, at the same time, to the lack of symmetry between birth and death. For what would be parallel, in the case of dying, to the interval between conception and birth? In fact, however, the distinction between conception and birth only pushes the problem back a step and leaves the origin of a living animal as problematic as its destruction. For it does not solve the mystery of what psychē is and how it is related to the body.

Socrates attempts to cover over these difficulties by relying on his proposed analogy. It is indeed a powerful one,[22] since sleep, at least a deep unconscious sleep, may be the closest experience we have of what death is. But Socrates must now conceal what the poets have long recognized when they imagine death as the long sleep from which we do not awaken. Being awake, Socrates proceeds, comes to be from its opposite, being asleep, just as the latter does from the former; and they are necessarily mediated by the geneseis of falling asleep, which, by definition, means being no longer awake, and re-awakening, which, by definition, means being no longer asleep.[23] Now Socrates wants Cebes to apply this model to "the other," the pair, namely, life and death. Since, however, these are opposites that do not seem to "have *genesis*" at all, Socrates does not ask about their necessary generation from each other but instead repeats their former agreement on the opposition between being alive and being dead. The analogy with the living animal that undergoes the cycle of being awake and being asleep should indicate that the psychē undergoes the cycle of being alive and being dead. But rather than ask about the geneseis mediating between these opposite states of one subject, Socrates transforms the question into one about the generation of one subject from its opposite.

What is it, he inquires, that comes to be from the living? Had Cebes thought about our most common human experience, he might have chosen this point to challenge the assumptions of the argument. He might have asked Socrates why they do not simply acknowledge that it is the living who come to be from the living, and that it is not the individual but the species that endures through the genesis.[24] But Cebes feels compelled by the argument to answer, "The dead." In response to Socrates' complementary question, "And what from the dead?", he betrays his sense of this compulsion: "It is necessary to agree that it is the living." As if to emphasize its inappropriateness as a demonstration of the existence of the human psychē after death, Socrates repeats only half the conclusion, while acknowledging its unlimited application: "Then from the dead, the living—both things and persons—come to be." With Cebes' unenthusiastic admission that it appears so, Socrates draws the consequence he first presented as its necessary condition: "Then our psychai are in Hades." Cebes admits, with the same reluctance, that it seems so. For if he sees no way to attack the argument, he must certainly feel dissatisfied: Socrates' conclusion in the present tense seems to describe not the fate of the psychē after death, but the nature of the psychē that is always "in the invisible."

[71e4–72a10]   Socrates reaches this conclusion without having established the actuality of two mediating geneseis. He now returns to that consideration with the claim that one of these processes can be accepted "For dying is surely evident, isn't it?". Since the existence of the psychē as dead is precisely what is in question, hence the genesis defined as a transition to that state, Socrates unexpectedly refers to the evidence of dying rather than of being born. What would have to be evident, however, is not birth as such, but a process through which something comes to be alive after first being dead. This genesis can be affirmed, therefore, only if the opposite genesis of coming to be dead is simply assumed. And even then it requires a hypothesis that is more a construction than discovery, as Socrates indicates by his question—the same one with which he began the argument (70b)—"What shall we make?". "Must we not deliver back in turn (antapodōsomen) the opposite genesis," Socrates inquires, "or shall nature be lame?".[25] Inspired by Socrates' model of reawakening (anegeiresthai) as the opposite of falling asleep, Cebes is willing to give back to dying its opposite genesis, "coming back to life again" (anabiōskesthai). He does not ask why nature must be symmetrical, nor why that requires the return to life as the opposite of dying in the cycle of one identical subject. Their agreement, Socrates soon confirms, was made "not unjustly." It projects the notion of human justice, Socrates implies, onto natural genesis. The translation of birth into coming back to life is thus shown to be motivated by the desire to construe it as a just punishment, the penalty for the crime of attachment to life.[26]

Socrates confirms the hypothetical status of their agreement—*if* there is coming back to life—while asking whether it would not constitute the genesis from the dead into the living. But he conspicuously avoids the question of what "the dead" are when he concludes that, in this way too, it can be agreed that the living come to be from the dead, no less than the dead from the living. Had he admitted that the latter has been simply assumed, along with the assumed self-evidence of the genesis of dying, he could not claim, as he does, to have established

a "sufficient witness" that "the psychai of the dead are somewhere from whence they come back again." Socrates has not
forgotten his own warning that the argument would require
mythologizing as well as investigating. For the being of the
psychai of the dead "somewhere" seems to be an opposite that
follows upon their existence in the body while living, like pleasure and pain joined in two heads, according to a mythos, such
that one always follows upon the other. The being, on the
other hand, of *our* psychai in Hades, the invisible place, must
represent that "practice of dying," which attempts to separate
psychē from body while alive, like pleasure and pain joined in
one head, according to the Socratic account, such that the pursuit of one is almost always accompanied by the other. The
two alternative conclusions in the first argument thus echo the
competing interpretations of Socrates' initial defense, construing purification as the fate of the psychē after death, on the one
hand, and as a mode of investigation not reducible to perception, on the other (cf. 70c–d). Of course, the first argument,
since it has never even raised the question of what psychē is,
could hardly make these alternative interpretations explicit. It
thus appears, to Cebes at least, to neglect his question about
whether the psychē possesses phronēsis after death, and hence
to be radically incomplete.[27]

[72a11–72e2]   Cebes is willing to admit only that it looks to
him as if their conclusion follows from previous agreements.
But since they have only hypothetically posited the genesis of
coming back to life, Socrates engages in one last effort to defend the justice—not necessarily the truth—of the agreements
on which that hypothesis was based. If genesis did not always
proceed in a circle,[28] Socrates reasons, from opposite to opposite and back again, then finally everything would have the
same figure (*schēma*), would suffer the same condition (pathos), and would cease coming into being at all.[29] Socrates does
not say why this consequence must be rejected. He intends,
presumably, only to present an argument for the conditional
necessity of a cyclical structure of becoming: it guarantees the

impossibility of genesis exhausting itself in a linear development toward one state that would preclude all determinacy.[30]
Socrates claims to be surprised when Cebes does not understand what he means; although he seems to have compressed
into a single statement his reflection on the fundamental principles of pre-Socratic thought, Socrates assures Cebes that it is
nothing difficult!

If, he explains, there were only falling asleep and no wak-
ing up, the myth of Endymion would be nonsense, the youth
who falls asleep forever would appear "nowhere." To be, Socrates implies, is to be something, and that is, in the language of
this argument, to be somewhere: Socrates preserves the contradictory character of an argument that never mentions the body
yet identifies something being *what* it is with its being in some
place. Now Socrates is presumably trying to prove that an irreversible process in a closed system leads eventually to a standstill in which no particular condition can be differentiated
from its opposite. He seems to argue only that Endymion
would be indistinguishable from everything in the same state
unless some one of the things that fall asleep were to wake up
again; he does not explicitly insist that everything that falls
asleep, including Endymion, must necessarily wake up again.
Yet, an eternally sleeping Endymion would have to be alive,
but without motion, without desire or thought. Endymion
seems to illustrate the genuine philosophers' paradoxical wish
for an eternally existing psychē that is transformed into a being
and is therefore no longer a psychē.

In the same way, Socrates continues, if all things were
mixed together and nothing separated, there would quickly
come to be that chaos—*homou panta chrēmata*—that Anaxagoras describes as the original state of the cosmos.[31] It is only,
according to the Anaxagorean cosmology, with the appearance
of mind (*nous*), which initiates motion, and hence separation,
that the determinacy of things is rendered possible.[32] In making his cosmic nous responsible for motion and discrimination,
Anaxagoras indicates the twofold function of psychē, though

without acknowledging the dependence of nous on psychē. Socrates himself, then, has just performed a combination guided by "mind": he has not by accident put together the eternally sleeping Endymion and the cosmic chaos of all things mixed together, which are linked by the absence of psychē. This juxtaposition is meant, furthermore, to illustrate the end state of an irreversible process: Socrates implicitly reproaches Anaxagoras for not recognizing that combination is itself a process that presupposes a prior state of separation,[33] and that, if mind is the cause of one genesis, it must be no less the cause of the other. In fact, as Socrates will argue in his later criticism of Anaxagoras, the operation of mind should be guided by the good; but it is the good and binding that truly hold all things together (99c). Yet, if the ordering of mind were unobstructed, and the goal of Anaxagorean teleology realized, Socrates seems now to suggest, it would have the same results as the mindless state of original chaos. For a closed system that progresses in only one of two opposite directions with no recycling must inevitably come to a standstill in which no further discrimination of one thing from another is possible.

Socrates has laid the groundwork for the final application of the principle of opposite geneseis. If all living things were to die, he inquires, and the dead were to remain in that condition without coming back to life, isn't it most necessary that in the end all things would be dead and nothing alive? To defend this necessity, Socrates asks what would happen if the living were generated from "the others." He presumably means anything other than the dead but tacitly points to the alternative that has been suppressed throughout the argument: that from which the living are generated are "the other living."[34] But Socrates must want Cebes to discover this alternative himself. If the living were to die, he repeats, and not be regenerated from the dead, is there any way out of the conclusion that everything would in the end by swallowed up in death? Cebes sees no way out: he is unwilling to accept what appears to be the only alternative, namely, that the living could come to be

in the strict sense, from nothing.[35] That the continuation of
genesis could be guaranteed by an infinite source, he simply
assumes to be impossible.[36]

But why does Cebes believe this is the only alternative?
Why does he not suggest that the function Socrates assigns to
coming back to life could be fulfilled by the generation of the
living from the living? Having submitted so thoroughly to the
premises of the argument and to its seemingly inexorable logic,
Cebes has become blind to the most evident facts of experience; having assimilated, perhaps without realizing it, the
genuine philosophers' disdain for the body, he has completely
forgotten about sexual reproduction, the process through
which life rejuvenates itself.[37] Socrates did preface the argument by recommending the consideration of plants, animals,
and all things that have genesis; but the principle that all opposites are generated from opposites has led to a suppression of
the essential characteristic of living things, which are as a
species self-reproducing. In the absence of that consideration,
Cebes has been forced to affirm coming back to life as the
opposite of dying, to preclude the possibility of everything ending up dead.

But is this to be regarded as a reductio ad absurdum because it contradicts our experience? It would seem possible at
any moment simply to claim that the source of genesis hasn't
been used up yet. Of course, it has been assumed all along that
something cannot come from nothing, hence that genesis has
no beginning, and an infinite stretch of time behind the present
moment would guarantee that the end state would already
have been realized. Socrates seems, however, to have conflated
a cosmological argument for the eternity of becoming with an
argument about the conditions for intelligibility in logos. For
he has emphasized another way in which it would be absurd to
speak of everything ending up dead. Since coming to be is
always coming to be something, if everything were to have the
same schēma or pathos, it would be impossible to speak of
anything becoming or being *what* it is. "Death" is significant,
then, only as the opposite of life and would be meaningless in

the absence of that opposition. But Socrates has only mentioned opposite determinations like life and death, the just and the unjust, the beautiful and the ugly, without articulating their status: his pre-Socratic argument, which eliminates coming to be in the strict sense—that is, from nothing—at the same time reduces being to eternal becoming.[38] Socrates intends to show, perhaps—although none of his interlocutors grasp this intention—that a coherent account of the genesis of opposite pragmata from each other depends upon the postulation of "opposites themselves," which are ungenerated and indestructible.[39]

Socrates offers this first argument about the coming to be and passing away of a living being as his response to Cebes' challenge about the existence of the psychē after death. The entire discussion that follows thus appears to be a digression until the final argument, called forth by another challenge from Cebes, which Socrates interprets as a demand for an analysis of the cause of coming to be and passing away as a whole (95e). Socrates will respond to an attack against the apparent contradiction between these arguments by distinguishing the mutually exclusive opposites themselves that are the subject of the last from the mutually generating opposite pragmata that are the subject of the first. He seems to contend that the two arguments that frame the entire series are complementary. But that contention conceals the fact that their presuppositions and conclusions are incompatible: while the argument on the cycle of opposites presumably demonstrates the existence of the psychē as alternately living and dead, that is precisely what will be denied by the final argument.

Socrates nevertheless concludes the first argument, as he will the last (107a), with the same expression of certainty:

> For it is, as it seems to me, Cebes, in this way above all, and we are not deceived in agreeing on these things, but there really is coming back to life, and from the dead the living come to be, and the psychai of the dead are.[40] (72d–e)

Socrates completes both arguments by affirming the existence of the psychē after death "really" (tō onti), literally "in being."[41] But the movement of the dialogue is an attempt to put any such claim into question. This is made explicit in the central interlude, which begins by describing the danger of resentment of logos and ends by introducing, as the only escape from that danger, the necessity of a turn from investigation of the beings to investigation through logoi. Perhaps it is only if reconstructed in accordance with this turn that the present conclusion ought to be affirmed: at the moment the dialogue is taken up by its reader, Socrates comes back to life—although not, as he agreed to demonstrate, "somewhere," not "in being" but "in *logos*."

CHAPTER FIVE

Anamnēsis

[72e3–74a8]   Cebes joins in immediately after the conclusion of Socrates' first argument but without saying a word about it. Instead, he reveals his dissatisfaction by simply introducing another argument; this one too, he believes will show that "the psychē seems to be something immortal." Perhaps Cebes realizes, despite his reference to another way of proving immortality, that Socrates never mentioned the word in the first argument.[1] If being born is nothing but coming back to life, Socrates has just argued, then our psychai must exist somewhere after death from whence they come back again. If, Cebes now adds, there is truth in Socrates' customary claim that our learning is nothing but recollection, then we must have learned in some prior time what we now only recall, and that would be possible only if the psychē were somewhere before coming into being in the human form (eidos).[2] That all birth is nothing but coming back to life revives Cebes' dormant memory that all learning is nothing but recollection: the denial that life comes into being in the strict sense—that something comes to be from nothing—brings to mind the denial that knowledge comes into being in the strict sense, from absolute ignorance.

Cebes introduces an argument that reproduces in its formal structure the argument he has just heard from Socrates. But Socrates' argument gave no indication of what the psychē is, or what it does, either in Hades or "here." It unfolded the

69

consequences of the genuine philosophers' belief in the separability of the psychē from the place it happens to inhabit; but it ignored their understanding of phronēsis as the condition of the psychē when released from the body and in contact with the pure beings to which it is akin. Cebes now intends to make up for that limitation. But while he might think that the teaching of the genuine philosophers is supported by the following argument, it is in fact completely undermined by it. Whereas they speak of death, or the separation of psychē from body, as the condition for the acquisition of phronēsis, the recollection argument supposedly accounts for the possibility of learning throughout life, when the psychē is united with the body, and particularly as a result of perception.

This is not the only difficulty of which Cebes is unaware. He seems to believe that recollection is awakened by both perception and Socratic questioning; but he is not concerned about how to understand the relation between these. He takes the recollection doctrine to be the perfect assimilation of Socratic inquiry and the genuine philosophers' notion of phronēsis, without recognizing the problematic assumptions he holds about each, let alone the fundamental incompatibility between them. Nevertheless—or rather, precisely because of this limited understanding—the recollection argument will turn out to be the only one in the entire conversation that both Cebes and Simmias wholeheartedly endorse. It is, therefore, *the* tool that Socrates shamelessly exploits: he need only appeal to the recollection thesis, and his interlocutors will immediately give up any opinions they believe conflict with it. Socrates takes advantage of their acceptance, despite the fact that it is based upon unexamined, and even preposterous, assumptions about the psychē, knowledge, and the objects of knowledge. In fact, Socrates even uses their acceptance of the argument to undercut the very assumptions on which it is based.

As soon as Cebes mentions the doctrine of recollection, Simmias interrupts to ask for the demonstrations that will remind him of it: he wants an enactment in deed of the theory about learning of which Cebes speaks. The sign, Cebes reminds him, that the learner possesses in himself knowledge

and correct logos—he does not say whether these are identical—is his ability to answer for himself when questioned
beautifully by another, an ability most clearly illustrated by
the use of mathematical constructions.[3] This very reminder
Cebes considers "most beautiful"; yet he certainly does not
ask any questions through which Simmias could discover the
truth for himself but simply expects him to trust a doctrine he
had heard before. Socrates naturally expresses concern, therefore, with Simmias' possible distrust of the proposition that
so-called learning is really recollection. And Simmias, not despite, but because of, denying his distrust, justifies that concern: he admits that he already begins to remember, hence to
be persuaded—not to learn.

Dissatisfied, apparently, with Cebes' enactment of recollection, Socrates takes over. But he does not bolster our confidence in the thesis when he seeks Simmias' agreement that, if
anyone remembers anything, he must have previously known
it. For knowing is here presented as the condition for remembering, when remembering is supposed to explain how knowledge comes into being. Socrates cannot, in any case, have a
precise sense of "knowing" in mind when he refers to it as a
condition for remembering: Simmias has just remembered a
doctrine he previously heard, without necessarily having understood it. Socrates nevertheless uses the word for scientific
knowledge (epistēmē). But he does not clarify its meaning
when he seeks Simmias' further agreement that, if someone
has seen or heard or perceived something in any way and recognizes not only that but also some other thing of which the
knowledge is not the same, he must recollect the other thing
that he has in mind. Socrates does not say only that the recollected object is other, but also that the knowledge of it is other,
distinguished, presumably, from the perception that awakens
it; he had originally claimed only that recollection requires
knowledge that is prior. This difficulty turns out to haunt the
entire argument, which is precisely an attempt to translate
knowledge other than, but related to, perception into another
time of acquiring it.

Although knowledge of a man, Socrates explains, is other

than knowledge of a lyre, whenever a lover sees the lyre or cloak or any possession of his beloved, the perception of it awakens in his thought the form (eidos) of the boy to whom it belongs. The term that we expect should designate the noetic "form" awakened by perception, refers in fact to the body of the beloved imagined by his lover at the sight of something that belongs to him. It is erōs or desire, Socrates implies, that forges the link between a present perception and an absent object of thought.[4] The lover's idealization of his beloved spreads from the eidos of the boy to all his possessions. He projects what is really his own longing for the boy onto the objects that awaken that longing, and his unawareness of that projection is the condition for his idealization. Socrates does not say why this should be the primary model for the recollection thesis. But it brings to mind his earlier account of the lover of phronēsis, based on the model of the human lover who would willingly follow his beloved to Hades in the hope of seeing and being with his pure psychē (68a). It is no accident, then, that Socrates' apparently arbitrary examples of the lyre and the cloak, which point beyond themselves to the beloved, happen to be precisely what Simmias and Cebes will choose as images of the body, which points beyond itself to the psychē (85e–86b, 87b–e).

Like the lover's recollection of his beloved, Socrates proceeds, the thought of Cebes is often awakened by the sight of Simmias; and thousands of other cases, Simmias swears by Zeus, thinking perhaps of countless other inseparable pairs of young men. This experience occurs mostly, Socrates admits, when the object has been forgotten through time or inattention. But the required "otherness" of the reminder and that of which it is a reminder is not dependent on temporal distance necessarily: recollection of a man can arise from seeing a picture of a lyre or horse, recollection of Cebes from seeing a picture of Simmias, or finally, recollection of Simmias himself from his own picture. In the cases preceding the last, the link between the present perception and the thought it awakens depends upon subjective associations in the observer; only in the last case does it seem to belong necessarily to the image itself. Of course, one would "know" the image only if one knows Simmias, and just for that reason, it is unclear how it could satisfy the condition that knowledge of what is recollected be other than knowledge of what causes the recollection.[5] In fact Socrates slides almost imperceptibly from speaking of the otherness of a present perception and absent object of thought to speaking of their likeness or unlikeness.

He seems to go out of his way to observe that recollection can be aroused by a reminder that is unlike that to which it points, as well as by that which is like it. But he concludes that only the latter case entails consideration of the adequacy of the likeness that serves as a reminder. Socrates thus confirms that his last example was the crucial one. In looking at the picture of Simmias, one is indeed reminded of what is missing: the image falls short of that which it imitates by the absence of psychē. If it were not for that absence, there would simply be two "Simmiases";[6] what distinguishes the portrait from that which it represents is life. Socrates speaks only of our awareness of the defectiveness of the image. But the example he chooses suggests just the opposite—that it is possible, namely, for an image to arouse resentment of the defectiveness of that which is represents:[7] in contemplating the perfection of the portrait, one would recognize the mortality of the living being.[8] What might indeed be aroused by this contemplation is the contradictory longing for an eternally existing psychē, as untouched by life as a portrait is.

[74a9–74d8]   Socrates invites Simmias to investigate whether any such defectiveness is at stake when we perceive equal pieces of wood or stone but speak of something other, "the equal itself." The argument, Socrates will shortly inform Simmias, is concerned just as much with any other "itself by itself" as it is with "the equal itself." Why, then, is this example given such prominence? If a present perception serves as a reminder, Socrates has just explained, because of its likeness to an absent object of thought, it may also be thought to fall short of it. The one is to be measured against the standard of the other; its aim is to be "equal" to that standard. Of course, the closer the image comes to being a perfect image, the more it approaches identity with that of which it is an image, thus annihilating itself as an image. Now Socrates might seem to have avoided this problem by translating identity into equality, a qualitative determination into a quantitative one. In fact he points to the problematic status of the notion of equality, which presupposes the simultaneous identity and difference of that which it relates. Since equality seems to require at least two relata, how can there be "the equal itself"?

But Socrates is not dogmatic. Shall we say, he asks Simmias, that this equal itself is something or nothing? Just as he first affirmed our belief that death is something before considering what it is (64c), Simmias now enthusiastically asserts, with an oath by Zeus, that we say the equal itself is something, before affirmatively responding to Socrates' subsequent question as to whether we know what it is.[9] Socrates proceeds to test that response, therefore, by asking whether it is from seeing equal pieces of wood or stone that we derive knowledge of the equal itself that is other—if, that is, it does appear other to Simmias. But since Socrates does not explain what it would mean for the equal itself to appear (*phainesthai*) at all, he gives Simmias no chance to answer. He proceeds instead to describe the way equal pieces of wood or stone, while being the same, sometimes appear equal to one but not to another.[10] He does not deny that phenomena that appear equal to each other can truly be so; for it is sufficient, apparently, to agree that they appear and really are equal in some, but not every, respect,[11] in order to distinguish them from "the equals themselves" (*auta ta isa*), which never appear unequal, like equality, which never appears to be inequality.

Simmias, who was confident of knowing what the equal itself is, does not seem disturbed at its sudden replacement by the plural, equals themselves, nor with the problem of their relation to equality. He does not question whether that "other" to which he claims equal pieces of wood or stone point is to be understood as the characteristic, equality, or as a paradigmatic instance of what is thus characterized, the equals

themselves. These equals themselves, which never appear unequal, are the product resulting from an operation of abstraction. To determine that the sticks and stones are equal requires
an act of counting or measuring; if one then "takes away" all
the other qualities that characterize the phenomena, all that is
left is the mathematical determination in regard to which they
are equal, their number or magnitude.[12] Yet, once the sticks
and stones have been stripped of every characteristic that
makes each one distinct, once they have been turned into the
pure members of the class of equals themselves, how can any
one be distinguished from another? How can there be a plurality of, say, one inches or ones?

As soon as the members of the class of equals themselves
are produced, they threaten to collapse into the unintelligibly
singular equal itself. This operation of successive abstraction
thus results in another version of the perplexity involved in the
thought of a perfect image, which would be indistinguishable
from what it represents. Simmias could be differentiated from
his portrait by the presence of psychē. But the problem underlying the series of arguments in the first half of the dialogue is
whether psychē itself measures up to the standard of the beings, with which it should display its kinship after death, when
it is freed from the contamination of the body. If, however, it
were to become "equal" to its desired object of knowledge, the
pure psychē would become a being "itself by itself" indistinguishable from any other and would cease to be psychē.

It is no accident that Socrates prepared for the discussion
of the equal itself by first offering the example of Simmias and
his portrait; but Simmias himelf is entirely unaware of the
questions implicitly raised by that move. And Socrates simply
takes advantage of his passivity when he asks whether the
equal itself is the same as "those equals," without specifying
whether he refers to equal phenomena or the so-called equals
themselves. When Simmias replies inappropriately, but following Socrates' lead, that they never *appear* the same to him,
Socrates repeats the question he at first suppressed—whether
our knowledge of "that equal" is conceived and grasped from

"those equals." Simmias agrees immediately to the derivative status of our knowledge of the equal itself, without inquiring whether it is from perceptible phenomena or from a mathematical model that such knowledge is said to be derived.[13]

Without resolving this ambiguity, Socrates inquires further about the way equal pieces of wood and "the equals of which we were just speaking" appear to us equal. Do they fall short of being like the equal itself or nothing? Socrates suggests the possibility, once again, that there is no unique being "itself by itself" of which members of the class of equals are an inferior likeness. For what is paradigmatically equal could only be the members designated as "the equals themselves,"[14] and their superiority would be nothing but their abstraction from every other aspect of equal phenomena. "The equal itself," on the other hand, is the formula Socrates is about to generalize when he refers to "the what it is" that we posit as the object of investigation in questioning and answering. Socrates suppressed recognition of the act of counting or measurement required for the designation of phenomena as equal; he only hints at the activity that is required for positing in logos the being of the equal itself.

[74d9–75d6]   Simmias is convinced, in any case—without needing any argument—that the others fall far short of the equal itself. Socrates proceeds, therefore, to describe the experience of someone who supposes that what he sees "wishes" to be like some other of the beings but is unable to and must remain inferior. Isn't this just what we have suffered, Socrates inquires, with regard to the equals and the equal itself? Despite Simmias' certainty, this is not at all the experience they have undergone. Socrates and Simmias have not perceived any phenomena that could be judged to be an inferior instance of equality; they have been simply constructing an account in speech. Simmias is utterly unaware of the effects on that account of their own speaking.

Socrates, meanwhile, has emphasized the pathos suffered by one who perceives things in this way: the characterization of phenomena as willing to be like a perfect paradigm of the determinations ascribed to them in a pathos undergone by the person who makes that ascription. And the paradigm to which he refers must, as Socrates will soon reveal, belong in some way to the psychē itself: to perceive phenomena as inferior to their perfect model betrays resentment of the inferior condition of the embodied psychē, suffering from forgetfulness of knowledge that is rightly its own (cf. 76e). Erōs does indeed seem to be the appropriate, if concealed, model for the recollection thesis, which has proven to be an account of the unwitting projection of the will onto that which is thought to be independent.[15] It is no accident that Socrates first describes this experience before arguing for the necessity of prior knowledge of the standard to which perceptible phenomena are allegedly referred.

Before we began to see or hear or perceive in any other way, Socrates will soon conclude, we must have somewhere grasped knowledge of "the equal itself, what it is," to which we refer the equals perceived through the senses, recognizing that they eagerly desire to be like it but are inferior. Before he reaches that conclusion, however, Socrates seeks Simmias' agreement that the deficiency of phenomena striving to be like the equal is brought to mind by nothing but sight or touch or some other of the senses. Simmias does not ask why prior knowledge of the noetic standard is required if the phenomena display their own defectiveness to the senses, all of which, he agrees, can be treated alike for the purpose of the argument. He does not notice Socrates' sudden omission of hearing from his list of the senses; but hearing is the condition of speech, and that is precisely what links the perceptible phenomena with the "much-babbled about" names that Socrates, like the poets, is constantly drumming into our ears (cf. 65b, 76d, 100b). It is, moreover, through hearing, not through sight or any other sense, that Simmias is being "reminded" of the recollection thesis; Simmias' self-forgetfulness calls our attention to the conspicuously absent consideration in the argument of speech or logos.

Socrates has good reasons, in any case, for gaining Simmias' assent to the claim that we possess knowledge of the
equal itself before using our senses, which we employ from the
moment of birth; for only then can he deduce that such
knowledge must have been acquired "as it seems" before we
were born. We must, in that case, have acquired before birth
and known at the moment of birth, not only the equal itself
and the greater and smaller,[16] but all such, for the present
logos, Socrates now acknowledges, is concerned no more with
the equal than with the beautiful and the good and the just and
the holy.[17] Yet just when he seems to have admitted the existence of a "second world" of noetic beings beyond that of
perceptible phenomena, Socrates suddenly articulates his own
understanding of the "itself by itself," which puts such an
interpretation into question. That which "it seems" we must
have come to know before birth is, according to Socrates' present formulation, nothing but that which we stamp with the
seal of "the what it is,"[18] through questioning in questions and
answering in answers.[19] What the recollection thesis identifies
as the object of a passive "noetic vision" by the pure psychē,
Socrates understands as the product of, and condition for, the
activity of inquiry. Yet he does transform the question, "What
is it?", the distinguishing mark of Socratic inquiry,[20] from the
interrogative to the indicative mode: the context of the recollection thesis calls for the replacement of a true question with
what seems to be an illusory answer.[21]

[75d7–76d6]   Had Socrates established the necessity of acquiring knowledge of the beings themselves prior to the use of our
senses, he could presumably have concluded that the psychē
must exist with phronēsis before birth, and that all subsequent
learning is really recollection. But one further condition has
yet to be guaranteed, for the fact that we acquired knowledge
before birth still leaves open an alternative: either we were
born with it and know throughout our lives, or we lost it at
birth and later regain it through the use of our senses. Only in
the latter case would it be possible to account for so-called

learning as really the recovery of knowledge that is our own. Even if it assumes an original acquisition of knowledge, then, the recollection doctrine still has to account for its loss: forgetting turns out to be as difficult to explain as learning. Now for the genuine philosophers, entrance into the body at birth is the sufficient condition for the self-forgetfulness of psychē, hence its release from the body at death is the necessary condition for its self-recovery. But the recollection doctrine faces the dilemma of having to affirm the former while denying the latter.

To defend the doctrine, Socrates must reassign all names in accordance with the truth of genesis and the falsehood of being: to know is simply to have acquired knowledge, to forget is to lose it, and there is no name for ignorance. The recollection argument thus translates into epistemological terms the argument on the cycle of opposites, which describes the coming to be and passing away of the living and the dead without ever defining what life or death is. But insofar as both arguments reflect the assumptions of the genuine philosophers, their juxtaposition leads to this striking result: being born (awakening) is parallel to forgetting, being alive (awake) to being ignorant, dying (falling asleep) to remembering, and being dead (asleep) to knowing. Yet the recollection thesis, while it depends upon this parallel sequence, nevertheless requires that the means by which the psychē recovers its own knowledge is not dying but perception, not separation from, but union with, the body.

Socrates wove together two alternative conclusions in the first argument: either our psychai are always in Hades, or the psychai of the dead must be there if they are to come back to life again. He has now offered Simmias two parallel alternatives: either we are always knowing, or we forget as the condition for recovering knowledge. In order to help Simmias with his justifiable perplexity over which to choose, Socrates finally offers a definition of knowledge independent of its genesis: to know is to be able to give a logos.[22] Given the alternatives Socrates has offered, Simmias feels compelled to conclude that, if and when men do come to know, they must recollect what they once learned; for without examining what it means to give a logos, he is certain that not all men can do this—indeed, he fears that by the following day, no man alive will be able to do so (cf. 77e). Simmias affirms, however unwittingly, that Socrates has just given a logos of learning as recollection, which is not itself the result of recollection: surely no object of perception has awakened it. Yet Simmias betrays the grounds for the persuasiveness of the thesis, despite its apparent lack of justification: if learning were in fact nothing but recovery of knowledge that is one's own, every man should be capable of this self-actualization.[23] The argument on recollection—which replaces the required analysis of "giving a *logos*" with an assumption about the inherent possession of knowledge by the separate psychē—is Socrates' response to the fear and anger his interlocutors expressed at his willingness to abandon them.

It is no wonder that, until confronted with the question of whether all men can give a logos, Simmias could not choose between the claims that either we are born with knowledge or we later recollect knowledge we had previously. For what Socrates seems to present as mutually exclusive alternatives in fact implicitly distinguish between our capacity for knowing and its actualization through learning. Simmias confirms this, without realizing it, when he objects to Socrates' conclusion that our knowledge of the itself by itself must have been acquired before birth; perhaps, he suggests, we might acquire this knowledge at the moment of birth, for that time still remains. Socrates compels Simmias to agree that he is saying nothing in suggesting that we gain and lose this knowledge simultaneously. But Simmias should not have given in as easily as he does, for his claim points to the nonmythological core of the recollection thesis: learning is intelligible only as the actualization of a potential that belongs to man as such.[24]

[76d7–77a5]   Socrates confirms this implication by his formulation of the conclusion of the argument. For the affirmation of the existence of the psychē before birth depends not only on an

undefended hypothesis about the existence of the beings themselves, but also on the claim that we refer and liken all our
perceptions to these, discovering that they were previously and
are now our own: the beings must belong, somehow, to the
psychē itself. Socrates refers to the beautiful and the good and
every such being (ousia):[25] he implicitly raises the question of
whether it is possible to perceive something as good in the
same way as it is possible to perceive something as beautiful.
Socrates describes the ousia, moreover, simply as that which
we are always babbling about: he recalls his earlier description
of the being itself by itself as that which we stamp with the
seal of "the what it is" in questioning and answering. The
ousia may indeed have some necessary relation to the psychē;
it is, however, not the object of a passive noetic vision before
birth but is, rather, posited in logos for the sake of logos.

Some other logos would be needed, Socrates admitted in
the first argument, to demonstrate the being of the psychē after
death, unless it could be established that the living are born
only from the dead (70d, cf. 106d). Some other logos would be
needed, he now admits to Simmias, to demonstrate that our
psychē is before we are born, unless it is established that the
beings are. The limitation of Simmias' understanding of the
beings is precisely the condition for deducing the prior existence of the psychē. What the recollection argument has in fact
shown is the common illusion that stands behind each. The
unrecognized projection responsible for the perception of
phenomena as "willing" to be like the beings is the genesis of
the "itself by itself"; and the motivation for that idealization,
Socrates has implied, is its application to the psychē, turned
into a permanent being itself by itself.

Socrates confirms this common ground by concluding the
argument with a return to, but reinterpretation of, equality: Is
it not equally necessary, he asks, that the beings are, and that
our psychai are before we are born, and if these are not, neither
is that? The "equal necessity" of which Socrates speaks is no
quantitative measure; it designates, rather, the relation between two logoi, neither of which has been proven necessary in

itself, but each of which implies the other. Simmias, on the other hand, sees only the "same necessity"; he must assume that each assertion itself, and only derivatively the relation between them, has been sufficiently demonstrated. For he finds nothing so clear as the existence of the beautiful, the good, and all the others of which Socrates speaks, and the existence of the psychē before birth must be guaranteed by its likeness with these. The logos, Simmias judges, "has taken refuge in the beautiful": Socrates' later insistence on the necessity of "taking refuge in *logoi*" is motivated precisely by the kind of illusory confidence Simmias displays here in the possibility of acquiring knowledge of the beings themselves (cf. 99e).

[77a6–77d5]   To Simmias' enthusiastic affirmation, Socrates makes no response, except to ask about Cebes, for he too must be persuaded. Although Simmias considers Cebes "the most obstinate of men in distrusting *logoi*," he is confident that they have been equally convinced by the argument but also share the same dissatisfaction: the demonstration of the existence of the psychē apart from the body before birth only intensifies their real fear as to whether and how it exists after death. The symmetry of logical possibility, which would make the claims of existence before birth and after death mutually supportive, does not converge with a symmetry of emotional concern, which is directed solely to the question of our survival. Only if the recollection argument had shown that the psychē is ungenerated, would it have offered hope that it is also imperishable.[26] But nothing has been shown, Simmias protests, to prevent the psychē, once set free from the body, from coming to an end and suffering corruption.[27] Cebes too finds the demonstration only half accomplished unless it can be shown that the psychē is after death as well as before birth: he joins Simmias not only in endorsing the recollection argument, but also in ignoring the argument on the cycle of opposites, which concluded with the claim that the psychai of the dead continue to exist.

Socrates, however, assures both his interlocutors at once that the complete demonstration has been supplied, albeit only implicitly: the recollection argument, with its demonstration of the preexistence of the psychē, must be "put together" with the argument on the cycle of opposites, with its demonstration that "all the living (every living being) come(s) to be from the dead." Yet this complete demonstration would have been furnished by the first argument alone, had it succeeded in establishing, as it was presumably intended to, that the living come to be from the dead no less than the dead from the living.[28] Socrates wants to take from that argument, however, only what seems to be another claim to the preexistence of the psychē; he thus indicates simultaneously the superfluous status of the recollection argument and the questionable validity of the first argument, which simply assumed the genesis of the dead from the living in order to prove the opposite genesis of the living from the dead. Socrates confirms this difficulty in elaborating the required combination: if the psychē is agreed to exist before birth, and if in coming to life, it necessarily comes to be from nothing and nowhere but death and being dead, how could it not be after dying, since it must come back to life again? Socrates argued originally only that coming back to life must be possible for at least one thing, unless everything were to end up dead; he now claims to have shown that every living being that dies must necessarily come back to life again.

The conjunction Socrates proposes would suffice only if it could overcome the qualified status of the conclusions derived in the first two arguments from hypotheses that remain undefended. But the strategy Socrates outlines does not itself defend the hypothesis of the existence of the beings, agreed on in the recollection argument, any more than the hypothesis of coming back to life, agreed on in the argument on the cycle of opposites. Just as problematic is the assumption that the psychē construed merely as the subject of the cycle of living and dying could be "put together" with the psychē construed as the possessor of phronēsis. While Socrates reduces his interlocutors' dissatisfaction to their fear (77d), he seems to betray his awareness of their justification through his willingness to conduct a third argument, either as a supplement or a replacement for the required combination of the first two.[29] If it were to succeed in its task, the ensuing argument would have to defend the unexamined hypotheses of the first two arguments and, at the same time, overcome the tension brought to light by their proposed combination: it would have to explain how the single nature of psychē accounts for its double function, animating the body as source of life and in contact with the beings as medium of cognition.[30] Socrates has yet to present an account of the psychē that would allow the philosophers' desire for death to be reconciled with the divine prohibition against suicide.

CHAPTER SIX

Likeness

[77d5–78b10]   Simmias and Cebes wish to continue the logos, Socrates charges, only because of their childish fear that the psychē may be dispersed in departing from the body, especially, he adds in ridicule, if the man happens to die in a high wind. Cebes, who first stated the common distrust that the psychē may be nothing more than breath or smoke, now laughs—betraying a momentary relief from fear[1]—at Socrates' mockery of just that understanding. Realizing that he can overcome his distrust only through self-persuasion, Cebes must separate himself from the fear attributed to him: he projects his internal dissension onto an autonomous and alien being by transforming Socrates' accusation of "childish fear" into "the child in us" who fears. The tension between Socrates' adjective and Cebes' noun points to the question of whether "the *psychē* in us" is anything other than a reification of the quality of "ensouled" body: it was only, indeed, by projecting all internal dissension onto the body as alien that the genuine philosophers could postulate the separability of the psychē as an autonomous being.

To free the child in us from that hobgoblin, the fear of death, it is necessary, Socrates advises, to sing daily incantations. But Cebes betrays his resentment of being abandoned by the one man able to do this, just as Simmias, when Socrates defined knowledge as the ability to give a logos, betrayed his resentment of being abandoned by the one man able to do so

(76b). Cebes, who attacked Socrates for his imprudence in running away from the care of the gods, considers Socrates indispensable for persuasion; Simmias, who attacked Socrates for his injustice in running away from his present companions, considers Socrates indispensable for the logos. While Simmias is impressed with Socrates' unique powers of argumentation, Cebes is impressed with his unique powers of enchantment. Perhaps it is not despite, but because of, that division that Socrates addresses the speeches that seem most enchanting to Simmias, those that seem most argumentative to Cebes—with the apparent exception, that is, of the present one. For while Socrates responded to Simmias' reproach by appealing to the universal capacity for recollection, he now responds to Cebes by recommending that, in quest of a good enchanter, he ought to search among all the Hellenes and the barbarians too, sparing neither money nor toil, and also among themselves, for perhaps he would find none more capable of such enchantment.[2] Socrates indicates, with this recommendation, the status of the argument that follows. Yet, at its conclusion, he in fact encourages Simmias and Cebes to share with the others their objections, which result precisely from the failure of their attempted self-persuasion. Socrates must hope, then, to accomplish just the opposite of what he allegedly recommends, for he leads his interlocutors to participate in their own persuasion only in order to awaken critical distrust.

The argument that is, at least by its conclusion, most evidently "mythological," thus proves to be most capable of stimulating reasoning. The mixture of opposites that underlies the series of arguments in the first half of the dialogue is thus emphasized by the argument in which that series culminates. The third argument is a culmination, at the same time, of the unfolding implications of the initial definition of death as a separation of psychē from body. That separation is here manifestly a performance in logos: the psychē, which is agreed to be "like" one principle, is separated from the body insofar as it is "like" the opposite principle. Yet the recollection argument has just established that a reminder that awakens an object of thought because of its likeness to it may, for just that reason, fall short of it. Psychē and body, Socrates will disclose, in their mere likeness to opposite principles, fall short of them. And the deficiency of each implies that their separability from each other is always a matter of degree. This continuum amounts, in turn, to a hierarchy of kinds of psychai: each is "like" the kind of life it leads, determined by the degree of its attachment to corporeal needs and related desires. When Socrates finally translates this likeness into identity, he turns the argument into an Aesopian fable: each psychē *becomes* in another life what it is like in this life, given its habits, its hopes, and its fears. The argument thus transforms what looks at first like a "physiological" analysis of the nature of psychē into a "psychological" one.

That transformation is anticipated by the outline Socrates provides for the strategy of the argument. He begins with a question: For what sort of thing is it fitting to suffer the pathos of dispersion, and for what sort is it not fitting? But he inserts at the center of this apparently ontological dichotomy a very different consideration: For what sort of thing would we fear suffering this pathos? After determining these matters, he inquires, must we not investigate, as the basis for our hopes and fears about our psychē, to which class it belongs? Yet the very order of this proposed outline casts doubt on the possibility of discovering an objective division of the dispersible and the indispersible that could be applied to the nature of the psychē independently of our hopes and our fears.

[78c1–79c1]   It is fitting, Socrates proceeds, "by nature"— since nature is not lame—for that which has been compounded and is composite to suffer decomposition in the same way that it was put together. If, on the other hand, there is something that happens to be uncompounded, that alone, if anything, would not fittingly suffer decomposition.[3] And it is most likely, he adds, that the uncompounded are always the same and unvarying, while the compounded vary from one time to another and are never the same. But Socrates can claim for this no more than likelihood, for he has not shown, on the one hand, that there is in fact something incomposite; and, on the other hand, while that which is composite might undergo the change of decomposition, he has offered no defense for the more radical claim that it *never* remains the same as itself.

To support this merely probable division, Socrates suggests that they return to those things under consideration in the preceding argument, namely the being itself (*autē hē ousia*) of whose being we give a logos in questioning and answering. Socrates does not, at this moment, explain what it means to give a logos of the being of the being itself.[4] He has acknowledged only that it is "the *what* it is" that we stamp with the seal of being in questioning and answering (cf. 75d); and when he now attempts to confirm the self-identity of something like the equal itself or the beautiful itself, he identifies "the being" (*to on*) with "each itself, *what* it is." None of these could undergo any alteration, Cebes agrees, being entirely monoeidetic.[5] But how could we ever know or state "what it is" if each has no relation to any other nor any internal articulation? Cebes is not troubled by this question; nor does he ask how, if each being is indeed "itself by itself," it could account, as Socrates proceeds to suggest, for the predication of the quality that it is to other things.

Nor does Socrates resolve this problem when he simply contrasts the monoeidetic ousia with "the many"—men or horses or cloaks—that bear the names of equal, beautiful, and all such. Not only do these "many" represent a plurality of instances in which beauty or equality are predicated, but each is in itself a plurality of the various qualities ascribed simultaneously to it. Socrates qualifies his claim, however, that they would be constantly other than themselves and each other and "so to speak" never the same; for this complete lack of identity seems to contradict our speech, in which we assign one name to each. Yet Socrates indicates the misleading character of our speech by avoiding the expected dichotomy between a phenomenal plurality of men, horses, or cloaks, and the ousia of each from which it would presumably gain its name. The monoeidetic form that never admits variance belongs only to the qualities equal, beautiful, and such, which we predicate of the many things, while no monoeidetic form "man," "horse," or "cloak" is postulated as the source of unity for the pragmata, each of which is always a "beautiful and large man," or horse, and so on.

Socrates proceeds to contrast the invisibility of that which is grasped only by reason through calculation with the tactility and visibility of the many, which are never the same (cf. 65e–66a): he is conspicuously silent about audibility. He emphasizes, moreover, the derivative status of the invisible as a mere absence of visibility. In making this the principle of his division, he betrays its subjective determination: the noetic objects are unseen by whom or what? With the apparently redundant description of the noetic objects as "not to be seen" (ouk horata) and "invisible" (aeidē),[6] Socrates slips in a double pun: he points to the paradoxical designation of the invisible eidē by a word that means the visible looks of things and then links it with the paradoxical "invisible place" to which the psychē is said to journey after death.[7] Hades, Socrates now suggests, is the invisible structure of the visible. He thus clarifies the alternative presented only obscurely in the first argument—that our psychai are always "there." It is for the sake of demonstrating that conclusion, Socrates reminds us, that he offers his present account of the monoeidetic beings.

Socrates invites Cebes to join him, if he wishes, in laying down two forms (eidē) of the beings—the invisible and the visible—although it is precisely as "the beings" that the members of one of the classes have been uniquely characterized. They lay down, further, that the invisible are always the same, the visible never the same, without defending the necessary connection between visibility and constant alteration, invisibility and self-identity. Socrates does not, in any case, present their division as a discovery of the nature of things, but as a hypothesis Cebes may wish to posit with him, an instrument useful for the purposes of the argument. Socrates points to that purpose when he asks whether "we" are anything other than, on the one hand, body, on the other, psychē; but his reference to the subject constituted by this dyad presupposes that "we" are indeed something other, namely living animals. Socrates

may have been justified in asserting only that this unified subject is characterized as, on the one hand, corporeal, on the
other, psychic, qualities "like and akin," as he is about to establish, to the visible and the invisible laid down as two eidē.

In agreeing, not simply that the body is visible, but only
that everyone would consider it more like the visible, Cebes
unwittingly points to the invisible source of motion in the
living body: what is most completely visible is the corpse.[8]
Socrates does not ask the parallel question, to which eidos the
psychē is more like, but rather whether it is visible or invisible.
And Cebes shows how hard it is to relinquish the identification of being with visibility when he agrees only that the
psychē is invisible to men at least; it might be, as the genuine
philosophers would maintain, visible "itself by itself" when
freed from imprisonment in the body. This is sufficient, in any
case, for Socrates to draw the moderate conclusion that the
psychē, because it cannot be seen by human vision, is more
like the invisible than the body is, and the body more like the
visible. Since it is the living animal that constitutes this continuum of more or less, only death would reveal the kinship
and likeness of the psychē with the invisible, the body with the
visible.

[79c2–80b7]   By contrasting the monoeidetic noetic object
and the multiform perceptible pragmata, Socrates was able to
characterize the invisible as always self-identical and the visible as always changing. He did not defend the assumption that
everything invisible is necessarily self-identical and everything
visible always changing. Agreement on the mere likeness of
the psychē to the invisible and of the body to the visible is not
sufficient, then, to ascribe to each the properties connected
with the two principles. But Socrates does not make the expected attempt to characterize the psychē in contrast to the
body; he attempts, rather, to establish opposing characteriza-
tions of the psychē itself, determined by its independence
from, or dependence on, the body. We have been saying for a
long time, he reminds his interlocutors, that whenever the

psychē makes use of the body, that is, the senses, for investigation, it is dragged down to those things that are never the same, where it wanders about, confused and dizzy, like a drunkard. The psychē seems to have no nature of its own but only to assimilate itself to its object. For when, on the other hand, it investigates alone by itself, departing into the pure and everlasting and deathless to which it is akin, it has rest from its wanderings and remains always the same and unchanging, since it is in contact with such.

Isn't it this condition (*pathēma*) of the psychē, Socrates asks, that is called phronēsis?[9] He recalls with this question the genuine philosophers' longing to escape from the dizziness of inquiry through the senses in the hope of acquiring phronēsis by the separate psychē after death. But Socrates' evaluation of this hope will be made clear only when he presents his own interpretation of that mode of inquiry through which he seeks escape from dizziness and blindness by taking "refuge in *logoi*" (cf. 99d–100a). Now, however, it is on the basis of his appeal to phronēsis as a condition of the psychē that Socrates raises the question he should have asked originally—to which eidos the psychē is more alike and akin. For Socrates' description of phronēsis saves Cebes from having to ask about the necessary connection between invisibility and self-identity in order for him to agree that the psychē is as a whole and completely more like that which is always the same than like that which is not. And while they should have contrasted with this the characterization of the psychē when it is not in possession of phronēsis, they conclude by agreeing that the body must be more like "the other."

To grant the likeness of the psychē to the invisible and unchanging, does not, of course, satisfy the challenge for a demonstration of its immortality and indestructibility. Socrates therefore supplements the proposed division with the distinction between the divine, which is by nature fit to rule and lead, and the human, fit to obey and serve.[10] To which should the psychē and body be likened, Socrates asks, if, when they are joined together, nature commands one to rule and be master, the other to be ruled and enslaved? Cebes ignores Socrates' reference to the "command" of nature, which implies the recalcitrance of body as well as of psychē to their assigned roles as ruler and ruled; he is confident that the body is like the mortal, psychē like the divine. While Cebes must assume the identity of the divine and the immortal, hence of the mortal and the human, he does not seem to realize that his agreement on the likeness of the psychē to the divine thus commits him to acknowledge the mortality of man as such.

Without making this consequence explicit, Socrates reaches the desired conclusion of the argument: the psychē is most like the divine and immortal and noetic and monoeidetic and indissoluble and that which is always the same, while the body is most like the human and mortal and polyeidetic and nonnoetic and dissoluble and that which is never the same.[11] Not only has the division of the invisible and visible, which provided the premise for the argument, disappeared altogether, but the original claim that the psychē is more like one eidos than the body is, and the body more like the other, has been transformed into the more radical conclusion that each is most like one of two opposing classes characterized by a presumably inseparable set of qualities. Through its function in ruling over the body, the psychē is like the divine and immortal; through its possession of phronēsis it is like the noetic and monoeidetic, hence like what is always the same and unchanging. But the indissolubility of the psychē—the crucial question at stake— would follow only from its being incomposite, which Socrates has not established, and he has argued only that, *if* there were something incomposite, it would most likely be that which is always the same and unchanging.

[80b8–82b9]   Having analyzed the relation between body and psychē as a continuum governed by greater or lesser degrees of likeness to opposite principles, Socrates draws the consequence that it would be fitting for the body to be dissolved quickly at death, and for the psychē to be completely indissoluble, or nearly so. It is precisely the consequences of this "nearly so" that provoke Cebes' dissatisfaction with the argument (cf. 87d–88b), just as the consequences of the mere invisibility of the psychē provoke Simmias' (cf. 85e–86d). Not only does Socrates reach a conclusion that confirms the fears of his interlocutors, but he draws out its painful implications in seemingly unnecessary detail. When a man dies, he observes, even the visible part of him, which we call the corpse, does not undergo decomposition at once. The Egyptians, in fact, can preserve the body for an incalculable amount of time,[12] and certain parts of the body, because they continue to "lie in the visible," are "so to speak, deathless." Having referred to the athanaton as that which the psychē is most like (80b) or that toward which it moves when it inquires alone by itself (79d), Socrates now uses it for the first time as a quality, not of the psychē however, as Cebes and Simmias might expect, but of the bones and sinews![13]

The invisible psychē, on the other hand, departs to another place that is like itself, noble and pure and invisible. This natural *telos* of the pure psychē is Hades, the name given by the poets to an invisible place in which the dead "live," and at the same time to the god who rules there.[14] It is a name that may inspire fear of one's fate after death, but only while overcoming the more fundamental fear of nonbeing.[15] Hades combines the obscurities about place in the first argument with those about time in the second. For it is the combination of a paradoxical place that is not seen and a paradoxical time in which nothing changes: its nonmythological equivalent are the unseen and unchanging "ideas." To this dwelling, Socrates concludes, his own psychē is about to journey, if god is willing, drawn by the attraction of likes. The desire for communion with Hades, the good and wise god,[16] transformed by a pun into the principle of the invisible, proves Socrates' prudence in his willingness to face death. Socrates' reconstruction of the creation of the poets thus provides precisely the reconciliation he seeks: Hades overcomes the tension between the greatest music and demotic music, between the desire for death and the divine prohibition against suicide.

Could the psychē characterized by its kinship with this invisible place, the good and wise god, be immediately dispersed, Socrates asks, and destroyed when released from the body, as the many fear? But he answers his own question without any claim about the physiology of the psychē as such. For apparently not every psychē leads a life in accordance with its "likeness to the invisible," but only the one that is pure because it avoided association with the body and gathered itself into itself alone. But this is precisely to engage in "correct philosophizing" and to practice really being dead; or wouldn't it, Socrates inquires, be the practice of death? It is no accident that this question reminds *us*, if not Cebes, of the ambiguity of Socrates' initial defense. For what his interlocutors may take to be the fate of the psychē after death is Socrates' description of a mode of investigation carried on throughout life: *whenever* the psychē engages in this activity, it departs into what is like itself, the invisible, divine, immortal, and phronimos.

Whenever, throughout life, the psychē practices dying in this way, it is freed from its wanderings and folly and fears and savage desires and all other human evils; but unless the latter belong to the body, as the genuine philosophers might insist, the desire for purification from these pathē is the desire of the psychē to escape from itself, to become like the noetic and monoeidetic. If it were freed from all these evils, it would dwell, according to Socrates' formulation, with the divine; it would dwell, as the initiates say, through all time with the gods (81a). That these might not be the same "place," appropriate for the same psychē, Socrates suggests in the myth he recites at the end of the conversation (cf. 111b–c, 114b–c); that myth, with this subtle correction, assumes in the second half of the dialogue the place and function of the present discussion as the conclusion of the first half.

But Socrates is concerned now only to distinguish the purified psychē from the one that departs defiled and impure. Because of its constant intercourse with the body, the impure psychē is bewitched by the body's desires and pleasures and thus becomes penetrated in its nature by "the somatoeidetic";

it is not the body itself, then, but the somatoeidetic nature of the psychē in its chosen attachment to the body that constitutes the hindrance to purification. Such a psychē is compelled to believe that nothing is true except what can be touched or seen—Socrates does not say "heard"—or drunk or eaten or used for "the *aphrodisia*," while it would fear and hate and avoid what is dark and invisible to the eyes but intelligible and comprehensible to philosophy. Just as the attraction of likes draws the purified psychē to its invisible dwelling, the natural gravity of the visible, which is burdensome and heavy and earthly, drags the unpurified psychē back into the visible place. What is said to be an account of the fate of the psychē after death, Socrates makes as clear as possible, is nothing but a description of what constitutes its purity or impurity in life.

"As it is said," Socrates qualifies his account, the spectres (*eidōla*) of those psychai weighed down by their attachment to the visible come to be visible, as *phantasmata* seen rolling around monuments and tombs. If Cebes wishes to believe that the purified psychē will dwell with the gods, he must believe at the same time that the impure will become ghosts.[17] But the latter must, in fact, be all human beings, whose psychai have been entombed in visible bodies.[18] Each psychē, "as is likely" (*hōsper eikos*)—or more appropriately, as a likeness—should be bound into a character corresponding to its practice in life: the gluttonous, violent, and drunk into asses and other beasts, the unjust and tyrants and robbers into wolves and hawks and kites. Socrates turns finally to those who practice by nature and habit, without philosophy, the demotic and political virtues called moderation and justice.[19] By contrasting such habitual practice with philosophy, he silently raises the question, once again, of what it means to engage in the practice of dying. Those who pursue it, in any case, do not belong in this fable; for it is the practitioners of the demotic virtues, Socrates insists, who go to the best "place" and are happiest. When Cebes expresses surprise, Socrates explains: these psychai enter into the political and gentle genos of bees or wasps or ants—Cebes does not stop to wonder about the inclusion of that gentle species at the center of Socrates' list!—or they return again to the human genos as moderate men. When Cebes admits all this is "likely," he must recognize by now that the argument on likeness has become an exemplification of image making.

[82b10–84b8]   Every human life can be characterized, apparently, through the image of a beast; for the psychē that departs pure does not return to human life at all. In ascribing this fate to the "lover of learning," Socrates recalls his imitation of the speech of the "correct lovers of learning" (67b), who were characterized by their opposition to the lover of the body, that is, of money or honor or both (68c). Unlike the many who refrain from bodily pleasures only because they fear poverty or dishonor, Socrates now repeats, the correct philosophizers do so only for the sake of entering the genos of the gods. In turning their backs on the body, they "bid farewell" (chairein) to other men as being ignorant[20] and turn instead to follow philosophy wherever it leads, believing it to be deliverance and purification. For when possessed by philosophy, the lover of learning realizes that his psychē is welded to the body, compelled to investigate the beings not in themselves, but through the body as if through prison bars. Condemning the body as the obstacle to his desire for direct contact with the beings, he never imagines that this very desire may be the true source of the systematic illusion he resents. Only philosophy, therefore, sees what is most terrible about the situation—namely, that it comes about through desire, so that the prisoner himself is responsible for his own incarceration.

In the course of constructing a model of "the best city in speech," Socrates depicts a cave, in which we human beings are imprisoned, as an image of the *polis*, in which we are compelled by laws and political opinion systematically to mistake images for reality.[21] In the course of defending philosophy as the practice of dying, on the last day of his life, Socrates identifies the prison no longer with the city but with the body. While an unnamed liberator leads the prisoner out of the cave of the polis by force,[22] a personified philosophy attempts to lead the psychē of the lover of learning by gentle encouragement and exhortation. The philosopher who escapes to the sunlight and no longer wishes to return is compelled by those who educated him for the best city to go back into the cave; but if he reentered any city other than the best in speech and tried to inform the other prisoners of their situation, he would be killed.[23] The psychē of the philosopher who longs to escape from the cave of the body, Socrates implied in his remarks on the divine prohibition against suicide, is compelled to remain imprisoned by the gods (62b). Yet his own imminent departure is justified, Socrates insisted, by some kind of divine necessity.

Socrates' description of the attempted liberation of the psychē from the body preserves, however, the ambiguity of his original account of the practice of dying. For philosphy does not encourage the lover of learning to terminate his life, but only to withdraw from investigation using the senses,[24] which is full of deception. It exhorts the psychē to collect itself within itself, to trust nothing but itself and the itself by itself of the beings, which it grasps by intellection itself by itself. Socrates' personified philosophy assimilates to the object of knowledge the act of intellection and identifies the psychē with the latter; it never attempts to account for the possibility of this perfect union of two independent entities. Yet the psychē of the "true philosopher," who sees in this exhortation a mirror of his own desire, considers it a deliverance not to be resisted. He attempts, therefore, to withdraw his psychē from pleasures and desires and pains and fears, realizing that the greatest evil resulting from them is the compulsion to believe falsely that their cause is most clear and true. Only, however, if one did not understand that these pathē belong to the psychē, so that its deliverance must be from itself, would he agree, as Cebes does, that the causes of intense pleasure and pain are "mostly the visible things."

In suffering the illusions produced by submission to the pathē, the psychē puts itself in bondage to the body. For every pleasure and pain, like a nail, Socrates explains, welds it to the corporeal, so that it takes as true whatever the body says to be so, adopting its manner and nurture because of sharing *its* opinions and gratifications. If the psyche becomes somatoeidetic in this submission, the body, as Socrates describes it, becomes capable of opinion and speech. The embodied psyche, which is indistinguishable from the ensouled body, is by definition unable to depart in purity to Hades, the invisible place; it has by definition no communion with the divine and pure and monoeidetic. It falls back quickly, Socrates adds, into another body, like a seed sown: he supplements the description of the nature of the impure psyche, characterized by its attachment to the corporeal, with an image of the cause of its coming into being.[25] Socrates' description of the practice of dying was open to a double interpretation: the separation of psyche from body, construed in the ordinary sense as the termination of life, meant in its reconstructed sense a mode of investigation pursued throughout life. The union of psyche with body that he now describes is open to the same double interpretation: what is apparently meant to explain the physiological origin of the living being is in fact the description of a mode of conduct in life.

Whereas Socrates first identified the motivation of the lover of learning as a desire to enter the genos of the gods, now, after describing philosophy's attempted liberation, he identifies the motivation for accepting this deliverance as a desire for communion with the divine and pure and monoeidetic, which may not be identical with the gods.[26] The psyche of the philosophic man, Socrates concludes, since it does not "calculate" as the many do (cf. 69a–b), would not think it right that philosophy should set it free so that it would then only enslave itself again to pleasure and pain. It would not want to reweave itself back together with the body, engaging in a labor like that of Penelope, who took apart each night the web she wove each day.[27] It is Cebes' understanding of this metaphor that must inspire the image he will shortly offer of the psyche as a weaver, fabricating the body with which it clothes itself (cf. 87b–e). But Socrates will soon clarify his concern for the separation not of the psyche from the body, but of the argument from all the fears and hopes that distort it. In his image of Penelope, then, Socrates must be thinking of the way in which logos or the greatest music is contantly being rewoven with, after having been separated from, mythos or demotic music. And there is no better reflection of that process than the present argument.

Socrates' own understanding of his image, however, is not shared by the psyche of the philosopher he describes to Cebes, any more than it would have been by the genuine philosophers he described to Simmias. The same illusion that motivates their desire for purification motivates the belief of the psyche to which Socrates now refers—that it must follow calculation (logismos) as long as it lives and thus arrive, when it dies, at what is akin to itself, freed from human evils. Socrates admits that the psyche is released from human evils only when *it* dies (cf. 77d). But what is this psyche that dies? Always abiding in logismos and thus actualizing its kinship with the monoeidetic, it seems to be no longer a psyche, but a being itself by itself. Of course, to identify this being with one's true self, as the genuine philosophers do, is to be entirely determined by the fear of annihilation and the hope of avoiding it, hence to be enslaved to, rather than liberated from, human evils. If that liberation is what it means to be dead, perhaps Socrates alone is capable of dying.

Simmias and Cebes could not possibly refute the conclusion Socrates addresses to both of them—that such a psyche would hardly fear being torn apart at its release from the body, scattered by the winds; having been purified of all pathe, it could not experience such a fear even if it were, after death, "no longer anything anywhere." Socrates ends this third argument, as he indicated in his original outline for it, by determining not what kind of being is naturally subject to dispersion, but what kind of psyche is naturally inclined to fear dispersion. His condemnation of the foolishness of this fear is entirely independent of any proof of the immortality of the psyche. Socrates thus completes the initial series of arguments, in the same way that he completed his opening defense (69d–e) and

will complete his final myth (114d–e), with an appeal to the
necessity of overcoming that attachment to the self manifest
in the fear of death.[28] But this is a self-overcoming, as Socrates
understands it, by and within the psychē, not by a pure psychē
of the body, and its basis is not the hope of eternal existence
after death but confidence in a particular mode of inquiry and
in the way of life devoted to it.

CHAPTER SEVEN

Images of the Psychē

[84c1–85b9]   The third argument, introduced as a magic charm to assuage the childish fear of death, concludes with Socrates' description of what the psychē passes into when it dies. With this disturbing conclusion, a long silence descends upon the entire company for the first time.[1] Socrates himself seemed to be absorbed in the prior logos, Phaedo reports; he cannot, of course, report the content of this internal conversation,[2] in which Socrates must have reflected on the unexamined assumptions underlying the preceding discussion. For Socrates admits, when he observes Simmias and Cebes conversing together, that there are many grounds for suspicion and accusation if anyone cares to work through the speeches sufficiently. But Simmias and Cebes, even in their dialogue with each other, do not seem to constitute the same self-sufficient whole as Socrates does in dialogue with himself. For they had been urging each other all along, as Simmias admits, to ask Socrates their questions; and while Socrates has been concerned, as he soon discloses, with the preceding series of arguments as a whole, Simmias and Cebes neglect the first argument entirely, as well as its recommended synthesis with the second, and raise their objections against the third argument alone. Socrates, therefore, invites himself along when he encourages them to continue the discussion; he seems to enter the second half of the conversation with more willingness than he displayed in the first half, which began with the compulsory apologia of his acceptance of death and continued with the compulsory defense of the presuppositions of that apologia.

They refrained from raising their objections, Simmias explains, in fear of displeasing Socrates in his present misfortune. Simmias and Cebes pity him for the failure of the prior arguments, which they must construe as Socrates' attempt to convince himself that death is not to be feared (cf. 91b). Yet the need that compels them to speak indicates that their pity is a veil covering unacknowledged anger: they resent Socrates' willingness to pursue his own self-interest while leaving them to rely on themselves. Socrates, however, only reasserts his conviction that death is no misfortune. But he recognizes how difficult it would be to make this belief persuasive to others, since he cannot persuade even Simmias, who fears that Socrates must be more fretful in his present circumstances than he was throughout his life. With that remark, Phaedo reports, Socrates for the first time smiled gently. Since it is questionable whether he ever intended merely to persuade his interlocutors, it is not surprising that Socrates betrays, with his gentle smile, that now familiar mixture of pleasure and pain.[3] When he insists that he in fact sings for joy in anticipation of his imminent release, Socrates tries to overcome the pity expressed by his companions; in doing so, he necessarily reinforces the resentment mixed with that pity. Socrates' present response thus echoes his initial defense, directed toward demonstrating the prudence of his desire for death, rather than his justice in running away from life (cf. 69d–e).

Simmias and Cebes do not recognize that they are listening to Socrates' "swan song." Perhaps they believe, like most men, that the swans sing for sorrow on their last day; but such a belief, Socrates charges, is just a projection of our own, uniquely human, fear of death. Men read in the natural sounds of the birds their own pathē; they neglect to "calculate" that no bird sings when it is hungry or cold or suffering from pain. The mixture of pain with the pleasure of expressing it may be as uniquely human as the fear of death. The swans, at any rate, sing most and best when about to die, in their joy at departing to the god of purification and prophecy, whose servants they are. Socrates has this privileged understanding of the swans, he assures his companions, because he is a fellow servant of the same god. He has already informed them, indeed, of the hymn to Apollo he composed during these last days, as a ritual of purification (61a–b); of course the offering to Apollo that Plato chooses to represent is, rather, the swan song of the *Phaedo*.[4] With this song, Socrates departs from life no more sorrowful than the swans, blessed with the gift of prophecy from the same master. At his public trial before the Athenian jury, Apollo's Delphic oracle provided Socrates' one link with the gods of the city, hence the only recognized support for his defense against the charge of impiety.[5] But it is with an ironic prophetic utterance that Socrates sanctions his claim to knowledge of what awaits him after death—that ultimate limit of human knowledge—[6]by appealing to the god who proclaimed him the wisest of men only because he had knowledge of his own ignorance.

Immediately after identifying himself as a servant of the *despotēs* Apollo, Socrates remembers his servitude to his present masters "here": Simmias and Cebes should not hesitate to ask whatever they wish—as long as the eleven do not prevent it. In contrast to his companions, Socrates has not forgotten that this conversation is circumscribed by the power of the city, manifest from the first moment, when Echecrates asks Phaedo whether the authorities allowed Socrates to speak with his friends or compelled him to die alone (58c), to the last moment, when the servant of the eleven announces the hour for Socrates to drink the hemlock (116c–d). When called upon by the Athenian jury to propose a penalty he considers fitting for himself, Socrates insists that he has no reasons to think of death as a great evil, but he has good reasons to think that of imprisonment, when one is compelled to live like a slave to those in power.[7] For imposing on him, however indirectly, just that punishment, Socrates should feel resentment of the Athenian dēmos. Yet just as Socrates turned the tables when he put the Athenian dēmos on trial in place of himself, so, on the day of his execution, he transforms them into unwilling benefactors. The authorities of the city have not compelled him to die alone, and Socrates therefore begins the second half of the conversation after paying respect to them; he reminds us, of course, that it was only because he refused to obey the warning issued by the man in charge of administering the poison that the entire conversation has taken place at all.

[85b10–85d10]   Encouraged by Socrates to speak, Simmias nevertheless begins with a defense of his boldness in continuing the inquiry. Although it is impossible or very difficult, Simmias believes, to know anything about these matters clearly in this life, anyone who wouldn't persevere in testing them until he was completely worn out would be a weakling. Simmias sees two alternatives, which turn, significantly, into three: either one must learn or somehow discover the truth; or, if that is impossible, one must take the best and most irrefutable human logos as a raft on which to sail through the dangers of life, unless one is able to sail on a more stable vessel, some kind of divine logos. Simmias believes that Socrates shares this opinion with him, and in some sense he does: having discovered the impossibility of obtaining clear knowledge of the beings, Socrates found himself, he later explains, compelled to proceed on a second sailing, on the safer vessel provided by the most irrefutable logos (cf. 99d–100a). But the procedure Simmias recommends, which could result equally in extreme dogmatism or skepticism, looks rather like a parody of the Socratic enterprise. For the safety Socrates identifies precisely with irrefutability in logos—for which he will present definitive criteria—is in Simmias' opinion only a means toward the goal of security in guiding one's life. Simmias does not clarify, moreover, how the divine logos that he thinks best provides this security would be distinguished from the most probable human logos; he does not define what makes the latter irrefutable, nor whether the former is identical with, or superior to, that discovery of the truth he considers difficult or impossible. While, on the other hand, it is knowledge of the beings themselves that Socrates considers impossible, it is precisely their truth that he claims to investigate by means of his second sailing through logoi.

[85e1–86d6]   Socrates consequently accepts Simmias' dissatisfaction but questions the way in which the preceding arguments appear insufficient to him. Having ignored the first argument and uncritically embraced the second, Simmias is disturbed only by the third: the invisibility of the psychē, upon which Socrates based its likeness to the divine and noetic and unchanging, does not seem sufficient to prove its immortality and indestructibility, nor even its independence from the corporeal. Socrates substituted for an analysis of the nature of the psychē a description of its mere likeness to the invisible objects of thought; Simmias now attempts to attack that description on the basis of a mere likeness. A harmony,[8] like the psychē Socrates has described, may be invisible and incorporeal and something altogether beautiful and divine in the harmonized lyre, yet the lyre itself and its strings are bodies and somatoeidetic and composite and earthly and akin to the mortal. And if someone were to shatter the lyre or cut and break its strings, the harmony would perish with the instrument; yet, according to Socrates' argument, one would have to maintain that the harmony continues to exist somewhere, that the wood and strings must decay before the harmony suffers destruction.

Simmias presents an analogy for the relation of psychē to body, whose traditional support is both a conditon for, and a result of, its persuasiveness, as Echecrates is about to confirm (cf. 88c–d).[9] His image is in fact so convincing that Simmias quickly forgets its status as an image, transforming it into an analysis of the physiology of the psychē. If the body is an instrument strung and held together by wet and cold and hot and dry, the psychē must be a harmony of these elements when mixed beautifully and in due measure;[10] but if the body is too relaxed or too tightly strung by diseases or other ills, then the psychē, no matter how divine, will necessarily perish. Simmias turns psychē into a mere quality, which could not come into being apart from, and would necessarily perish with the destruction of, the living body. He offers this proposal in the belief that Socrates too must consider the psychē to be something of this sort. That belief is, in fact, never explicitly refuted; for Socrates never directly attacks the image as such but only shows Simmias' interpretation of it to be incapable of accounting for the psychē as a medium of cognition, which Simmias himself has enthusiastically endorsed (cf. 76e–77a).

Socrates tacitly suggests that Simmias' interpretation of harmony, as a likeness of psychē, is not the only possible one.[11] For Simmias has not in fact distinguished between the silent instrument, the audible harmony produced when the instrument is being played, and an autonomous "noetic" harmony of mathematical proportions;[12] yet the latter would not be affected in any way by the destruction of the instrument and consequent cessation of the harmony produced in sound. In presenting his Pythagorean account of psychē as a harmony, with no separation of the noetic from the aesthetic, Simmias unwittingly reveals the fundamental problem of the Pythagorean account of reality as a whole.[13] But while the separation of noetic harmony might seem to imply the separation of an "idea of *psychē*" from its embodied instances, that is precisely what Socrates implicitly rejects. He indicates instead the proper interpretation of the noetic level when he refutes Simmias' objection on the basis of the demand for maintaining harmony of logoi (cf. 92c). Simmias' image thus suggests, through Socrates' implicit interpretation, that the invisible, incorporeal, beautiful, and divine harmony is that produced through a technē of logos,[14] separable from the embodied psychē, which is itself one with the ensouled body.

But Simmias, who is satisfied with his analysis of the psychē as a harmony of corporeal elements, draws its unwelcome consequence: it must be the psychē that is the first to be destroyed in what is called death.[15] What is called death, Socrates first argued, is the release and separation of the psychē from the body, and that is in fact the practice of the philosophers (67d). Simmias has now anticipated, however, the redefinition of death as nothing but the destruction of the psychē, which Socrates will construe as the point of Cebes' objection (cf. 91d, 95d). Simmias "seems to have grasped the *logos* in no trifling way," Socrates admits and, at the same time, Phaedo reports, stared, wide-eyed, straight ahead and smiled.[16] Phaedo, in his own habitual way, interprets Socrates' gaze as nothing but his customary gesture (cf. 117b); yet his interpretation may be no less questionable than his initial interpretation of the customary separation of pure pleasure and pain (59a), which was put into doubt by Socrates' subsequent analysis of their necessary union. For if Socrates' smile betrays his pleasure at Simmias' discovery of the limitation of the prior argument, perhaps the stare that accompanies it marks a moment of fear, either real or pretended: Simmias' objection has, at least momentarily, for everyone but Socrates, completely shaken confidence in the power of logos (cf. 88c–d).

[86d7–88b3]   Socrates admits that he himself is at a loss in confronting Simmias' challenge and calls upon anyone else more prepared to do so. Without waiting for a volunteer, however, he recommends that, before addressing Simmias' objection, they first listen to Cebes' and then either agree with them if they seem to be "in harmony" or, if not, continue to plead for the logos. Socrates cannot apparently accept or refute the separate objection of Simmias or Cebes but can only accept a harmony or reject a contradiction that might obtain between them (cf. 95a). He will refute Simmias' objection in regard to those presuppositions—concerning the derivative status of psychē from body—with which Cebes disagrees (cf. 87a); and he will respond to Cebes' objection, in turn, on the basis of an analysis of the meaning of harmony in logoi, which is the unstated implication of the image Simmias has offered. While this strategy might seem to be a refuge in despair, it in fact illustrates just that procedure Socrates will describe in the account of his philosophic development as a turn from investigation of the beings to investigation of their truth through logoi (cf. 99d–100a).

　　Encouraged to report his own disturbance before the battle to defend the logos can begin, Cebes objects that the argument seems still to be open to the original attack (cf. 77c): although it has been cleverly and sufficiently demonstrated that our psychē existed before entering the human form, no demonstration has established that it will exist somewhere after we have died. This is just the question Socrates claims to have taken up in the argument on the cycle of opposites that he conducted with Cebes, whereas the preexistence of the psychē, which Simmias denied through his image, is the question Socrates took up with him in the argument on recollection. It was Cebes, however, who introduced that argument in order to persuade Simmias of something he himself accepted; he now addresses his objection to Simmias in order to persuade him of his error in suggesting that the psychē is weaker and less enduring than the body. But Cebes thus launches what he believes to be a more fundamental attack on Socrates' argument: even granting the superiority of psychē to body will not guarantee its indestructibility.

Why, Cebes has the personified logos ask, should he distrust the claim that, if the weaker part still exists after a man dies, the stronger part must necessarily be preserved? Like Simmias, Cebes can express his distrust only through a likeness; yet, unlike Simmias, he is not misled into ignoring its status as an image, perhaps because it seems to be such a preposterous one.[17] To say, Cebes argues, that the psychē lives on after death because it is stronger than the body, which does not perish immediately, would be like saying that an old man who had died did not perish but must be safe and sound somewhere if the cloak that he wove and wore was still safe and had not perished, since a man must last longer than a cloak. And yet, although the weaver is not weaker than the cloaks he produces, he must nevertheless have woven and worn many cloaks throughout his life, so that even if he outlasted many of them, he might perish before the last one. Cebes proceeds to spell out the analogy that is meant to explain the physiology of the living organism. The psychē is always weaving anew the body,[18] which is constantly changing and being destroyed. But eventually the psychē exhausts itself in this toil and, however many deaths it has survived, in one of them, it is finally destroyed. Now the last garment it was wearing, the final condition of the body, survives it; but once the psychē has been destroyed, the body displays its natural weakness and decays.

Cebes thus transforms the notion of the psychē enduring through a cycle of many lives, which Socrates introduced in the first argument, into an analysis of the constant passing away and reproduction of the body by the psychē within what we consider one life span.[19] But he is willing to concede—since the structure of the argument is no different—that the psychē might endure through a repeated cycle of births and deaths as ordinarily understood; for even this concession would not prove that the psychē could not be altogether destroyed in one of its deaths. Cebes thus reproaches Simmias for his denial of the possible survival of the psychē beyond the destruction of the body; and if "immortality" means the capacity to endure through what we call death, Cebes is willing to grant it. But he does so only to render more explicit the common fear he shares with Simmias: if death is redefined as the destruction of the psychē, which finally occurs in one particular dissolution of the body, Socrates has not yet proven that the psychē is incapable of meeting that fate.

Simmias and Cebes think they have brought to light Socrates' failure to demonstrate that the psychē cannot be destroyed at death. Simmias attempts to do so through an apparently reasonable image that reduces psychē to nothing but a quality resulting from the mixture of elements of the body. Cebes' more laughable image, on the other hand, reduces body to nothing but a product of the psychē, though it does not explain why the psychē requires this protection or adornment. It is now clear why Socrates insisted on combining their two objections before responding to either. For one amounts to the claim that there is in truth only body, the other that there is only psychē; their juxtaposition thus results in the separation of psychē from body that Socrates first presented as the definition of death. But while their combined objections perform this separation in logos, each one alone is an attempt to account for psychē as a principle of life. What they have unwittingly brought to light is the true problem underlying the first series of arguments: not only have they failed to demonstrate immortality, for which we have no evidence, but in assuming the identification of psychē with mind, they have also failed to account for life itself.

Now Simmias' image of the derivative status of psychē, as Socrates will shortly argue, simply contradicts his acceptance of the identification of psychē with mind. Cebes' image, on the other hand, because it makes body derivative from psychē, raises this question: Why, if psychē is mind, should it take on its ministerial role in producing the body, especially since that toil is the cause of its own destruction? Cebes must have been convinced by now of Socrates' prudence in wanting to run away from his masters, the gods. But wouldn't it be better, then, not to be born at all? If it were, the genuine philosophers' desire would be reasonable, even if it is not fulfilled. Of course in that case, the recollection thesis, which requires perception as the condition for learning, would have to be rejected; and this Cebes is no more willing to do than Simmias. Yet, while the recollection thesis thus presupposes the necessity of life, it cannot explain its possibility. In his response to Cebes, which occupies the second half the dialogue, Socrates attempts to meet his objection by accepting and unfolding its implications. He must replace the recollection thesis with an account of thinking and knowledge that does not depend on the identification of psychē as mind. Life remains inexplicable, Socrates acknowledges, unless it is simply assumed to belong to the essence of psychē.

The question raised by Cebes' image thus points to the transformation that will be accomplished by the second half of the dialogue. But as Cebes himself understands it, his objection only shows the necessity of completing what he thinks the first series of arguments was meant to accomplish: Socrates has yet to demonstrate, Cebes insists, that the psychē is altogether immortal and imperishable (*pantapasin athanaton te kai anōlethron*). And in the absence of that demonstration, Cebes concludes, anyone who feels confident about death displays his utter foolishness. But Cebes thus betrays his lack of understanding of Socrates' confidence in the face of death, which has nothing to do with an illusory belief about the character of the psychē as a natural phenomenon. Socrates would presumably show no more fear in his present circumstances even if he in fact accepted the account of the relation between psychē and body that Cebes has just presented.[20] Both Cebes and Simmias recognize Socrates' failure to demonstrate that the psychē cannot perish or be destroyed, and is in that sense immortal. But neither entertains the possibility that this is the fulfillment, rather than the failure, of his intention.[21] Socrates himself, however, has spoken nowhere of the imperishability of the psychē, and he referred to the athanaton only as a principle to which the psychē may be likened insofar as it engages in a particular mode of inquiry. He made it painfully clear that he has never characterized the psychē as deathless by ascribing that quality, however loosely construed, only to the bones and sinews (80d). His interlocutors seem to be proud of having discovered objections that take Socrates by surprise. But Socrates must have smiled for the first time precisely because they have grasped—even if they don't realize it—the intended implications of the first series of arguments.

CHAPTER EIGHT

Misology

[88c1–89c13]   The objections raised by Simmias and Cebes launch a double attack on the argument in which the first half of the dialogue culminates. Simmias objects to the consequences derived in the third argument from the mere invisibility of the psychē; his image of the psychē as a harmony of corporeal elements requires a reconsideration of the argument on recollection that Socrates addressed to him. Cebes objects to the consequences derived in the third argument from the mere superiority of the psychē to the body; his image of psychē as source of genesis and destruction requires a reconsideration of the argument on the cyclical genesis of opposites that Socrates addressed to him. Their objections thus disclose—even if unwittingly—the relations among the preceding arguments,[1] as well as the deficiencies from which they suffer, at least insofar as they are meant to demonstrate the unceasing existence of the psychē. It should be a benefit, then, when this double attack throws the entire company into confusion and despair. But they suffered a loss of confidence, Phaedo recounts, not simply in a demonstration of the immortality of the psychē, but in regard to all future inquiry.

Simmias' and Cebes' twofold attack on the argument creates an experience of pain in everyone present. But they do not think of their pain as merely an indication of their own fears and hopes; they take it to be, rather, sufficient evidence of the truth of what Simmias and Cebes propose. The painful, Socrates' listeners believe, is a sign of the true; they were perfectly willing, after all, to accept the antihedonism of the genuine philosophers, for whom philosophy is identical with asceticism. Socrates saw far ahead when he indicated, in his opening remarks, the need for an examination of pleasure and pain and their relation to each other. In the absence of that examination, all those present with Socrates interpret their own disappointment to mean either that they are worthless judges or that the pragmata themselves are untrustworthy. It is precisely such an experience that Socrates is about to identify as the source of the hatred of logos that he considers the greatest evil. The failure of the logos to serve as a satisfactory weapon against the fear of death calls attention to its own need to be rescued from an even greater danger.

This danger is manifest in the effect that emanates from the original participants and spreads to the frame conversation: Echecrates interrupts Phaedo's report for the first time, and thus marks the beginning of the central interlude that divides the dialogue into two halves. Echecrates sympathizes with the response Phaedo describes; for he too thought the arguments seemed entirely persuasive, yet now they have suddenly fallen into distrust. What is so disturbing to Echecrates, however, is not simply the apparent defeat of Socrates' arguments, but his realization of what he would have to give up if he were to accept Simmias' image of the psychē as a harmony. For although that doctrine, as Echecrates now recalls, always had, and continues to have, a marvelous hold on him,[2] he had not recognized that it implied the denial of immortality. And while he believes that he must now begin all over again, he too fears that after this no logos can be trusted. Whether the reader of the dialogue should share this despair depends, of course, on whether he too seeks only persuasion to confirm comforting beliefs. Motivated by this desire, Echecrates is eager to hear how Socrates defended the logos, and whether he was as disturbed as the others, just as he asked to hear, in the opening exchange, what Socrates said and how he died (58c): he betrays the incomplete separation of

deed and speech, pathos and logos, and thus appropriately introduces the interlude in which Socrates attempts most explicitly
to accomplish that separation.

Yet Phaedo describes that attempt, paradoxically, by expressing his admiration not for the argument itself, but for the
pleasant, gentle, respectful way in which Socrates listened to
the young men. Phaedo was impressed with Socrates' quick
recognition of how they were affected by the speeches, with his
skill in curing them, and with his ability, like a brave general,
to call his men back from cowardly flight.[3] When Echecrates
asks, finally, how he accomplished this, Phaedo reports not the
logos Socrates presented, but the deed he performed and its
emotional effect. While he was sitting on a low couch at Socrates' feet, Phaedo recounts, Socrates stroked his long hair and
held it tightly at the back of his neck—as if imitating his intention of cutting it off the next day as a traditional sign of mourning. Socrates will warn Crito, at the conclusion of the conversation, not to be concerned with his burial, since the corpse
will be something entirely other than "this Socrates" with
whom they are conversing (115c). He now warns Phaedo not to
cut off his hair on the morrow in mourning for him, but to cut
it off today, as Socrates would his own, if the logos dies and
cannot be brought back to life.[4] Socrates admits that he is
neither the corpse nor the argument; in doing so, he betrays his
awareness that "he" will indeed be absent on the morrow, and
thus indicates the urgent necessity of his alliance with Phaedo
for the preservation of the logos.

Faced with the challenge of confronting the joint attack of
Simmias and Cebes, however, Phaedo protests, "Even Heracles
is said to be no match for two." And he insists, understandably
enough, when Socrates offers to come to his aid as Iolaus serv-
ing Heracles, that the relation must be the other way around.
Engaged in the battle to cut off the nine heads of the Hydra,
Heracles was met by two new heads for each one slaughtered,
while being attacked at the same time from another direction
by a large crab emerging from the sea. Only by calling Iolaus to
his aid was Heracles able to burn away the heads, while burying under a rock the central one that was immortal.[5] In the

mythical context first established by the dramatic frame of the dialogue, Socrates/Theseus engaged in a heroic mission to overcome the Minotaur, which consists in the fear of death. But the labyrinth of logoi in which that monster lies has become itself a more forbidding monster, a Hydra whose multiple heads each double to meet any attack against it. The initial problem of the relation between body and psychē, for example, turned into a more complicated problem of the relation between two functions of psychē. And even if any one of the heads of this Hydra were slaughtered, its immortal one is that distrust of logos itself that is always a potential threat, not only at this particular moment of despair. To confront this monster, Socrates/Heracles must transform the fear of death, and of his death in particular, into the fear of the death of the logos. He addresses for that purpose not Simmias and Cebes, but his potential ally Phaedo and speaks no longer of the psychē, but of men; not about purification, but about a technē of logos; not about the practice of dying and being dead, but about the difficulty of maintaining love of men and love of logos.

[89d1–90d8]   Socrates takes Phaedo as his ally in the mission of subordinating concern for himself to concern for the logos itself. But in analyzing the threat against the latter, Socrates begins by articulating not the correlative distinction between hatred of men and hatred of logos, but rather their common root. Misology, Socates explains, is like the misanthropy that comes into being when someone with intense trust but no art believes a man to be altogether true and healthy and trustworthy but soon finds him to be wicked and untrustworthy; and when one undergoes this experience again and again, particularly among those nearest and dearest, one ends up hating everyone. Socrates describes the experience he himself might have undergone in pursuing his examination of the Delphic oracle, approaching everyone reputed to be wise and discovering nothing but pretense.[6] He could have been saved from misanthropy, however, only if he did not begin with complete trust in the soundness and truth of those he examined: his knowledge of human nature must have warned him that the majority of men lie between the extremes of the perfectly good and the perfectly bad (cf. 113a, d–e).

Socrates' observation on the mediocrity of most human beings does not seem very startling. What is startling is that Phaedo does not understand it. It is unusual, Socrates must explain, to find a very large or very small man or dog, or anything quick or slow, beautiful or ugly, black or white. But while this explanation is enough to satisfy Phaedo, Socrates does not support it by articulating the distinction between the "opposites themselves" that represent those extremes and the pragmata, the many things that are always more or less characterized by such qualities.[7] Socrates speaks loosely when he says that, even in a contest for wickedness, the extreme would be most rare; strictly speaking, perfect wickedness, no less than perfect virtue, in human character would be, in principle, impossible.[8] But Phaedo considers the absence of these extremes only "likely"; we know he believes, after all, that, with the exception of this unique occasion, every experience of pleasure or pain is always an unadulterated instance of each, with no mixture of them (59a). If Phaedo thinks this true even of pleasure and pain, there must be no limits to the array of separate beings he imagines. Phaedo is a genuine philosopher, and, in choosing him to preserve the conversation, Socrates seems intentionally to have invited misunderstanding. But in representing this strange alliance, Plato must have had another end in mind: the portrayal of Phaedo's crucial misunderstanding is the necessary condition for illuminating the character of the Socratic turn that is its correction.

Socrates introduces his account of misanthropy and elaborates the illusion that produces it only, presumably, as a model for misology: when someone, without possessing a technē of logos, has complete trust in the truth of an argument and later believes it to be false, and undergoes this experience time after time, he must end in distrusting and hating all logoi. This is precisely the case among those who pass their time in disputation and come to believe that they are the wisest of men because they alone have discovered that there is nothing sound or firm in any logoi, nor in any pragmata whatsoever. Socrates

seems again to describe his own experience, identifying himself as the wisest of all men because he knows that he knows
nothing.[9] He looks like the disputatious (*antilogikoi*), who
spend their time in refuting arguments without finding anything to take the place of what is rejected; but whereas the
disputatious discover the untrustworthy character of all logoi,
as well as of pragmata, Socrates discovers only knowledge of
his own ignorance, without abandoning trust in the soundness
of logos itself. Precisely that knowledge of human nature that
saved Socrates from misanthropy must save him at the same
time from misology, for only by recognizing his own deficiency
can he escape from blaming his ignorance on logos itself.

Misological, like misanthropical, resentment arises from
hope based on an illusory standard, followed by inevitable disappointment, directed not against oneself and one's own illusions, but projected onto something alien. But while this
analysis of the pathē uncovers the common structure of misology and misanthropy, the very possibility of escape from this
double danger requires recognition of the tension between
them. For logos does not share with human nature the character of always being somewhere between the extremes of
truth and falsehood. The man who suddenly appears to be base
and false may indeed be so, at least in part; but the logos that is
first considered sound and true and then suddenly appears to be
base and false may only appear to be so. Recognition, however,
of the criteria that determine the soundness of logos would
require a technē, which Socrates has yet to introduce; its
analysis will bring to light the distinction between "opposites
themselves" and the pragmata characterized by their participation in the opposites (cf. 103b), which explains the necessity of
the continuum of degrees displayed by human character. It is
such a technē, then, that at the same time prevents misanthropical resentment arising from illusory standards of human
character and the misological projection of our own deficiency
onto the logos itself.

The experience of misology, Socrates concludes, is the
greatest evil that can befall a man; he recalls his claim, at the
conclusion of the preceding series of arguments, that the great-

est evil resulting from submission to pleasure and pain is the compulsion to believe falsely that the source of the pathos is most real and true (83c). The pleasure of hope for immediate knowledge of the beings, Socrates implies, and the pain of frustation in obtaining it cause a man to believe in the clarity and truth of the pure wisdom he desires, hence the insufficiency of what is accessible through logos. This illusion, however, is in fact his own self-imposed obstacle: like the prisoner who incarcerates himself through his own submission to desire (82e), the misologist suffers the greatest evil, since he deprives himself of the only possible means to "the truth of the beings and knowledge." But the ambiguous status of this "and," which links truth with knowledge and does not clarify whether the "beings" are the object of one or both, points to the limitation of Socrates' present account of misology. It will be overcome only in his analysis of the technē of logos that provides the escape from this danger; for, as Socrates will disclose in the course of that analysis, avoidance of misology depends precisely upon abandoning the desire for knowledge of the beings themselves, in order to preserve trust in the possibility of discovering "the truth of the beings" through logoi (cf. 99d–100a).

Socrates confirms, in this central interlude, his distance from the genuine philosophers in whose voice he delivered his initial defense. For his understanding of misology as the greatest evil could not be shared by those preoccupied with resentment of the body as *the* obstacle to the attainment of phronēsis, construed as direct contact of the pure psychē with the pure beings. Given that goal, the genuine philosophers should direct no less resentment against logos than against the body, since it seems no more capable than sense perception of furnishing a receptive noetic vision of the beings themselves. The genuine philosophers thus appear to be the source of the disputatious; and just as the first half of the dialogue was determined, however implicitly, by the beliefs of the genuine philosophers, the second half will be no less determined as a reaction against the disputatious. The unwillingness of the disputatious, like that of the genuine philosophers, to admit their own deficiency results in the cynical belief that there is nothing firm or sound in logoi or pragmata. Yet Socrates concludes his account of misology by warning Phaedo of the need to guard only against the belief that there is nothing sound in logoi: he suggests that maintaining trust in logos, over against the cynicism of the disputatious, might require admitting, like the disputatious, the unsoundness of the pragmata—recognizing, that is, that the pragmata are not the beings themselves.

[90d9–91c5] Even when repeatedly disappointed by arguments, Socrates insists finally, we must assume that it is not the logos—from which we perhaps demand something impossible in principle—but we ourselves who are not yet sound, and who must therefore strive eagerly and manfully to become so. Socrates addresses this exhortation not only to the young men, but to himself as well, for, as he now admits, he fears he has not conducted the preceding arguments in a spirit of disinterested objectivity. He suspects that he has not spoken philosophically but rather, like "uneducated lovers of victory," who carry on disputation with eagerness not for the truth, but to make their opinions appear true to their listeners; Socrates differs only insofar as he is eager to make his opinions appear true primarily to himself. But Socrates thus enacts that self-accusation that he just declared to be the necessary condition for maintaining trust in logos: he shows his distance from the motive of self-persuasion, which would stand in the way of concern for the truth, at the very moment when he stands back to accuse himself of that motive.[10]

Socrates elaborates this warning against the self-interest that has made the discussion thus far a reasonable wager. If what he says happens to be true, it would be beautiful to be persuaded of it:[11] even if it were true, Socrates implicitly admits, he does not have knowledge of it. The fundamental assumption of which he remains ignorant must be the agreement that "death is something" (64c); for Socrates contrasts the first part of his wager with the alternative that "there is nothing for the dying man."[12] But even in this case, Socrates reasons, there would be a double benefit. For, on the one hand, his arguments based on the contrary assumption have allowed him to avoid being unpleasant to his companions; and, on the other hand, if death were indeed an absolute end, his own ignorance or foolishness would not last forever, which would indeed be an evil. With his insistence that he would appreciate death even, or precisely, if it meant nothing but the termination of his ignorance or foolishness,[13] Socrates responds to Cebes' preceding charge against the foolishness of those who are confident in dying without possessing a proof of the immortality of the psychē (88b).

Socrates defends both his justice and his prudence by asserting the coincidence between concern for his companions and his own self-interest. Yet this alleged coincidence conceals the tension present from the outset of the conversation; for, while encouragement of his companions requires the attempt to prove the immortality of the psychē, Socrates has just admitted that he himself has no such need. To satisfy his own self-interest, Socrates would have to persuade himself only that knowledge of ignorance cannot be beneficial, that perpetual philosophizing without acquisition of wisdom would be an evil.[14] Socrates seems to express in his present self-accusation not his fear of death, but his fear of desiring it, of having grown weary of his own ignorance.[15]

After warning Phaedo of the interests leading him to argue as a lover of victory, Socrates turns to warn Simmias and Cebes of the need to fight against him, as he must fight against himself. Socrates first responded to Simmias' and Cebes' perplexities about the prohibition against suicide by advising them that they must be eager (prothumeisthai), and perhaps they might hear something (62a). He now advises them that they must raise any possible objections to the argument, lest Socrates in his own eagerness (prothumia) deceive himself and them alike. They must beware lest he, like a bee leaving his sting in them, prick them with arguments motivated by eagerness for self-persuasion and then depart without defending the assumptions or implications of those arguments.[16] The objections that they offered only reluctantly in the fear of disturbing Socrates, must be continued not because of Socrates' philosophic indifference, as he first seemed to suggest (84e), but because of his urgent involvement. Just as Phaedo is to cut off his hair in mourning not for the death of Socrates, but only for the death of the logos, Simmias and Cebes must separate from all self-interest their examination of the logos: only through this separation can they participate with Socrates in the practice of dying.

CHAPTER NINE

Harmony

[91c6–92a6]   Socrates encouraged his interlocutors to express their reservations about the argument by describing the conversation as his joyful swan song; he is now prepared to respond to them after issuing a warning about the distorting effects of his own self-interest. Socrates asks quite reasonably, therefore, to be reminded of anything he seems to have omitted from his summary of their objections. Simmias' distrust, as Socrates understands it, arises from his fear that the psychē, although more divine and beautiful than the body, may nevertheless be destroyed first, being "in the *eidos* of a harmony." Cebes, on the other hand, appears to agree with Socrates that the psychē is more enduring than the body but claims that no one can know whether, after wearing out many bodies, it might not finally be destroyed in departing from its last body, so that death would be nothing but this perishing of the psychē. While Socrates drops altogether the image with which Cebes introduced his objection, he emphasizes the image that Simmias inadvertently turned into an account of the nature of the psychē. Of course it was Cebes who spoke of the eidos into which the psychē enters (87a), and he meant the human body, while Simmias never called the harmony an eidos. Nor did he declare it to be more beautiful than the body, but only to be the result of a beautiful mixing of the elements of the body, about which Socrates is now entirely silent. Nevertheless, Simmias and Cebes accept Socrates' formulation with no revision, for it sufficiently stresses their primary concern: the prior arguments have failed to supply a proof of the unceasing existence of the psychē after death.

Socrates, however, does not announce any intention of attempting to satisfy that challenge. He seems interested, rather, only in discovering some inconsistency between their objections or between those objections and the presuppositions accepted in the preceding arguments. He finds the required basis in the one argument he himself did not initiate; for the logos that identifies learning as recollection, and thereby demonstrates that the psychē must be "somewhere" before being imprisoned in the body, is the one argument that both Simmias and Cebes wholeheartedly endorse.[1] Since, however, their affirmation of the persuasive power of this argument may be for different reasons, Socrates must separate the objections he has put together. Turning first to Simmias, with the address "Theban Stranger," he foreshadows the conclusion of his refutation (cf. 95a).

[92a7–92e3]   That Simmias has affirmed the recollection argument on the basis of an unexamined assumption concerning the existence and nature of "the beings" does not concern Socrates, at least not immediately. For, however inadequate his grounds may have been, Simmias has accepted a demonstration of the preexistence of the psychē; he cannot maintain, consequently, that harmony is a composite pragma, and that the psychē is some kind of harmony of elements of the body, which could never exist prior to that from which it is put together. Simmias does not take the opportunity to argue that perhaps harmony is not a composite pragma, or that the psychē is a harmony, but not of corporeal elements,[2] despite Socrates' explicit, if mysterious, remark that harmony is not that to which Simmias likens it. Socrates offers a clue to what he has in mind by reformulating Simmias' image: the lyre and strings and sounds come into being unharmonized, and harmony is the last to be put together and the first to be destroyed.

Whereas, according to Simmias, the lyre and strings are the material elements from which harmony is produced, Socrates makes the crucial addition of "sounds." He thereby separates from the instrument itself the noise produced by it and, at the same time, separates from that noise the harmonic order imposed upon it. If the instrument, then, represents the body and the strings its elements, what is represented by the sounds produced by the strings and capable of being brought into harmony? It is precisely what Simmias left out of his image, Socrates implies by the conclusion of his response, that represents the psychē and its pathē.[3] While the coming into being and perishing of the psychē is thus dependent on the instrument of the body,[4] the harmonic order imposed on the psychē is not itself necessarily dependent on the body.

But what then is this harmony itself separate from psychē? Socrates offers a sign in his subsequent question to Simmias, as to how there can be harmony between the two logoi, that which identifies the psychē as a harmony and that which identifies learning as recollection. Socrates seems to offer Simmias a free choice of which logos he prefers, as if neither could be shown to be more true than the other, as long as both are not held at once. But since he suggests only that certain presuppositions underlying Simmias' particular interpretations of each logos might have to be qualified or discarded in order for them to be reconciled, they may be no more a set of mutually exclusive alternatives than the alleged alternative Simmias was offered in the recollection argument—whether we are born with knowledge, or whether we recollect afterwards that of which we acquired knowledge before birth (76a–b). Simmias was indeed so perplexed by that choice that Socrates was compelled to replace it with the alternative that either all men can give a logos of the issues being discussed or they recollect what they once learned (76b–c). If Simmias is now being confronted with a parallel set of alternatives, the proper understanding of harmony would be connected with the capacity to give a logos, for both have been forced to compete, in an allegedly mutually exclusive opposition, with the identification of learning as recollection. This suggestion is confirmed by Simmias' response:

he is willing to give up his image of the psychē as a harmony because of his natural acceptance of the demand for harmony between logoi—his refusal, that is, to admit self-contradiction.

Simmias introduced his image of the psychē as a harmony after a methodological reflection concerning the need to rely on the most irrefutable human logos, unless a more safe, divine logos is available (85c–d). He now justifies the abandonment of his image by admitting that it appealed to him, as to most men, not through demonstration, but through mere likelihood and plausibility, which can always be deceptive.[5] It is no wonder that Simmias still expresses such skepticism at the conclusion of the last argument (107a–b), or that he considers Socrates so indispensable for giving a logos (76b), if even the human logos that appears most irrefutable is convincing only because of likelihood and plausibility. And yet, Simmias is led to admit the deficiency of the harmony thesis by seeing its apparent conflict with the recollection thesis, and he is entirely convinced that the latter was based on a hypothesis worthy of acceptance. Now Socrates is about to elaborate a procedure for positing a hypothesis, examining its consequences, and attempting eventually to defend the original hypothesis. But Simmias' remarks are, once more, a parody of Socratic procedure. For the premise in which he places so much trust is his unexamined assumption that nothing is so clear as the existence of the beautiful, the good, and the others of which Socrates always speaks (cf. 72a). Simmias' confident belief in the existence of "the beings," which are "seen" by the pure psychē before birth, prevented him from investigating the meaning of giving a logos, just as it now prevents him from investigating a possible meaning of harmony other than his own image of the psychē as a mixture of corporeal elements.

Socrates leads Simmias to give up that image without explicitly supplying an alternative answer to the question, "What is psychē?". He nevertheless accomplishes two purposes at once. He attacks Simmias' unrecognized self-contradiction in conceiving of the psychē, on the one hand, as naturally akin to the pure beings it contemplates apart from the body and, on the other, as a mere quality derived from a particular mixture of

elements of the body. In what may seem to be a rather arbitrary
refutation of Simmias' particular self-contradiction, Socrates
points to the fundamental problem of the relation between
psychē as medium of cognition and psychē as source of life. In
using the recollection thesis, moreover, to reject the harmony
thesis, Socrates exemplifies through the very form of the refutation his alternative interpretation of the meaning of harmony. Yet this interpretation of harmony as consistency of
logoi—which Socrates will elaborate in the course of responding to Cebes' objection—proves to entail a denial of the assumption on which the recollection thesis depends; it denies,
that is, the understanding of the beings as the object of a passive vision by the pure psychē.

[92e4–93b7]   This initial refutation seems to satisfy Simmias,
in any case, more fully than Socrates.[6] Some implication of
Simmias' image was, after all, apparently devastating enough
to stop Socrates in his tracks when he first heard it, although
only, perhaps, because it brought into the open what Socrates
himself already recognized. Socrates' initial refutation of Simmias' image turns on the incompatibility between maintaining
the autonomy and separability of the psychē, on the one hand,
its status as a derivative quality of the body, on the other.
Socrates now adds a supplement to intensify that conflict. He
begins by asking whether a harmony, like anything composite,[7] could ever be in any condition other than that of the
elements of which it is composed, whether it could ever do or
suffer anything other than what its elements do or suffer. Simmias offers no counterexample, although he might have proposed the relation between a word and its letters, a sentence
and its words, an argument and its propositions; he is unaware
of the nature of logos as a composite whole that has qualities
other than those of its component parts.[8] Simmias agrees immediately that it would not be fitting for a harmony to lead,
but only to follow, its elements, so that it would be unable to
move or produce a sound in opposition to its own parts. He
divines that a harmony is not some other thing alongside its
parts but believes, unjustifiably, that this commits him to

denying any special status to the ordered arrangement of those parts.

Rather than explore this question directly, however, Socrates adds a supplement to this supplement; before applying to the case of psychē Simmias' agreement on the passive status of a composite harmony, he tries to support the latter with a new premise. If every harmony is by nature a harmony insofar as it is harmonized, Socrates reasons, it would be more and more fully a harmony insofar as it is more and more fully harmonized—if possible—[9]less and less fully a harmony insofar as it is less and less fully harmonized. Although Simmias had spoken of the psychē as the harmony that results when the body is strung together neither too tightly nor too loosely, implying that psychē is somehow itself a matter of degree, he is puzzled by Socrates' present suggestion. For what Socrates seems to propose is not the reasonable claim that the sounds produced by the strings of an instrument can be more or less harmonized, but that this is true of the harmony itself,[10] although every harmony as such, while it might be different from another, would seem to be necessarily no less a harmony than any other.[11] Socrates is proposing the reduction of all differences to those of degree. "Harmony," he implies, may be our unjustifiable construction of a substance that misrepresents the more or less harmonized quality of sound, just as "the child in us" who fears death was Cebes' construction of a being that misrepresents the mere quality of childish fear (cf. 77d–e).

If "psychē" were of the same character, it would be only our name, which we mistakenly construe as an independent being, for the more or less "psychized" quality of living body. Now if Simmias had really understood his original image, he should have agreed to this consequence: the being of psychē is as relative as a state of health. But Socrates appeals to Simmias' ordinary understanding of psychē as a substance, which might be exemplified by different kinds, none of which, however, could be more and more fully a psychē or less and less fully a psychē than another.[12] Each would be equally a member of the same class, not simply relatively characterized by its participa-

tion in the principle of "the psychic." While Socrates gains
Simmias' agreement without having to offer any further defense, he does not immediately draw the consequence that
psychē could not then be a harmony. He has argued, in any
case, only that each harmony is more or less a harmony *if* it is
possible for it to be more or less harmonized, and he does not
attempt explicitly to affirm or deny that possibility.[13]

[93b8–94b3]   Socrates proceeds instead to bring to light the
consequences of the agreement about the nature of the psychē
by reinterpreting the meaning of its likeness to a harmony.
One psychē, Socrates reminds Simmias, swearing by Zeus,[14]
is said to possess mind and virtue and to be good, another to
possess mindlessness and wickedness and to be bad. Since
these are, of course, characteristics of human beings, they
seem to differentiate not one kind of psychē from another, but
a hierarchical range within one kind—at least this would be
self-evident if Socrates had not just sworn by the highest god.
But what is it, in any case, to which these characteristics are
ascribed? They certainly don't appear to have anything to do
with the excellence of the mixture of hot and cold and wet
and dry. Socrates, in fact, simply replaces Simmias' doctrine
with another traditional image, according to which virtue is a
harmony and vice a discord; he does not acknowledge that it
is an image, nor does he clarify exactly what it is that is
thought to be harmonic in the virtuous psychē or discordant
in the wicked one. He assumes, rightly, that Simmias will
accept this traditional image and will find himself, consequently, in a dilemma.

Will someone who claims that the psychē is a harmony,
Socrates asks, have to admit that the good one that is harmonized has within it a harmony while being a harmony, and that
the other is disharmonic and has no other harmony within it?
Although Socrates has just asked about the possibility of a
harmony being more or less harmonized, Simmias cannot figure out how anyone could justify this allegedly absurd claim.
He might have proposed that a certain mixture of bodily elements provides the necessary conditions for life—that is, the

harmony constituting the psychē that is just psychē and never more or less so—while the human psychē has an internal structure that may be characterized as more or less harmonious or discordant, which we call being virtuous or wicked. But Simmias proves unable to defend the proposal offered to him. He has given no thought to how his physiological account of the psychē as the vital principle in any living organism is related to the ordinary understanding of the moral character differentiating one human psychē from another, any more than he thought about how either is related to the cognitive function of the human psychē.

Since Simmias does not take advantage of his implicit proposal, Socrates simply reminds him of their agreement that one psychē is no more nor less a psychē than another, which would be equivalent to the claim that one harmony is no more nor less a harmony than another, hence no more nor less harmonized.[15] With an apparently superfluous consideration, Socrates leads Simmias to agree, further, that whatever is no more nor less harmonized "participates" not to a greater or lesser degree in harmony but to an equal degree.[16] Yet, with this addition Socrates corrects his original reduction by acknowledging that "more or less" applies only to the degree of participation, the degree to which something is characterized by a particular quality, but not to that in which it participates in order to be so characterized at all. Socrates thus implicitly lays down the principles required to establish that every psychē, which as a kind cannot be more nor less of a psychē, can nevertheless participate more or less in harmony, and hence would be a more or less fully harmonized psychē. Although he claims to conclude, on the analogy with a harmony, that every psychē that is no more nor less a psychē can be neither more nor less harmonized, he would be justified in concluding only that one psychē could be no more nor less "psychic" than another.

If, Socrates infers, wickedness is disharmony and virtue harmony, one psychē could participate no more in wickedness or virtue than another; or, more precisely, no psychē could participate in wickedness at all, for if harmony is itself wholly harmony, it could not participate in discord, and likewise the psychē, being wholly psychē. That which is "wholly harmony" could participate in disharmony no more than in harmony, for it would *be* harmony "itself by itself." But Socrates has spoken nowhere of that which is more or less psychic because of the degree of its participation in psychē itself. And whereas harmony has as its opposite disharmony, so that whatever is not wholly harmony would participate in that opposite, psychē has no opposite in which whatever is not wholly psychē could participate. Socrates states the conclusion that follows, as he emphasizes, "according to this *logos*": if all psychai were by nature equally psychai, so that none could participate in evil any more than harmony could participate in disharmony, then all psychai of all the living—not even restricted to human beings—would be equally good. Compelled by the logos, Simmias reluctantly agrees. But since his desire to distinguish the good from the wicked prevents him from willingly affirming this conclusion, he feels obliged to abandon his claim that the psychē is by nature a harmony.

[94b4–95a5]   Socrates himself, however, seems to be no more satisfied by this refutation based on an appeal to Simmias' moral standards than he was by the original one. He has drawn attention to Simmias' conviction of the hierarchical range of human psychai by reducing the substance harmony to the quality of being harmonized, but without ever connecting that to their previous agreement on the nonautonomy of a composite whole. That agreement, it seems, could not alone provide the means of refuting Simmias' image without some understanding of the psychē implicitly introduced by the apparent digression on virtue and vice. Socrates now brings that connection to light by asking Simmias whether anything in man is fit to rule other than the psychē (cf. 80a), especially if it is prudent (phronimos). Socrates brings to light, with this reminder the limitations of any physiological account of the psychē as such. The question of its autonomy, he indicates, is specifically concerned with the conduct of human beings, and the description of the harmonic or discordant psychē must be relevant to that concern.

Simmias originally agreed that a composite harmony could never produce a sound in opposition to the tension and relaxation of the strings of an instrument. Reminded now of the standard of phronēsis, however, he readily agrees that the psychē is not always and necessarily compelled to follow the pathē of the body: it may prohibit the body from drinking even when it is thirsty or from eating when it is hungry and may oppose the body in countless other ways. The psychē, however, does not oppose the dryness of the throat, only the desire for drink, not the emptiness of the stomach, only the desire for food.[17] Socrates' simple examples, intended presumably to reveal the struggle of the psychē against the body, in fact reveal the struggle of the psychē against itself, and thus illuminate what it means to characterize the psychē as internally harmonious or discordant. Even if the psychē were understood as a composite harmony, Socrates implies, its components would not be the hot, dry, cold, and wet, as Simmias proposed, but its own pathē. Simmias is compelled to admit, in the light of Socrates' examples, that the psychē actually leads those elements from which it is said to be composed; in fact it opposes them, he agrees, in almost everything throughout life, sometimes inflicting harsh and painful punishments, sometimes milder ones, sometimes threatening, and sometimes admonishing. Socrates identifies the harsher punishments with medicine or gymnastics, and thus reinforces the explicit claim that the psychē is involved in an effort to rule over the body, which is alien to it. Yet the only thing that the psychē could "threaten" or "admonish" would seem to be itself. The attempted tyranny of the psychē, Socrates implicitly indicates, results from its misdirected resentment of the body, which should be directed against its own pathē in their recalcitrance to reason.

The psychē attempts to gain control, Socrates elaborates, by "conversing with" (dialegomenē) its desires and angers and fears as if they were alien pragmata. This is how Homer describes Odysseus: "He smote his breast and rebuked his heart in speech: 'Endure, heart, you have endured a more outrageous thing than this.' "[18] Through a personification, Homer represents an internal struggle in which Odysseus addresses his own heart—that is, his passionate anger—as if it were another subject with a will of its own. Now Socrates uses Homer's image of opposition within the psychē in order to illustrate the opposition of the psychē to the body; he can do so, of course, only by ignoring its status as an image. In fact, it is just this passage, supplemented by another with the same structure, that Socrates employs on another occasion in order to establish a division—presumably tripartite—within the psychē, based on the principle that the same thing cannot do or suffer opposites at the same time.[19]

Odysseus' self-reproach, which Socrates interprets as the struggle of reason against *thumos*, is juxtaposed with Leontius' angry reproach against his own eyes—"There ye wretches, take your fill"—which Socrates interprets as the struggle of thumos against the desire to see. Moved by anger, a part of the psychē identifies itself as the whole and regards any conflicting internal force as a personification of some part of the body. The psychē, consequently, is understood as monoeidetic, and its own self-control as despotism over the alien. Socrates appeals to an image of this psychological struggle to "rule" oneself in order to refute Simmias' image of the psychē as a composite harmony derived from elements of the body. But what Socrates tacitly shows, is thumos at work in constructing the ideal of the pure psychē separate from the body and compelled to tyrannize it.[20] The construction of the pure psychē, moreoever, has been shown all along to be parallel to that of the pure beings: their origin, Socrates now seems to hint, is willfulness and moral indignation.

If Socrates has not suppressed recognition of Homer's image as an image, it would have indicated the difference between an internally harmonized, rather than discordant, state of the pathē within the human psychē. This potential would suggest how it can be, in contrast to the derivative harmony to which Simmias likens it, "a far more divine kind of *pragma*"—to which Simmias agrees, by Zeus, with an unconscious irony. He accepts Socrates' conclusion that we cannot speak beautifully of the psychē as some kind of harmony, since we would be in harmony, it seems, neither with the divine poet Homer nor with ourselves. Yet he does not seem to grasp Socrates' implication that the common ground of harmonization, understood as the well-ordered state of the parts of the psychē in relation to the whole, and harmony, understood as consistency of logoi, must be the law of noncontradiction.[21] Having suffered, in any case, from an unrecognized state of discord, based on the inconsistency of unexamined presuppositions, Simmias, the Theban Stranger, has finally been harmonized, thanks to Socrates' "musical" skill, with Homer, as well as himself. But Socrates has refuted Simmias' particular interpretation of the psychē as a harmony, without ever showing that the psychē could not perish before the body—the intention that, according to Socrates, motivated the image Simmias proposed (cf. 91d). Socrates is understandably thankful to Harmonia, the Theban goddess, for being, so it seems, measurably gracious to them.[22]

[95a5–95e6]   But what kind of logos is now needed, Socrates asks, to propitiate Cadmus? He joins the challenge of Cebes with that of Simmias through the image of husband and wife,[23] and thus seems to confirm his original plan of attacking the objection of each by discovering some contradiction between them. But while Cebes has experienced such encouragement from Socrates' sudden overturning of the distrust engendered by the logos of Harmonia that he would not be at all surprised if the logos of Cadmus suffered the same defeat, Socrates now expresses his lack of confidence, admitting that he has conquered one threat only to confront a more imposing one. After warning Cebes not to boast, lest the coming argument be routed, he entrusts the logos to the care of the god and gathers up his strength, in Homeric fashion, to mount the attack.

Socrates offers once more a summary of Cebes' objection and asks him to make sure that nothing escapes their examination. What you really seek, he explains to Cebes, is a truly worthy demonstration that our psychē is imperishable and immortal. That it has been shown to be strong and divine and to exist before birth implies, according to Cebes, only that it may endure for an immeasurably long time, capable of knowing and performing other deeds; but this does not preclude the possibility that its entrance into the human body is the beginning of its destruction, as if life were a disease. That human life is a long illness from which the psychē wishes to be healed Socrates has not explicitly denied.[24] It is the basis of the resentment he ascribed to the genuine philosophers and the assumption justifying their longing for death as the separation of the psychē from the body. But it is precisely that understanding of death, Cebes argues, that avoids the crucial question of destruction. "Death" is the name we apply to the termination of any particular life, but, according to Cebes, it should really apply only to the termination of that life in which the psychē finally perishes with the body. And since no one knows what particular occasion of separation from the body will bring destruction to the psychē, one would be altogether foolish not to experience fear at the end of this present life.

Socrates clarifies, in this final repetition, the grounds of Cebes' demand for a proof of immortality *as* imperishability. Yet he puts into question, at the same time, the worth of Cebes' physiological account as an attack against the philosopher's confidence in dying. For the latter, Socrates has repeatedly implied, must be identical with confidence in the way one has lived one's life. Whether it is prudent or foolish depends, then, not on possessing a truly worthy demonstration of the imperishability of the psychē, but on understanding the criteria that make any demonstration truly worthy; for, without that understanding, one would be threatened by the danger of losing all trust in logos. And to deprive oneself, in that way, of the only means for investigating "the truth of the beings" is to destroy the basis for confidence in the one life worth living. Before he confronts Cebes' challenge, Socrates points to the direction that confrontation must take if it is to be sufficiently fundamental.

CHAPTER TEN

The Technē of Logos

[95e7–96e7]   While Cebes was eager to hear Socrates' response to his objection, Socrates himself fell silent for a long time, Phaedo reports, investigating something in relation to himself. Absorbed in his own thoughts, Socrates prepares himself not simply to refute Cebes' objection, but to explore the fundamental question it raises. What Cebes seeks, Socrates now informs him, is no trifling matter, for it requires a complete investigation of the cause of coming to be and passing away as a whole. For the sake of this inquiry, Socrates offers to relate the history of his own experiences; Cebes, of course, is free to use it for the persuasion of which he speaks. After identifying concern with one's own pathē as the obstacle standing in the way of concern with the logos (cf. 90d, 83c–d), Socrates offers a report of his own pathē. But this report turns out to be the unfolding of a technē that generates trust in logos, and Socrates' own intellectual development a reflection of the necessary progression of philosophic thought itself.[1]

Socrates offers this intellectual autobiography to Cebes, because he sees in him, perhaps, a mirror of himself when young, when he was wonderfully eager for that wisdom called "investigation of nature." He thought it magnificent to know the "causes" of each thing,[2] why each comes to be and perishes and—as if it belonged to the same inquiry—why it is. "I used to toss myself up and down,"[3] Socrates admits, investigating these questions. He wanted to know whether it is heat and cold, by some kind of fermentation, that result in the organization of living animals, then whether it is because of blood or air or fire that we think, or rather, because the brain furnishes sensations from which memory and opinion arise, from which, in turn, knowledge comes into being.[4] Despite Socrates' professed desire to discover the causes of everything, his examples reveal a particular focus: by investigating the causes of life and knowledge, what Socrates really wanted to know was the human psychē.[5] But he could not have been aware of that goal since, he claims, he continued to study the conditions of heaven and earth. What he in fact discovered, however, was his own natural unfitness for this sort of investigation; for he felt "intensely blinded" by inquiries that put into question even those matters he formerly believed he had grasped. Not only did Socrates pursue the investigation of nature to learn about the human psychē, but the result of his inquiry was the acquisition of what seems to be the familiar Socratic knowledge of ignorance.

That distinctive "human wisdom" is typically represented in the Platonic dialogues as the result of Socrates' examination of the moral and political opinions of others; but it does not appear to be those sorts of opinions that Socrates now claims to have held before, and to have questioned after, his investigation of nature. Rather, Socrates confesses, he believed he knew, like most others, that the cause of a man's growth is eating and drinking, since when flesh is added to flesh, as like to like, the small bulk becomes greater, and the small man great. Cebes innocently agrees to the reasonableness of this belief in a physiology of addition, without realizing the threatening perplexities lurking behind it, which Socrates attempts to indicate through an increasingly abstract series of examples. He believed he knew that a big man or horse standing next to a smaller one is greater "by a head," or turning to even clearer matters, that ten is greater than eight by the addition of two, and a two-cubit length greater than a one-cubit length because it exceeds it by half.

Cebes, who wants to know what Socrates thinks now, must still find these claims self-evident. But Socrates, swearing by Zeus for the third and final time in the conversation,[6] admits he is far from thinking he knows the cause—no longer the causes—of these matters. Socrates' former opinions were put into question, it seems, by the goal of discovering one comprehensive cause, at least of becoming and being greater, applicable to growth, magnitude, and number; yet he still has not achieved that goal on the last day of his life. Socrates may have been "awakened from his dogmatic slumbers" by his attempted investigation of nature; but it was that pursuit, he confessed, by which he was intensely blinded. If that is the same blindness that results from any attempt to look directly at things and grasp them through the senses (cf. 99e), it is not at all evident how it could have brought to light the perplexities concealed in Socrates' prephilosophic opinions, or in the logical structures they presuppose.

[96e7–97b7]   What then are the puzzles that led Socrates to knowledge of his own ignorance? He cannot even understand, he explains, when one is added to one, whether the one to which the addition was made becomes two, or the one which is added or both together become two by the addition of each to the other. He finds it amazing that, when separated, each was one and not two, yet mere juxtaposition is the cause of their becoming two.[7] Socrates cannot take for granted what appears to be the most simple arithmetic operation. Is addition, he wonders, a performance executed in space? And, if not, how is it to be understood? To give a physiological account of how someone grows larger requires an understanding of what addition is; but to give an account of addition requires, in turn, an understanding of the relation between "each" and "both." And Socrates sees in the grammatical problem of what the subject is to which we ascribe the predicate "comes to be two" the ontological problem of how a common quality comes to characterize a whole whose elements are not characterized by it separately.[8]

These perplexities throw Socrates into a state of wonder— the beginning of philosophy.[9] No less amazing is the claim that one becomes two by being divided in half. Is division too, Socrates wonders, a spatial operation? But isn't the one on which the operation is performed thought to be an indivisible unit? And if, somehow or other, the operation is performed, does it transform halves of one into two ones? But in that case—if no further qualifications are stipulated—addition and division would be opposite causes of the same result. And as long as they are taken to be the cause of *what* something becomes or is, these opposites would appear to violate the law of noncontradiction and thus fail to satisfy the minimal condition for intelligibility.

The juxtaposition of two accounts of how two comes to be, through the division of an original unit or through the addition of originally separate units, was just the perplexity Socrates introduced in his opening description of pleasure and pain, which seemed to him wondrously related to each other (60b–c). And that description furnished in turn the model for a double account of the relation between body and psychē. Does body become alive, then, by having psychē brought near to it, or does psychē become thereby embodied? And if both together become two by mere juxtaposition, how can they also become two by the separation of one from the other? In fact, as Socrates realizes in conclusion, he cannot yet persuade himself that he knows how one comes to be. For not only do there seem to be opposite causes that both produce two, but the same causes, and the same opposition, could also produce one: if body and psychē are really united, they make a single living animal, but if they are really separated, each is a single entity—the corpse, at least, is a unit, whether or not the psychē proceeds by itself on its journey to Hades.

Socrates has now reached the extreme stage of his knowledge of ignorance. Since he does not know how one comes to be, and since, furthermore, whatever is, is one,[10] he cannot claim to know how anything comes to be or ceases to be or is at all. His perplexity about two deepened to a perplexity about one; but since to be is to be something, and to be something is to be one, the perplexity about one pushed him beyond the problem of numbers to the problem of being. Socrates tried to think about being by thinking about becoming and perishing, and about that in turn by thinking about combination and separation; but in doing so, he discovered contradictions that he lacked any means to avoid, let alone resolve. Having set out with the desire for knowledge of nature, Socrates was compelled by the perplexities of the logos to investigate the presuppositions of his own reasoning.[11] He draws a radical conclusion, therefore, from the wonder-inspiring puzzles he has described. He must consider the mathematical operations of addition and division a paradigm for all mechanistic explanation; for once he recognized the perplexities of how two and one come to be, he claims, he found himself no longer able to follow "the way of the method" of natural science.

Socrates turned instead to another way of his own that he "mixes up at random" (eikē phurō). He seems to allude to the mixed-up condition of human life before Prometheus' introduction of the arts: men had eyes but saw nothing, they had ears but did not understand, and, like shapes in dreams, throughout their lives, they mixed up everything at random.[12] Socrates' mixed-up way of his own is designed to deal with the threat of contradiction in logos, which he discovered by reflecting on the problem of the cause of two and one and being; but the allusion with which he refers to his own path identifies it as a regression behind all knowledge of cause, a reversal of the apparent progress Prometheus brought when he bestowed his fateful gift of numbers, letters, and the arts. The very order of Socrates' presentation, moreover, seems to reflect his own mixed-up way; for after simply referring to it, he returns to the recital of his philosophic development, without clarifying whether this subsequent stage followed from, or preceded and perhaps inspired, his discovery of the perplexities to which his own procedure should provide an answer.

[97b8–99c9]   Once, Socrates continues, he heard someone reading from a book said to be by Anaxagoras, claiming that it is mind (nous) that arranges and is the cause of all. Socrates seems to go out of his way to identify the communication of this teaching in a written work: he arouses our suspicion about teleology as a questionable application to nature of the character of a human work of art. The Anaxagorean position pleased Socrates in any case; for to say that mind arranges all must mean, according to Socrates' interpretation, that it does so with a view to what is best.[13] To discover the cause of how anything comes into being and perishes, therefore, one need only discover how it is best for it to be or suffer or do, and by the same knowledge, one would necessarily know what is worse as well;[14] knowledge of what is best and what is worse, of course, would not entail knowledge of what is actual, unless the good could be shown to operate unlimited by any conditions of necessity. Socrates points to that problem when he admits his delight in finding Anaxagoras a "teacher of the cause of the beings to my liking" (kata noun), literally "in accordance with mind." The pun Socrates constructs out of a colloquial expression discloses why the claim of teleology should be suspect: a universe constructed "in accordance with mind" is so pleasing to us, just because it projects onto the whole the operation of the human mind, without necessarily acknowledging that projection.

From Anaxagoras Socrates hoped to discover whether the earth is flat or round or in the center of the cosmos, with an explanation of the necessity of its being as it is, based on an account of what is best. Teleology identifies the good and the necessary without confronting the possibility of a tension between them.[15] Socrates expected that Anaxagoras would, in assigning the cause of each and of all in common, go on to explain the best for each and the good for all in common. Teleology cannot treat a part except as part of a whole; but the possible tension between them reflects the tension between the necessary and the good, since what is best for the particular, considered alone, may not be good for the whole of which that particular is only one part among many.[16]

Teleology could be saved, one might conclude, if reflection on the relation between part and whole led to recognition of the distinction between the good and the necessary, the former identified with purpose, the latter with the means through which it is carried out. In that case, however, an explanation would still be required of how the one functions as the condition for the realization of the other. But if means and end had to be added together or separated from an original unity, teleology would lead back to the same perplexities Socrates discovered in all mechanistic explanation. A comprehensive teleology would require a defense of the superiority of life, or of death, not merely for one individual but for that individual as a single part of a cosmic whole. And to defend the belief that life is good even for one individual, a teleological account would have to answer this question: Does union with the body serve as the means by which the good of psychē can be realized, and, if so, how? But if, at least for some and on some occasions, death is preferable to a life not worth living, teleology would have to account for the goodness not only of the union, but also of the separation of psychē and body. To be guided by the good teleology requires mind, and mind requires psychē; but psychē, with its apparently incompatible ends, seems to make teleology impossible.

Socrates reveals the attraction of teleology, despite these difficulties, with his admission that, if he could be shown what is best, he would no longer yearn for any other kind of cause.[17] But he silently points to the danger of such satisfaction. To possess knowledge of the good would put an end to all inquiry: the impossibility of teleology is, paradoxically, the hidden good that renders philosophy necessary and possible. The implicit irony with which Socrates first expressed his great hope in discovering the teaching of Anaxagoras is repeated, therefore, in his description of being let down by it. If mechanical explanation is open to the danger of self-contradiction, teleological explanation is open to the inevitable disappointment that results from reliance on inappropriate standards: each alone and both together threaten to produce that experience of misology that Socrates considers the greatest evil. Their common ground is indicated by the failure of the Anaxagorean promise, which consists in its regression to mechanical cause. For Anaxagoras in fact made no use of mind, Socrates complains, to explain the ordering of things but assigned as causes air and ether and water and many other absurdities; despite his assurance of an intentional design of the whole, Anaxagoras could present only the means, without revealing their status as mere means.[18]

Socrates alluded, in the first argument, to the Anaxagorean cosmology, according to which the appearance of mind is preceded by an original condition of chaos. He introduced that argument with a reference to the Aristophanic portrayal that made him appear indistinguishable from Anaxagoras. But Socrates distinguished himself by admitting how much the present discussion would be motivated by self-interest: he implicitly criticized Anaxagoras for constructing a cosmological theory of mind without reflecting on his own human perspective in doing so. Socrates now confirms that attack when he turns, for the first and last time, to the silent context of the entire conversation. He likens Anaxagoras' teleological cosmology to an explanation of his own present situation, sitting in the Athenian prison and talking with his companions.

It is as if someone—not Socrates himself—were to claim that Socrates does all that he does "by mind." But what Socrates, in contrast to Anaxagoras, must have understood, is that mind requires psychē; and since psychē is no less the locus of desire, fear, anger, and all the other passions, it would seem impossible for any human being to do all that he does "by mind." Anaxagoras' teaching, in any case, would be equivalent to someone claiming that Socrates acts by mind but then proceeding to argue that the cause of his sitting in prison is the operation of his bones and sinews—of which Socrates gives a surprisingly detailed description—[19]or to argue that the cause of his conversing is the operation of voice and air and hearing. Having indicated the problematic assumptions of teleology, which treats natural phenomena on the model of human action, Socrates criticizes its reversion to mechanism, which treats human action on the model of natural phenomena. Such an account, Socrates charges, necessarily neglects what are truly the causes of his situation, namely, that the Athenians believed it better to condemn him, hence he believed it better to sit there, more just to remain and undergo whatever penalty they commanded.

Socrates assigns equal responsibility to the Athenians, who thought him guilty of injustice and impiety, and to himself, whom he called a divine gift to the city and its greatest benefactor;[20] he is willing, in this case, it seems, to accept opposite causes of the same effect. Nor does either of these causes express the operation of mind based on knowledge of the good, for each is simply an opinion of what is better; such opinions were apparently of no interest to Anaxagoras, but they are decisive for Socrates. At the same time, however, that Socrates juxtaposes his own opinion with that of the Athenian dēmos, he indicates the difference between them. His own opinion of what is better is based on a consideration of what is more just and would otherwise indeed have been in conflict with the latter: his bones and sinews might have been in Megara or Boeotia long ago, carried away by an opinion of what is best, had he not believed it to be more just and more beautiful to undergo the penalty ordered by the city instead of, or at least before fleeing and running away.[21]

Socrates brings to light the inseparability of mechanism and teleology, and with that of body and psychē; for his opinion of the best, which should represent the intention of psychē in contrast to the mechanical operation of the body, would have been carried out not only through the bones and sinews but in their service. What he believes to be good, Socrates makes clear enough, is life and its preservation; he was motivated to face his death sentence only because of reflection on the just and the beautiful, which are not only distinct from what is simply good but apparently incompatible with it. The just and the beautiful are examples of the eidē, which Socrates is about to introduce as *the* cause "in *logos*"; but since they do not in themselves lead to any action, only the particular intention based upon them can be designated truly a cause "in being" (*tō onti*), which must be distinguished—despite its inseparability—from that without which it would not be a cause. To fail to do so, Socrates charges, is to be groping in the dark,[22] to be as blind as those who mistake the pragmata for the beings themselves (cf. 99d–e).

To illustrate this danger, Socrates returns to his critique of cosmology. One theory after another offers a mechanical account of the position of the earth,[23] without searching for the power that causes things to be placed as is best. No such theory satisfies the principle of sufficient reason,[24] for none explains why the cosmos *must* be ordered as it is, since they all ignore the good and binding that truly binds and holds all together.[25] Anaxagoras identified mind as the cause of separation; but if it is to operate in the service of the good, Socrates now stresses, it must be just as much a cause of combination. It must unite, Socrates reminds us, the good with the necessary; but he thus confirms the problematic status of teleology, even while using it as a standard to criticize the insufficiency of mechanistic physics. Socrates could explain his own deed of remaining in prison by articulating the combination of mechanical cause and an opinion of what is better; to account for why the earth remains in place in the center of the heavens, however, requires an analysis of mechanical cause in conjunction with the intention of mind based on knowledge of the good. Socrates would gladly have become the pupil of anyone who possessed knowledge of such a cause, he tells Cebes, but he could neither find a teacher nor discover such knowledge himself.

[99c9–100a3]   Having shown that teleological cause, even if it seems desirable, is not available, Socrates asks Cebes if he wishes to hear a demonstration of "the second sailing in search of the cause" with which he has busied himself.[26] Since this would seem to represent a third mode of inquiry, only the common ground of mechanism and teleology as "investigation of the beings" can explain why Socrates' replacement of that enterprise constitutes what is presumably a second-best alternative. But Socrates' second sailing would be a compromising alternative only if the first way were both desirable and possible, and that is precisely what he proceeds to deny in his subsequent consideration of the danger inherent in all investigation of the beings.[27]

Socrates likens this danger to the misfortune that befalls those who attempt to look directly at the sun during an eclipse: they risk the destruction of their eyes, which they might have avoided by investigating the sun through an image in water or something of that sort. The image of blinding one's eyes instills fear in Socrates, by leading him to conceive of the danger of blinding his psychē. Visual blindness thus serves as an image for noetic blindness, but the image for "noetic vision" cannot be aesthetic vision, since the latter, or at least a certain attitude toward it, is in fact the cause of noetic blindness: the danger of blinding one's psychē arises precisely from looking at things (pragmata) with one's eyes and trying to grasp them with one's senses. Those who will be visually blinded because of their unwillingness to look at a reflection in water, mistake the concealed sun for the sun itself; those who will be psychically blinded by their unwillingness to rely on reflections, in accordance with the analogy, mistake the pragmata grasped through the senses for the beings themselves.[28] If these pragmata were simply perceptible objects as such, the senses would be the source of the eclipse, and the body the only obstacle to direct contact of the psychē with the beings. But that is precisely the belief against which Socrates' image is meant to be a warning. It is the belief that Socrates ascribed to the genuine philosophers (cf. 66e). But Socrates' indications of his own distance from them suggests a very different understanding of the cause of the eclipse: it is not the body, but the needs and desires, and hopes and fears of the psychē—our attachment to "the visible" for example (cf. 83c–d)—that lead us to mistake the pragmata for the beings themselves.[29]

Striving for direct contact of the psychē with the beings is not, then, the means of escape from, but rather the cause of, this deceptive condition, as Socrates confirms by explaining his own way of overcoming it: just as it is necessary to observe the sun through a reflection in order to avoid blinding one's eyes, it is necessary, in order to avoid blinding one's psychē, to "take refuge in *logoi*" and to investigate through them "the truth of the beings." This second sailing on the vessel of logoi might appear to be a compromising alternative to direct observation of the beings themselves. But the necessity of observing the eclipsed sun through its image in water is itself a visual image for the necessity of turning from vision to logos; it is an image, therefore, whose very content demands that, in leading beyond itself, it deny itself.[30] Socrates attempts to correct its possibly misleading implication by insisting that investigation through logoi is no more a compromising reliance on mere images than investigation "in deeds" (*en tois ergois*) would be:[31] his own deed of remaining in prison, which Socrates chose in order to illustrate the problematic character of teleological cosmology, was no less an image than the logoi about the just and the beautiful that provided its motivating grounds.

Socrates does not, therefore, present his turn to investigation through logoi as a complete replacement for investigation in deeds but suggests, rather, their complementary relation. The model for the turn to logos that does not ignore the necessary connection of logoi and erga as equally images of the beings is the Platonic dialogue: Socrates' deed of remaining in prison provides in the *Phaedo* the proper context for the speeches on immortality. What it would have meant to investigate deeds alone is illustrated by Echecrates' opening remark—the Phliasians know only that Socrates drank the poison and died. To look directly at things, without turning to speeches, would be to look directly at the corpse of Socrates and expect to understand everything at stake in this last conversation. But if, on the other hand, investigation of logoi were sufficient in itself, the *Phaedo* would have consisted in a treatise outlining several possible arguments for the immortality of the psychē, without illuminating their context, the effects they produce, and the interests from which they arise, nor, consequently, the clues for determining the intention behind any unsoundness in the arguments. Yet, what is dramatized in the *Phaedo*, of course, is only the representation of deeds in speech: the dialogue points to the limitations of logoi, without violating that turn to logos that Socrates presents as the only way to escape the danger of blinding one's psychē.

To pursue the Socratic second sailing is to replace investigation of the beings themselves with investigation of their truth. Like the light, in Socrates' image, that serves as a bond between the eye and the visible object, the truth must be the bond between the mind and the noetic object. Just as the light makes possible the visibility of the phenomena, as well as the capacity of the eye to see, truth makes possible the knowability of the beings, as well as the capacity of the mind to know:[32] investigation of the truth of the beings is investigation of what makes knowledge possible. To neglect the latter because of having blinded one's psychē is to suffer the same danger as that of misology, through which one deprives oneself of the possibility of discovering the truth of the beings (cf. 90d). But what it means exactly to investigate the truth of the beings through logoi, and thus gain protection against the psychic blindness of misology, Socrates has yet to clarify.

[100a3–100e4]   He begins in each case, he explains, by laying down (hupothemenos) the logos he judges the strongest. Then whatever seems to him to harmonize (sumphōnein) with that, he posits as being true—concerning both cause as well as everything else that is—and whatever does not harmonize, he posits as not true.[33] Socrates first asked Cebes if he wished to hear about his "second sailing in search of the cause." But he seems to have demoted the importance of that particular object when he now claims to pursue this mode of investigation in regard to "all the beings." The procedure he describes indicates, nevertheless, what it means to give up the attempt to gain knowledge of the beings themselves; for it seems to define truth as nothing but consistency of logoi, without suggesting any possibility of overcoming the positivity of the premise in accordance with which such consistency is determined. Socrates' description of hypothesizing the logos judged to be the strongest, which presents no criteria for that judgment, echoes

Simmias' reflection on the necessity of accepting the most irrefutable human logos, given both the impossibility of discovering the truth and the unavailability of a divine logos (85c–d). But in contrast with Simmias, Socrates does not deny the possibility of determining the truth, although he does stress the status of his hypothetical starting point when he claims to posit as true whatever is consistent with it.

Socrates quite reasonably expects Cebes not to understand fully; yet he insists that what he says is nothing new, but only what he is never ceasing to say, both elsewhere and throughout the preceding conversation. He attempts to thematize what has already been in practice apparently by showing Cebes the kind of cause with which he has been occupied: this eidos of the cause is the eidos as cause—not, however, of the coming into being and perishing of something, but of its being *what* it is. To treat the eidos, or "the what it is" (cf. 75d, 78d), as the cause of the determinacy of something else would seem to demand that we inquire what it itself is, and that in turn to presuppose that it is "itself by itself" something. Socrates first asked Simmias if he believed that death is something before offering a definition of it (64c); and he first asked Simmias if he thought "the equal itself" was something before asking if he knew what it is (74a–b). The being of the eidos, Socrates now clarifies, is not given in some "noetic vision" but must be laid down in a hypothesis as the necessary condition for inquiry. If the eidē, then, are "the truth of the beings" that must be sought through a second sailing, the hypothetical method of reasoning and the particular hypothesis of the causality of the eidē are not so arbitrarily connected as Socrates' presentation has led some readers of the dialogue to think.[34]

To illustrate the hypothesized causality of the eidos, Socrates informs Cebes, he must go back to those "much-babbled about things" (cf. 65b, 76d, 78c) and, in returning, set out from them: "the much-babbled about things" are what language renders always already familiar, and Socrates has appealed to them throughout the conversation, but without yet presenting his interpretation of their status. He begins to do so by laying down the hypothesis that the beautiful itself by itself is some-thing, and the good and the great and all the others. Socrates speaks as if each itself by itself were entirely independent; yet his list of examples raises the question of their relation to each other.[35] Included in this list, moreover, is the good, although Socrates has just admitted that it was lack of knowledge of the good that compelled him to abandon the Anaxagorean project in favor of the procedure he is now describing.[36] Socrates intro-duced this technē of logos in an attempt to turn attention away from all self-interest, particularly the urgent self-interest aroused by the present situation, which was determined, Soc-rates acknowledged, by his "opinion of what is better." The good, it would seem, cannot be divorced from self-interest; and if it cannot, for that reason, be treated hypothetically, it would be incapable of being assimilated to the Socratic technē of logos.

But Socrates does not explore these questions. He is eager to gain Cebes' agreement to the hypothesis that each itself by itself is something; for he can then attempt, Socrates promises, to demonstrate the cause and to discover how the psychē is immortal. While we would expect, instead, a demonstration of the immortality of the psychē and a discovery of the cause, Socrates' interlacing of words suggests that the final argument for immortality will be in the service of his demonstration of the eidos as cause, rather than the other way around.[37] Cebes, in any case, quickly offers his assent—and Socrates just as quickly accepts it—to the hypothesis that the beautiful itself is something; it furnishes the required basis for the further claim that, if anything else is beautiful other than the beautiful itself, it is only because it participates (metechei) in that beautiful. Cebes again immediately agrees, without raising the question of the difference between the being of the itself by itself and its being the cause of something other having the quality that it is.[38] In fact, however, Socrates seems now to have identified the cause of such an attribution not with the eidos, but with the relation of "participation." Of course, he is unwilling to make any confident claim about how it works, whether by presence (*parousia*) or communion (*koinōnia*) or whatever else one wishes to call it—just as, in public prayers, one addresses the gods, because of ignorance of their correct names, by whatever name is pleasing to them.[39]

If someone tries to fill in this formula for an unknown "how"[40]—to suggest that something comes to be beautiful because of a lovely color or shape or anything of that sort—Socrates claims to be confused, compelled to bid farewell to all these other wise causes.[41] He insists only on the explanation that "all the beautiful come to be beautiful through the beautiful." This is the safest answer Socrates can give to himself and to others, but not absolutely safe, since, as a claim about genesis, it betrays its ignorance of cause in the ordinary sense. It implicitly raises the question as to whether anything can come to be beautiful simply or whether, rather, it only comes to be more beautiful than it was previously, or more beautiful than something else with which it is compared. Socrates confirms the limitation of his first claim with an apparently superfluous repetition: the claim that "through the beautiful the beautiful (are) beautiful"—because it is restricted to the question of something *being* what it is—provides an answer that is safe, Socrates promises, not only for him but for anyone else to give. The safe raft on which to sail through the dangers of life that Simmias sought in some divine logos (85d), Socrates has now replaced with a safe raft on which to sail through the dangers of logos. But the price he pays for this safety is restriction to a "simple and artless and perhaps foolish" answer that is indeed pre-Promethean, an eidos of cause that abandons any falsifiable claim to knowledge of how something comes to be or ceases to be what it is.

[100e5–101d1]   Socrates seeks Cebes' acceptance of this safe answer before extending it, for, in doing so, he points to certain perplexities concealed by his original model. Through greatness, Socrates inquires, are the great great and the greater greater, and through smallness the smaller smaller? Socrates does not mention "the small" but only "the smaller"; he calls our attention to the fact that "greatness" is the name not only for one member, but for the pair of opposites. That something said to be small is actually only smaller than something else, however, makes one wonder how anything could be said to be great without further qualification. The latter ascription seems, rather, to be a misleadingly abbreviated way of expressing the relation of one thing being greater than another. When, in fact, Socrates just described his perplexities about greatness, he spoke of one man or one horse being greater than another; his reference to members of two species suggests that, even if something were said to be great, it would be relative to the kind of thing it is. Socrates does not go back to ask, although perhaps he should have, whether any of the so-called beautiful things is only more beautiful by the relative absence of ugliness, either in comparison with other members of the same kind or as a superlative instance of one kind, which would have to be compared to other kinds.[42] To be beautiful, then, would always be a matter of being more or less so.

Socrates' example of greatness and smallness recalls, in any case, the difficulties he eventually came to recognize in his prephilosophic opinions about cause—how a man grows larger, "by what" one man or one horse is greater than another, or ten greater than eight, or a two-cubit length greater than a length of one cubit (96c–e). He is preparing to instill in Cebes the very perplexities he himself experienced when he found himself blinded by the investigation of nature and recognized that he could no longer claim to possess knowledge of how something becomes greater, or how anything comes to be at all. Socrates must replace the fear of death, which led Cebes to seek a demonstration of the imperishability of the psychē, by the fear of self-contradiction, which must compel Cebes, as it does Socrates, to maintain the safety of logos at all costs.

Cebes would not accept the claim, Socrates advises, that one man was greater or smaller than another "by a head" but would insist that one thing can be greater than another only by greatness and because of the great, one thing smaller than another only by smallness and because of the small. Socrates emphasizes that Cebes would *speak* in this way—he may apparently *think* otherwise—for if he were to speak of one man as greater or smaller than another by a head, Socrates warns, he would fear the attack of an opposing logos, charging, first, that the greater would be greater and the smaller smaller by the same thing, and further, that the greater would be greater by a head, which is small, and that would be monstrous! Cebes quite understandably laughs at Socrates' warning: the laughter that has all along accompanied the fear of death is being transformed, along with that fear, into the laughter appropriate to the fear of self-contradiction. What Cebes is to fear is an attack against the claim that one cause could produce opposite results, or that one result could be produced by a cause opposite to it. This is precisely the structure Socrates outlined for Simmias in describing that exchange of greater and lesser through which courage and moderation come into being from their opposites (68d–69a).[43] From that irrational "shadow-painting," Socrates assured Simmias, the true character of virtue together with phronēsis is a "purification." He must now spell out for Cebes exactly what is required for such "purification": he must disclose the means of avoiding any apparent contradiction that could be exploited by the disputatious to arouse distrust in logos (cf. 90c, 101e).

Socrates proceeds to warn Cebes of the danger in claiming that ten is greater than eight by two and because of this, or that a two-cubit length is greater than a one-cubit length by half; he must seek safety, rather, in the claim that ten is greater than eight by number and because of number, a two-cubit length greater than a one-cubit length by magnitude.[44] But the fear motivating these answers is only "somehow" the same as in the previous case, Socrates admits; for Cebes would now have to claim, in following Socrates' advice, that ten is greater than eight and eight smaller than ten by the same thing, number, or a two-cubit length greater and a one-cubit length smaller by the same thing, magnitude. Since, indeed, Socrates has just established that everything greater must be so only because of the great, everything smaller only because of the small, number should be the cause, presumably, only of something being countable, magnitude only of something being measurable.

Socrates does not stop to explore these difficulties concerning number or magnitude and the relations of being greater or smaller. He approaches, rather, the final perplexity that led him to recognize the deficiency of the whole series of his prephilosophic claims to knowledge of cause. If one is added to one, or if one is divided in half, he warns Cebes, you would not say that addition or division is the cause of two coming to be; but "in a great voice"—not apparently in thinking—you would say you know of no other way each comes to be than by "participating in the proper being (ousia) of each in which it participates." Cebes must accept no cause of the coming to be of two other than participation in the dyad, while whatever is to be one must participate in the monad. Cebes does not ask whether whatever is to be two participates at the same time in number, or whether, in being greater than one, it also participates in the great. Socrates supposedly wants Cebes to stick with the safe answer he has proposed when he commands him to bid farewell to additions and divisions and all such refinements, leaving these for wiser men to deal with; but whether the safe answer is truly free from these refined perplexities has been put into question by the very examples Socrates furnished to illustrate it.

Whatever perplexities Socrates may have concealed from Cebes, however, he has reasons for doing so. For Cebes must learn, Socrates warns, "to distrust his own shadow and inexperience." It is the inexperience that, without a technē of logos, would lead to the danger of misology, for the disputatious who would attack his self-contradictory claims are voices that Socrates compels him to internalize. Cebes must undergo a risky development, becoming, on the one hand, similar enough to the disputatious to take seriously a purely verbal contradiction, while remaining, on the other hand, unlike the disputatious, whose discovery of contradiction leads them to abandon all confidence in logos as a means for pursuit of the truth.

Socrates can use their attack against any claim to knowledge of cause in the ordinary sense in order to overcome their simultaneous attack against logos itself only because of his discovery of the safe raft that consists in a technē of logos. Of course, the art of reasoning Socrates has described, and the final argument in which it will be applied, thus seem to be as dependent on the disputatious as the series of arguments in the first half of the dialogue was on the genuine philosophers. Socrates has satisfied Cebes, in any case, with his proposed solution to the problem of the cause of two and one; he has presumably completed a model invulnerable to any disputatious attack exploiting the perplexities that compelled him to abandon his original claims to knowledge of cause. He is prepared on that basis to return to his account of the procedure of hypothetical reasoning; that general account seems to have been merely interrupted, although it will in fact be significantly affected, by the consideration of its application to the Socratic eidos of cause.

[101d1–102a1]   With the fear of the disputatious instilled in him, Cebes must hold fast, Socrates warns, to that "safety of the hypothesis" that precludes the possibility of self-contradiction. And if someone were to attack the hypothesis itself, Socrates continues, you would bid farewell to him and would not respond until you had investigated the consequences of the hypothesis, whether they harmonize (sumphōnei) with each other or are in discord (diaphōnei).[45] Socrates' account might appear to agree thus far with the initial statement that he feared was not yet clear enough for Cebes to understand (100a). But Socrates has now transformed a description of his own practice into a recommendation for Cebes' practice; and he no longer speaks of laying down as true whatever harmonizes with an accepted hypothesis, but rather, of determining the harmony or discord with one another of the consequences that follow from it. In his initial account, Socrates identified truth with consistency, since his primary concern was to confirm the impossibility of trying to grasp the pragmata through one's senses, and to replace it with the safety of investigating the truth of the beings in logoi. But the safety of consistency with a given starting point did not necessarily extend, in Socrates' first account, to the starting point itself, which was simply whatever logos he judged to be strongest. That starting point is now specified, in Socrates' present elaboration, to be a hypothesis safe in itself from all possible contradiction.[46] Yet Socrates only now seems to admit the possibility that consequences that contradict each other might be entailed by the one hypothesis with which they are severally in accord.[47] He has, after all, just offered the example of number as a safe answer to the question of the cause of ten being greater than eight as well as of eight being smaller than ten. He can no longer claim, therefore, to identify as true whatever follows from the hypothesis, and in fact ceases to speak of truth at all.

Socrates confirms this adjustment by the further step he now adds: when it becomes necessary to give a logos of the initial hypothesis itself—Cebes is not told when that would be—he must give it in the same way, laying down another hypothesis that would appear best among the higher ones. According to the original account Socrates presented, the hypothesis laid down as strongest could not itself be rejected, for whatever comes to light as inconsistent with it is simply identified as not true. But Socrates now acknowledges the necessity of defending that hypothesis "in the same way": once the consequences of the initial hypothesis have been shown to harmonize with it and with each other, the initial hypothesis must be defended by showing that it harmonizes with a hypothesis from which it can be derived, as well as with other consequences derivable from the same hypothesis. Since the call for justification of the initial hypothesis follows upon the examination of the harmony of its consequences, that very examination must be capable of bringing to light the presuppositions of that hypothesis not yet recognized or thematized in the initial agreement on it. The "higher hypotheses," then, to which appeal is made for justification, must be those implicit presuppositions of the initial hypothesis;[48] and the "best" among them would seem to refer to that which would entail the most comprehensive set of consistent consequences, including the initial hypothesis itself.[49] The ascending movement to a higher hypothesis is thus an archeological movement uncovering the deeper levels of assumption concealed in the initial hypothesis: every step forward would actually be a step backward in recognizing an apparently self-evident starting point to be in fact derivative.

This process must be carried on, Socrates concludes, until reaching "something sufficient," a starting point that is alone self-justifying, presumably, because it conceals no more implicit presuppositions from which it could be derived. Socrates' description of this procedure as a dialogic activity, however, suggests that "something sufficient" is nothing but that higher hypothesis that would defend the initial hypothesis against a particular questioner and thus silence any further attack. Simmias was persuaded of the preexistence of the psychē because he was so certain of the existence of the beings themselves that no further examination seemed to him necessary (77a, 92d–e). Cebes is about to be persuaded by Socrates' final argument on immortality because of consequences drawn from the hypothesis, with which he is completely satisfied, that things are what they are by virtue of participating in the proper ousia of the various qualities ascribed to them. He demanded no further examination, therefore, when Socrates insisted that he could not yet consider whether this participation was to be construed as parousia or koinōnia or in some other way. It is an anonymous interlocutor who will bring just that problem to light by "attacking the hypothesis," questioning the relation between the eidē and the things said to participate in them (103b). And Socrates, in accordance with his own recommendation, will delay an adequate response—until it is too late!—before establishing the immortality of the psychē as a consistent consequence of his hypothesis.

The point of sufficiency Socrates reaches in his conversation with Cebes and Simmias thus seems to be only a provisional stopping point: while Cebes' satisfaction with the final argument brings the discussion to an end, Socrates confirms the truth behind Simmias' dissatisfaction by insisting that they would have to examine more clearly their first hypotheses (107b). Socrates would have to show, in accordance with the procedure he has outlined, how the causality of the eidē could be derived from a higher hypothesis: he would have to confront the problem of participation to which the objection of the anonymous interlocutor points. Were Socrates directing the conversation toward this anonymous interlocutor, he would be challenged, then, by a different determination of "something sufficient"; and in that case, as the dramatic action of the dialogue suggests, he might not have succeeded in accomplishing a demonstration of the immortality of the psychē. Not the *Phaedo* alone, but every Platonic dialogue, points to this tension between the meaning of "something sufficient," on the one hand as a provisional stopping point determined by the subjective satisfaction of particular conversants and the contingencies of the occasion, and, on the other, as that asymptotic standard of presuppositionlessness toward which all examination of hypotheses by way of higher hypotheses ought to proceed.[50] The formula for the impossible reconcilation of this tension is "the good": no further inquiry would be needed, Socrates admitted before introducing his second sailing, if only he possessed knowledge of the good.

Socrates concludes his address to Cebes with the advice that he must not mix up the starting point and its consequences as the disputatious do. Socrates might seem to allude to his own "mixed-up" way (97b), according to which examination of the consistency of consequences derived from a given hypothesis leads to the discovery of a presupposition from which that hypothesis is itself a consequence. But the disputatious—those, apparently, whom Cebes was warned to dismiss when they attack the hypothesis itself before considering its consequences—do not recognize the difference between the way from, and the way to, first principles.[51] Instead of aiming at a truly sufficient starting point, they believe their own wisdom so sufficient, Socrates charges, that they are content even when mixing everything together (*homou panta*): they are satisfied with the epistemological equivalent of Anaxagorean chaos, the state of the cosmos before the appearance of mind, in which the one genesis of combination is not balanced by the opposite genesis of separation (cf. 72c). Refusing to abandon confidence in their own wisdom, the disputatious cast blame on the weakness of logos itself; their assumption that logoi have no more stability than the pragmata is precisely the belief that, Socrates warned, is the source of misology, the greatest evil (cf. 90c).

Cebes must proceed in the way Socrates has described if he wishes "to discover something of the beings." Such a wish would hold no attraction for the disputatious, who are content with their undefended claim to its impossibility. Yet, once again, it is Socrates himself who seems to hide behind the mask of the disputatious.[52] For he admitted that, confronted with the verbal contradiction lurking behind all claims to knowledge of cause, he was forced to abandon the desire to discover the beings themselves; he did so, however, precisely because of recognizing the necessity and possibility of investigating "the truth of the beings" by means of the technē of logos he has just elaborated. Cebes will do as he says, Socrates concludes, if he is "one of the philosophers." Socrates intends, perhaps, to test Cebes' awareness of the difference that should by now be evident: Does he belong to the class of the "genuine philosophers" who desire knowledge of the beings, or is he one who recognizes the need to abandon that impossible pursuit in favor of a second sailing?

[102a2–102b2]   Cebes provides no explicit evidence of whether he has passed this test. Moved, apparently, simply by the appeal to their status as philosophers, Cebes, in union with Simmias, assures Socrates, "You speak most truly." Yet their enthusiasm is suspicious: they have never even asked if the hypothesis of the causality of the eidē is only one illustration among others of the general procedure of hypothetical reasoning, and, if not, what the necessary connection between them is. Their sudden affirmation of clarity calls to mind the sudden disillusionment they expressed in common at the conclusion of the first series of arguments. Indeed, just as Echecrates interrupted then to announce his sympathy with Phaedo's description of the confusion and mistrust generated by the objections of Simmias and Cebes (88c–e), he now interrupts to confirm the satisfaction of "we who were absent" and are simply listening to Phaedo's report. The boundaries marked by this intrusion thus constitute a frame around the core of the dialogue, which moves from the threat of misology to the security of Socrates' technē of logos.

Imitating the enthusiasm of Simmias and Cebes, Echecrates praises Socrates for having made these matters wonderfully clear, even to a man with little sense (*smikron noun*)! Echecrates' mere figure of speech confirms the independence of the Socratic technē of logos from any account—teleological or otherwise—of psychē as mind. But since Echecrates shows no awareness of the significance of his figure of speech, he makes us wonder whether Plato intends his reader to share in this feeling of clarity. Socrates does seem to have succeeded in turning attention to the logos itself: whereas Echecrates first requested to hear both what Socrates said and what pathē he suffered (88e), he now requests simply to hear what was said next. But whether Socrates has been equally successful in explaining the technē of logos illustrated by the hypothesis of the causality of the eidē is put into question by Phaedo's response to Echecrates. After imitating in detail the speeches of a daylong conversation and and narrating the matter between them,[53] he suddenly turns to indirect discourse and merely summarizes the discussion providing the grounds for the application of Socrates' methodological reflections to the final argument on immortality.

Socrates went on, Phaedo thinks, after these matters had been granted "and it was agreed that each of the *eidē* is something, and the others, participating in them, take their names from these very things." What should presumably constitute the philosophic peak of the dialogue, Phaedo presents as a mere conclusion with no argument in defense, introduced by the qualification, "I believe." His only prior moment of hesitancy was in expressing his belief that Plato was sick on the day of Socrates' death, and the only subsequent one his admission that he cannot remember the name of the interlocutor who raises the question of the relation between the eidē and the pragmata—the very problem he now passes over so quickly in a single summary statement. Phaedo's insufficient report of the discussion on participation, which might have pointed to the higher hypotheses justifying the first hypotheses of the conversation, seems to cast doubt on his trustworthiness as narrator; yet precisely that deficiency allows him to proceed with his report of the final argument on immortality. Exemplifying, however unwittingly, the inevitable "impurity" of the procedure of hypothetical reasoning,[54] Phaedo shows himself to be a most appropriate Iolaus to Socrates' Heracles in the battle for the salvation of the logos.

CHAPTER ELEVEN

Immortality

[102b3–103a3]   Having summarized the agreement on the be-ing of the eidē and their relation to the pragmata, Phaedo re-sumes direct discourse to report the argument based on that agreement, through which Socrates has promised to discover the immortality of the psychē. To say that things receive their names from the eidē in which they participate might seem to suggest, as its paradigmatic illustration, the individual person designated by his proper name. The proper name operates like the Athenian logos that each year declares the sacred ship, despite its being worn away part by part, to be the very "ship of Theseus" that once made its legendary journey to Crete (58a). Socrates points to the rhetorical power of the proper name when, just before drinking the poison, he tries to comfort Crito by commanding him not to say, as he buries the corpse, that he is burying "Socrates," for to speak in that way produces terrible effects (115e). By means of this restriction, Socrates hopes to convince Crito of the identification of the self with a psychē that is unaffected by death and burial; the proper name betrays the pathē that motivate our particular interest in positing the identity of the self that remains the same through all change. But while Socrates now chooses Simmias as an example of a pragma, he does not ask in which eidos he must participate in order to receive the name Simmias. Socrates suggests, by this silence, that what the proper name in fact illustrates is the mistake in construing any pragma as a neutral substratum that remains the same despite the plurality of eidē in which it participates. Rather, each pragma is an inseparable unity of a subject and a quality ascribed to it, and when the opposite pragma is ascribed to that subject, that inseparable unity constitutes the opposite pragma.[1]

Socrates therefore chooses an example in which Simmias is nothing but the accidental center of two opposite relations. In calling Simmias greater than Socrates but smaller than Phaedo, Socrates asks Cebes, would he be saying that there is in Simmias greatness and smallness? Socrates emphasizes the speech through which this predication is made. For the greatness or smallness in Simmias is the product of our act of comparing him with another. While, therefore, the two relations in which he stands might seem to exist at the same time, that may be an illusion that results from forgetting the two acts of comparison, which cannot, perhaps, be performed simultaneously. Only an observer who suppresses his own acts, when he looks at Simmias standing in the middle of Socrates and Phaedo, can grant Simmias "the eponym, to be great and small."[2] The independent status of the two opposites in which Simmias participates disappears in the name referring to one continuum of more and less, along which Simmias occupies a particular position.[3]

Even to speak with the proper qualification, however, and to say that Simmias is greater than Socrates and smaller than Phaedo, is not true "in these words," Socrates explains. For it implies that Simmias is greater or smaller because of being Simmias, or because of Socrates who is smaller being Socrates, or Phaedo who is greater being Phaedo. But none of them is great or small apart from the relations between them, or rather, as Socrates now insists, between the opposite qualities themselves. Expressed correctly, therefore, it is only the greatness in Simmias that exceeds the smallness in another, while the smallness in him is exceeded by the greatness in another. Of course, the greatness in Simmias that exceeds the smallness in another is simply his height, the very same height that constitutes the smallness in Simmias exceeded by the greatness in

another. Just as Cebes laughed at Socrates' warning of a potential disputatious attack (101b), Socrates now laughs at the pre-
cision of a speech that sounds like a written legal contract,
which is designed, presumably, to provide protection against
the same threat of verbal contradiction.

Socrates hopes, consequently, to make it appear to Cebes as
it does to him, that not only would the great itself never wish to
be great and at the same time small, but also greatness in us
would never admit the small nor wish to be exceeded. While
Simmias can become smaller, having been greater, greatness in
him, since it is unwilling to admit its opposite, must, when the
small approaches, either flee and withdraw or have already
been destroyed.[4] Now the alternative of flight or destruction is
not applicable to the great itself, since it is presumably not
present in the first place in the pragma characterized as greater;
and it is not clear how, when *we* become smaller, greatness *in
us* could withdraw rather than be destroyed. But this alternative, which will turn out to be crucial for the argument, Socrates is not yet prepared to explore. He must establish only that
greatness in us does not wish to abide and admit smallness,
thus becoming other than what it was, nor does the small that
is in us wish to become or be great, but rather, like any opposite, it must either depart or be destroyed in the change. Greatness or smallness in us, according to Socrates' formulation,
only "wishes" to remain what it was: it might be compelled,
against its inclination, to admit its opposite, which would constitute its own destruction. The "wishing" of greatness or
smallness not to coexist with its opposite—not to violate, that
is, the law of noncontradiction—looks like the "wishing" of
pleasure or pain not to become present in a man at the same
time as the other (60b). But such a personification, Socrates
suggested in his opening remarks, is the unrecognized projection onto apparent opposites of the human will to separate
them.

Socrates might appear, in any case, to contrast the mutually exclusive opposite qualities with the subject that can per-
sist through the change from one opposite to the other while
remaining what it is: "I (*egō*), having admitted and abided

smallness, and still being what I am, am this same one, small."
But his formulation does not in fact affirm the identity through
this change of a neutral subject; it suggests, rather, that "Socrates great" is one pragma and "Socrates small" its opposite.[5]
How, then, can the immanent qualities, greatness and smallness in something, that determine the opposite pragmata generated from each other, at the same time preserve the safety of
logos, which requires that no opposite "dare" to be or become
its opposite? Socrates describes this battle of opposites in us
metaphorically, by borrowing the military language of advance
and attack, flight and withdrawal, destruction or abiding.[6] But
his obscurity about the status of that mediating level on which
genesis is actualized only confirms his own silence in specifying the nature of "participation" (100d); it suffers from the
same incompleteness as Phaedo's report on the discussion concerning the relation between the eidē and the pragmata said to
participate in them.

[103a4–103c9]   The claim that no opposite that is still what it
was can ever become or be its opposite brings the discussion
full circle round to the first argument, although Cebes, to
whom the two arguments have been addressed, seems unaware
of it. But someone whose name Phaedo does not remember
expresses surprise—he swears by the gods—at Socrates' apparent denial of their original premise, according to which the
greater comes to be from the smaller and the smaller from the
greater, exemplifying the necessary genesis of all opposites
from each other (70e). The anonymous interlocutor, who
seems to be the only one following the conversation with sufficient attention,[7] enacts a Socratic second sailing: he brings to
light the fact that the two arguments concerned with the relation between opposites are themselves the manifestation in
logos of the relation between opposites.

Listening most attentively to this objection, Socrates,
Phaedo reports, threw his head to one side, looking away perhaps from the speaker. Socrates commends the speaker's
manliness while reproaching him for neglecting the difference
between the two arguments; that difference is rendered ex-

plicit, nevertheless, only as a result of this objection. The first argument, Socrates now contends, was concerned with the coming to be of one pragma from its opposite, whereas the present one is concerned with the opposite itself, either in nature or in us, which cannot come to be from its opposite. Whereas the first argument dealt with those things possessing the opposites and named by their names, the last deals with the things themselves according to which the pragmata are named. In presenting this response, Socrates addresses his anonymous interlocutor "dear one"; he addressed Cebes in the same way when he completed his argument for the necessity of a cyclical genesis between opposites (72c). Socrates claims now to clarify the distinction between opposite pragmata and opposites themselves, though without specifying any further consequences of the division within the latter, between those "in us" and those "in nature." Yet the qualities in us through which genesis is actualized would seem to belong on an intermediate level between that of opposite pragmata, on the one hand, and opposite eidē, on the other. Despite Socrates' affectionate address to his anonymous interlocutor, his response seems to repeat once more the insufficiency of Phaedo's summary of the fundamental hypothesis on the participation of the pragmata in the eidē.

The anonymous interlocutor has put into question the compatibility of the premises of the first and last arguments; an adequate response to his objection would seem to require, therefore, a more thorough examination than Socrates conducts of the relation between the two halves of the dialogue. But such an examination is in tension with the immediate challenge of providing a demonstration of the immortality of the psychē. It is a task assigned by Plato to his reader, therefore, not by Socrates to his companions. Socrates is able to avoid it, because he answers the anonymous interlocutor while at the same time looking up at Cebes, who admits he is not disturbed by the objection. Socrates is eager to agree with Cebes on "this simply"—that no opposite will ever *be* its opposite. He transforms the claim, uttered just before he was interrupted, that no opposite will ever be or *become* its opposite;

and since the question of becoming is relevant not to opposites in nature, but only in us, Socrates thus avoids having to clarify the status of the latter.

[103c10–104c6]   Having established, however dogmatically, their fundamental premise, Socrates asks Cebes to investigate whether he will agree that he calls something hot and cold, qualities which are other than fire and snow. Yet in accordance with what was said previously, it must seem that snow, though other than the cold, will never admit the hot while still being what it was but will, when the hot approaches, either withdraw or be destroyed; and again fire, though other than the hot, will, when the cold approaches, either go away or be destroyed but will never dare admit coldness while still being what it was. Socrates seems to have complicated the argument unnecessarily with these examples. In fact, however, they raise a crucial question for the application of this model to the conclusion of the argument: If fire as carrier of heat is equivalent to psychē as carrier of life, what is the equivalent to snow as carrier of cold? The drama of the dialogue indicates an answer—the poison (cf. 63d, 118a). But Socrates will be as silent about a carrier of death, parallel to that of life, as he will be about an eidos of death, parallel to that of life. This is, of course, no arbitrary silence. For the poison brings death simply by chilling the body—an effect that will be portrayed most vividly; it thus points to the fundamental mystery of how psychē can be affected by this corporeal change. Socrates is understandably silent about the causality of the poison, for to know how that operates is to know what psychē is.

Socrates' description of snow and fire, characterized essentially by the cold and the hot, seems to be parallel to his previous description of the immanent qualities of greatness and smallness in us. While these latter, however, are themselves opposites that derive their names from the great or the small while coming to be present in some other thing, fire and snow are not themselves opposites, but each seems to be a pragma characterized by one opposite quality. On the basis of this transition from a triple-level to a double-level analysis, Socrates can conclude that there are some cases in which not only the eidos itself is worthy of having the same name for all time, but also something other that always possesses the shape (morphē) of that eidos, whenever it is. Whereas Simmias would never deserve for all time the name "great" or "small," because he is always greater or smaller in relation to some other, fire or snow always deserve the names "hot" or "cold," since each always— as long as it exists at all—possesses the shape of the eidos hot or cold. Of course, since being hot or cold is a matter of degree, fire would be only hotter than something else, and snow colder, even if it does appear to be contradictory to speak of cold fire or hot snow.

Socrates hopes to make the argument clearer, as he did previously (cf. 96d–97b, 101b–c), by considering the example of numbers: since every number is determined by participation in one of two opposites, the even and the odd, it could never admit the other and still be what it was.[8] When Socrates formulates the principle in terms of names, however, asking whether the odd must somehow always have this name we now utter, Cebes agrees immediately, without considering the fact that, if Socrates referred to whatever is characterized as odd, it might just as well be called "uneven" (cf. 104e). But Socrates clarifies the status of "the odd" as a principle when he asks whether "this alone among the beings" or also some other that is not itself the odd must nevertheless always be called this, together with its own name, since it is of such a nature that it is never separated from the odd. The triad (hē trias), he suggests, can always be addressed by its own name as well as by that of the odd; the pentad also, and indeed half of all numbers, are by nature such that each, while not the same as the odd, is nevertheless always odd; and again, two and four and the whole other row of numbers, while not the same as the even, is each nevertheless always even.[9] Socrates articulates for Cebes the point he wanted to clarify through the example of numbers: not only do opposites themselves *appear* incapable of admitting each other, but also those things that, while not being opposites always possess opposites, *seem* incapable of admitting the *idea* that is the opposite of that which is in them,[10] so that when this comes, they must either be destroyed or withdraw.

Three (*ta tria*), Socrates suggests as an example, will be destroyed or suffer anything else before submitting to becoming even while still being three and odd. Socrates necessarily shifts, although almost imperceptibly, from the triad to three; for, like the monad or dyad in which anything that is to be one or two must participate (101c), the triad, in which anything that is to be three must participate, could not be destroyed, since it would not enter into arithmetical operations at all. Three, by contrast, must be a countable collection that would be destroyed as three if, for example, one were taken away; yet Socrates could not refer to an actual collection of objects, for while they might be said to be three, they could not themselves be called "odd."[11] The passage must point, then, to the distinction, which Aristotle reports, between two kinds of number:[12] while the mathematical number, like the eidetic number, could be characterized as essentially even or odd, it could also be said, unlike the eidetic number, to be destroyed when involved in an arithmetical operation that produces the opposite of the idea it always possesses. As an intermediate between a collection of objects and the eidetic number, it would allow for the "generation and destruction" of numbers in arithmetical operations, while remaining subordinate to the safe answer, that the cause of any countable collection being what it is, is participation in its proper ousia (cf. 101c).

[104c7–105b4]   The ambiguity of the conclusion Socrates draws from his consideration of numbers—that not only opposite eidē but also "certain others" do not abide the approach of an opposite—justifies his subsequent invitation to define what sort these are. Yet Cebes is quite understandably confused by Socrates' new formulation: the nonopposites that refuse to admit opposites must be those things that always compel whatever they occupy to have not only their own idea but also that of some opposite. For the exclusion of an opposite is here assigned to something that is intermediary between an eidetic opposite with which it is inseparably connected and some other thing that it occupies; it has, moreover, its own idea that it imposes, together with that of the eidetic opposite, on that which it occupies. To clarify this new formulation, Socrates renders explicit the implied distinction between the triad and three: the triad in its intermediary role is the idea of three that compels whatever it occupies to be three as well as odd.[13]

Just when Socrates seems to have arrived at an adequate clarification, however, he exploits the ambiguity of his original formulation by expanding, while apparently merely repeating, it: such a thing—now, presumably, whatever is occupied—would never admit the idea that is the opposite of the shape (morphē) responsible for producing its own characterization.[14] A collection of three units occupied by the idea of three would never admit the idea of the even, for the latter is the opposite of the odd, which is, as Socrates goes on to confirm, the morphē that produced its characterization as three and odd.[15] And since three has no part in the idea of the even, Socrates concludes, the triad is uneven. Socrates seems to have pursued a rather circuitous route merely to establish that the idea of any odd number must be uneven. In doing so, in any case, he casts doubt on his original claim that not only the odd itself, but also some other—the triad, for example—must always have the name "odd" whenever it is (104a). He has, furthermore, implicitly put into question the appropriateness of applying the model of numbers, with its division into two kinds, to the case of psychē: Socrates will never speak of an idea of psychē, in which each particular psychē must participate, corresponding to the eidetic number that is itself an idea, imposed together with the idea of the even or the odd on any mathematical number participating in it.[16]

Rather than explicitly raise this question, however, Socrates proposes to define once more, with further unacknowledged variations, what sort of nonopposites do not admit opposites themselves. The triad, though not the opposite of the even, not only refuses to admit it, but also brings forward against the even the opposite with which it is always connected; and in the same way, the dyad always brings forward the opposite of the odd, and fire the opposite of the cold, and all the numerous others.[17] Socrates has expanded his military metaphor, for the intermediary is now not only an occupying force, but it actively brings forward the opposite, with which it is allied, in self-defense against the approach of the hostile opposite. Socrates asks Cebes to examine the revised formulation that results from this addition: not only do opposites themselves exclude each other, but also that which always brings forward some opposite to that which it approaches will never admit "the opposition" of that which is brought forward. Socrates no longer speaks of the opposite itself approaching— either its own opposite, or something that always possesses its opposite, or something that compels whatever it occupies to have its own idea as well as that of an opposite, or whatever is occupied by that which always possesses an opposite. He points ahead to the problematic application of this principle. For when his silence about the poison as the carrier of death compels him to speak of death itself as approaching a man, we do not know what this active agent could be. At the moment, in any case, the opposite itself is treated as passive, and its own opposite is said to be excluded, not necessarily by what is approached, but by the active intermediary that brings forward an opposite to whatever it approaches.

After transforming the general principle through so many twists and turns, Socrates offers to refresh Cebes' memory, since it cannot hurt to listen to it over and over again! Just after this warning, however, in response to an alleged repetition that in fact puts into question the application of the general principle,[18] Cebes claims to be following Socrates and to agree "most intensely." Socrates is therefore saved from having to specify whether the exclusion of an opposite has been attributed to the nonopposite that always brings forward an opposite to something it occupies or to that which is thus occupied, or to both at once. The argument has progressed from the example of Simmias great and small, through the example of hot fire and cold snow, to the example of odd three and even two. There is, in the first case, nothing in the nature of the subject that connects it inseparably with one opposite or the other, since Simmias can become greater having been smaller, or he can be greater in one relation, smaller in another. The principle of exclusion of opposites applied, consequently, not to the subject that admits both contraries, but to the greatness in him, which is in fact an abbreviated expression for one relation, and the smallness in him, which is an abbreviated expression for another. In the case of fire and snow, by contrast, each subject is essentially characterized by one of two opposite qualities, although its being so characterized is a matter of degree; heat can be transferred by fire, moreover, to some other thing, which is not itself essentially hot or cold but can change from one to the other. Only in the third case is each subject not only essentially even or odd, but never merely more or less so; and in this case there is no neutral subject that can change from one opposite to the other. Socrates does not clarify which is the proper paradigm to be applied to the case of psychē and its characterization, which is presumably the point of the argument.[19]

[105b5–105d5]   Socrates is prepared, without that clarification, to offer Cebes a model for a "more refined" answer that goes beyond the first "unlearned" one, whose own safety is nevertheless guaranteed by the preceding argument. If Cebes were to ask, "By what coming to be present in something will it be hot?", Socrates would no longer be restricted to the simple answer, "By heat," but could now give the more refined answer, "By fire." And if he were to ask, "By what coming to be in a body will it be ill?", Socrates would no longer cling to the simple answer, "By illness," but would boldly respond, "By fever." If Cebes were to ask, finally, "By what coming to be in a number will it be odd?", Socrates would no longer be compelled to answer, "By oddness," but can now reply, "By the monad." Socrates' refined answer represents an advance in knowledge of cause in the ordinary sense, but only at the price of giving up irrefutability. It assigns a cause that is neither sufficient—since its safety depends upon its essential connection with some independent opposite—nor necessary—since the result it produces might just as well have been produced by some other cause.

The argument that prepares for this refined answer has established that fire can be the cause of heat only and not of cold, but it did not and could not have established that fire is the only cause of heat; conversing might just as well be the cause of heat (cf. 63d), or even fever, as Socrates suggests by adding it between his original examples of fire and number. And cooling might just as well as fever be the cause of illness, or at least of death (cf. 118a). That it is the monad that renders some number odd may seem to be an advance over the simple answer, "By oddness"; yet it is no longer a necessary answer, for Socrates has just admitted that the idea of the odd can be brought forward by the idea of any odd number. The monad, moreover, which is now identified as the refined cause of any number being odd, was first presented as the safe answer to the question of the cause of anything—apparently even or odd, or perhaps not to be construed in a mathematical sense at all— being one (101c).[20] While the monad, in its mathematical function as an intermediary, is subordinate to oddness, the latter may be subordinate to the monad as the eidetic cause of unity. Socrates thus points with this last example, to the problematic subordination of psychē, which will soon be assigned a merely intermediary function as the cause of life in the body.[21]

The model for the refined answer, furthermore, preserves, rather than resolves, the equivocation of the preparatory argument on the exclusion of opposites; for it does not indicate whether the quality in question characterizes only that which is approached or that which brings it forward, or both. Fire, which is essentially hot and therefore never admits the cold, can also bring forward heat to whatever it approaches, making it too hot. But fever, though it brings forward illness to the body it approaches, could not itself be said to be ill any more than healthy. And even if the monad were to make the number in which it comes to be present odd, it is questionable whether it is itself necessarily odd and not also even,[22] or neither odd nor even. Socrates thus distinguishes between a cause that is capable of transferring to something the quality by which it is characterized and a cause that transfers to something an opposite quality that is not its own characteristic: he does not specify which is the proper model to be applied to the case of psychē, which he is finally about to introduce.

Since Cebes believes he has followed the model "very sufficiently," Socrates instructs him to imitate by answering in turn the question: "By what coming to be in some body will it be alive?" Socrates connects his question about the cause of life "in the body" most closely with his example of fever as the cause of illness in the body: he recalls Cebes' image, with its implication that the entrance of the psychē into the body is the beginning of its destruction, as if life were a long disease (95d).[23] Socrates' formulation implies, furthermore, that psychē could not itself be characterized as living any more than fever could be characterized as ill. By asking about the cause of life "in the body," finally, Socrates compels Cebes to answer, "By psychē." He precludes the answer, "By the union of body and psychē," which would have recalled the original definition of death as their separation, while clarifying that the attribute "living" belongs properly only to the compound being.

Socrates asks Cebes the one question he never raised in the preceding model when he inquires whether psychē is always the cause of life in the body. Cebes is convinced that it is, without considering the possibilities, suggested by the first series of arguments, that psychē could be understood as the cause of death no less than of life, or that body no less than psychē could be understood as the cause of life. In giving up the nonfalsifiable answer—that the body comes to be alive by participation in the eidos of life—for the sake of answering "by what" that participation takes place, the refined answer might thus seem to lose the safety Socrates sought, motivated by a proposed disputatious attack. But to overcome that attack requires, as Socrates has shown, not a nonfalsifiable answer but only a noncontradictory one; and to account for something being what it is by referring to one possible refined cause, which is not itself the opposite of another such cause, might be empirically wrong but could not be logically contradictory.[24] A threat to the logos would be constituted, therefore, not by a claim that something besides psyche is the cause of life, but by the claim that, in causing life, psyche produces a result opposed to its own essential nature, or that psyche is both the cause of life, through its attachment to the body (cf. 81d–e, 83d), as well as of its opposite, death, through its longing for phronēsis (cf. 67c–e). Socrates defends himself against this possible attack, once more, by the way he formulates his question, whether the psyche always comes to whatever it occupies bearing life. His repetition manages to avoid, at the same time, the unsettled question of whether the quality "living" characterizes the psyche or the body it occupies, or only both together.

[105d6–105e9]   To apply the general principle on the exclusion of opposites to the case of psyche as the cause of life, Socrates must establish, first, that there is something that is the opposite of life and not, as he goes out of his way to suggest as an alternative, nothing. That this alternative is not explored depends upon the unquestioned premise of the entire discussion—that we believe death is something (64c)—which was agreed upon before the subsequent consideration of what it is. Death was then defined as a double separation—the body becoming separate from the psyche and the psyche being separate from the body; and it was with that definition in mind that Cebes originally posited the opposition of "being alive" and "being dead" (71c). When Cebes now affirms death, without further specification, to be the opposite of life, Socrates does not raise the question of whether this opposition is equally intelligible on the basis of the ordinary understanding of death as annihilation. The opposition between being alive and being dead looks like the opposition between even and odd, not like that between hotter and colder, which is a matter of degree, or greater and smaller, which is a relation dependent on an act of comparison. But this range of examples has been introduced, presumably, precisely because of the questions it raises. Physiologically, of course, a man is either alive or dead. But isn't it by allowing us to "witness" Socrates dying that Plato has led us to understand what it means to be "more alive"?

However that may be, Socrates simply accepts Cebes' claim about the opposition of being alive and being dead in order to draw the desired conclusion from the final formulation of the principle of exclusion of opposites (cf. 105a): psychē, which always brings forward life to the body it occupies, could never admit the opposite, which has been identified as death. If the original definition of death were read into this conclusion, the impossibility of "dead psychē" would be tantamount to a denial of its possible existence apart from the body. The present argument was introduced, however, in response to Cebes' objection, which amounted to a redefinition of death as the perishing or destruction of the psychē (91d, 95d). It must demonstrate, accordingly, that psychē cannot admit death, understood as its own destruction.[25] But this interpretation does not necessarily conflict with that based on the definition of death as separation; for it makes no claim at all about the possibility of the separate existence of the psychē. The impossibility of psychē remaining what it is and becoming dead may look like the impossibility of three remaining what it is and becoming even. Yet, while three cannot become even because it is itself odd, psychē cannot become dead not because it is itself alive, but only because it is the cause of life in the body.

Before stating the expected consequence of the claim that psychē will never admit the opposite of life, Socrates introduces an apparent digression on the names we give opposites. By asking what we *now* call "the non-admitting of the *idea* of the even," he encourages Cebes to remember the characterization of the non-opposites that do not admit the idea opposite to that which is in them (104d–e); Cebes does not, therefore, refer to "the odd" itself, but rather to the characteristic of a number that is "uneven." But Socrates does not specify whether he is thinking of a characteristic or of the subject characterized by it when he proceeds to ask what names we give to "the non-admitting of the just" and to "that which does not admit the musical"; and Cebes only confirms that ambiguity when he answers in reverse, "Unmusical, the other the unjust." Socrates seems, in any case, to have introduced a rather superfluous pair of examples. He recalls, without any immediately evident reason, his description of the guilt from which he sought purification—namely, the possible injustice of his neglect of demotic music (cf. 60d–61b). Yet it is in fact no accident that these examples appear at just this point, for Socrates is finally prepared to overcome that guilt: he is about to establish a perfect harmony between demotic music and philosophy, by showing how both maintain—though construed in very different ways—the immortality of the psychē.[26]

Socrates asks finally what we call that which does not admit death, and Cebes, imitating the established model, replies "*athanaton.*" But this characterization could be ascribed, on the basis of the preparatory argument, to the body as long as it is occupied by psychē no less than to the psychē as long as it occupies a living body.[27] Body as such, of course, has no essential connection with one opposite eidos; it is therefore capable, in contrast with psychē, of still remaining what it is while undergoing the genesis from being alive to being dead. It is only the ensouled body, then, that participates in the eidos of life, since it is not by virtue of being body that it does so. But it is equally true that only embodied psychē can be called "deathless."[28] For psychē earns this ascription by virtue of being the cause of life in the body it occupies, and to say that it cannot be dead is to deny the possibility of its existence apart from that defining function.[29] Nevertheless, when Socrates reaches the conclusion, "Then the psychē is something *athanaton,*" what Cebes hears is the ordinary understanding of the term *athanaton,* which would be ascribed only to the gods, who are deathless because they never cease to exist. Cebes enthusiastically assures Socrates that the demonstration has been "very sufficient."

[105e10–106b3]   Cebes seems to be entirely satisfied that Socrates has at last fulfilled the demand for a demonstration of the immortality of the psychē as imperishability (cf. 88b, 95b–c). But it is precisely the nonidentity of these qualities that compels Socrates to pursue the argument beyond its present conclusion. He has established the immortality of the psychē only as an inability to abide the approach of death, the opposite of life, which the psychē always brings forward to the body it occupies. But Socrates originally specified a subsequent alternative for something that cannot remain behind and admit an opposite; the supplement he now adds to his argument must attempt to demonstrate that the psychē that cannot admit death necessarily withdraws rather than allow itself to be destroyed, at its approach.

To accomplish this purpose—or to show that it cannot be accomplished—Socrates returns to the original examples in his preparatory model. If the uneven were necessarily imperishable, he asks as a counterfactual condition, would three be anything but imperishable?[30] When Cebes responds, "How could it not be?", he points, however unintentionally, to the unresolved ambiguity of the argument. For the imperishability of three would follow necessarily, only if the uneven referred to a class, each of whose members would be imperishable; if the uneven were construed, on the other hand, as a class characteristic, nothing would prevent the number three from perishing, while the quality of unevenness would "withdraw," coming to be present in some other odd number.

Socrates proceeds to expand his model, but in so doing reveals the uniqueness of the numerical example. If the unhot were necessarily imperishable, he asks, whenever someone brought heat against snow, wouldn't the snow withdraw, safe and unmelted? For it would not be destroyed, nor could it remain and admit heat. Before giving Cebes a chance to answer, Socrates affirms the parallel case:[31] if the uncoolable were imperishable, whenever something cold came against fire, it would never be quenched nor destroyed but would depart, going away safe. Here, in contrast with the previous example, Socrates goes out of his way to stress the absurdity of snow taking off unmelted or fire departing unquenched. He seems to differentiate, furthermore, between the possibility of three being imperishable (*anōlethros*) and that of snow or fire not being destroyed (*ouk appolusthai*). Snow or fire, like three, cannot remain what they are and admit the opposite of their essential qualities. If, however, their essential qualities were not in fact imperishable, at the approach of an opposite, three could not turn into something else but would simply cease to exist, whereas snow or fire would turn into something else, being melted or quenched. To perish, Socrates seems to suggest, is simply to cease to exist altogether, whereas to be destroyed is to turn into something else because of losing an essential attribute.[32]

Having established the consequence entailed for a member of any class hypothetically taken to be imperishable, Socrates asks finally if it is necessary to say the same about the athanaton.[33] If it is also imperishable, he reasons—dropping the "unreal" form through which the premise of the previous examples was expressed—then it is impossible for the psychē, when death comes toward it, to be destroyed. For it will not admit death, nor will it be dead, Socrates concludes, thus confirming the meaning of destruction as the fate of something essentially characterized by one opposite that becomes other than what it was by admission of the other opposite. Yet, if the immortal psychē cannot become other than what it is, it may, at the approach of death, have to cease to exist altogether. If the psychē cannot be dead, what indeed would it mean to say that it "withdraws," presumably to Hades, when it ceases to occupy a living body?

[106b3–106d1]   Just as the psychē will not be dead, Socrates continues, three will not be even, nor again will the odd be even, nor will fire be cold, nor the heat in fire. But the distinction Socrates now suppresses—between the odd or the hot, which never become even or cold, and three or fire, which cannot be even or cold as long as they are at all—leads him to imagine the objection of an unnamed critic. It was the objection of an anonymous interlocutor at the outset of the argument that compelled Socrates to articulate the distinction between opposite pragmata that come to be from each other and opposite eidē that exclude each other. But Socrates has now extended the principle of exclusion of opposites beyond the safe answer to a more refined one, which is neither an opposite pragma nor an opposite eidos. Unlike the opposite eidos itself, however, the refined cause that always possesses an opposite whenever it exists may have to be destroyed or cease to exist when approached by the opposite it cannot admit while remaining what it was.

Motivated, apparently, by that thought, Socrates' imaginary critic is willing to admit, in accordance with their prior agreements, that the odd does not become even at the approach of the even, but he sees nothing to prevent it from being destroyed, while the even comes to be in its place. Socrates does not clarify the ambiguity of "the odd" by distinguishing the characteristic of being odd, which does not become even, from the number that is odd, which can be replaced by one that is even. Nor does he confront the question of what it would mean for three to be destroyed, in the sense of turning into an even number. He has argued only that three would be imperishable if the uneven were imperishable; and though he now rejects the truth of that premise, he insists that, if it were true, three and the odd would withdraw together at the approach of the even. In the same way, fire would withdraw from the cold if the hot were imperishable, and so for all the rest. Since the same reasoning should be applicable, Socrates implies, to pyschē, if the immortal were imperishable, he need only distinguish that case from the former ones by establishing the truth of its premise.

If the immortal is agreed to be imperishable, Socrates had argued before he interrupted himself with an imagined objection, then the psychē could not be destroyed when death approaches it. But he now transforms that consequence, in accordance with the model of three and the uneven, when he claims that psychē would be, with regard to the immortal, also imperishable. "With regard to the immortal" must mean insofar as psychē is a member of the class of the immortal. For if the latter were simply a class characteristic, it could be objected that, when the man dies, his psychē, although it could not remain psychē and become dead, could indeed cease to exist, while its deathlessness would "withdraw" and come to be present in some other psychē occupying a living body.

Socrates must demonstrate, then, that it would be a self-contradiction to claim that what cannot be dead could nevertheless cease to exist. He must establish the identity of life and existence, which was not presupposed by the first part of the argument and was denied by the series of arguments in the first half of the dialogue. Unless this necessary connection between immortality and imperishability can be affirmed, Socrates concedes, some other logos would be needed (cf. 70d, 76e). Those agreements, however, that represent "something sufficient" to the interlocutors who accept them, on the basis of which further consistent inferences may be drawn (cf. 101d–e), represent, for the reader of the dialogue, precisely those points at which an affirmation of self-evident truth must be transformed into a question for further examination.

[106d2–106e4]   But Cebes does not hesitate to grant Socrates his agreement: if there is anything at all that would not admit corruption, he believes, it must be the immortal, which is everlasting. Cebes replaces the question about imperishability with a claim about what is subject to corruption (*phthora*), which would seem to be especially applicable to natural things: perhaps he still has not forgotten the common human fear that the psychē is something like breath or smoke (70a). Nor does Cebes specify how he understands "the immortal" whose invulnerability to corruption he affirms simply by asserting that it is everlasting (*aïdion*),[34] thus presupposing exactly what is in question. He must consider this justified by the necessity of rejecting the consequence he thinks would otherwise follow, namely, that everything would sooner or later cease to exist. Cebes seems to remember the conclusion of the first argument, in which the assumption that there must always be something living, unless everything were to end up dead, led, as its necessary condition, to the agreement that there must be something always capable of coming to be alive again, namely the psychai of the dead (72c–d). The assumption that there must always be something that escapes destruction now leads Cebes to conclude that there must be something that always escapes destruction, namely the immortal, which is everlasting.[35]

Socrates offers Cebes his qualified support: it would be agreed by all that the god at least and the eidos of life itself and anything else immortal, if there were such, could never be destroyed. That it is something immortal only in the ordinary sense, rather than in the reconstructed sense at stake in the first part of this argument, that could be characterized as everlasting, Socrates confirms by his reference—for the first time in the argument—to the god, who is by definition always living. Yet this would hardly constitute the grounds for the indestructibility of the eidos of life itself. Socrates is silent, in any case, about the human psychē. But he does put the ordinary understanding of its immortality into question when he emphasizes the hypothesis that if there were anything else immortal, it too would be indestructible. With an irony he himself is not likely to recognize, Cebes affirms the universal acceptance of Socrates' claim, "By all, by Zeus, men, and even more, I believe, by the gods."

Eager, apparently, to reach the conclusion of the argument, Socrates immediately accepts Cebes' agreement and poses on that basis his final question: Since the immortal is incorruptible, would the psychē, if it happened to be immortal, be anything but imperishable? The model for this question was the imperishability of three, if the uneven were imperishable. But that model serves only as a reminder of their failure to estab-

lish the imperishability of the immortal. It is a reminder, moreover, that while three was said to be determined not only by
the idea of the odd, but also by its own idea, Socrates has
nowhere established a parallel idea of psychē. When Cebes
responds to Socrates' question, "Most necessary," he must ignore its optative mood and the hypothetical condition con-
tained within it. But Socrates' stress on that hypothetical condition suggests that what is required for a demonstration of
imperishability is not the immortality established in the first
part of the argument, but rather immortality in the ordinary
sense. Socrates would have had to demonstrate—but he did
not—that psychē could not cease to be alive, because it could
not cease to exist.[36] The imperishability of the psychē has not
been, and could not be, established, that is, without assuming
what is supposed to be deduced from it.

[106e5–107a1]   Socrates manages, nevertheless, to reach a justifiable conclusion that avoids just this problem: "When death
approaches the man, the mortal, as it seems, of him dies, while
the immortal departs, going away safe and incorruptible, with-
drawing from death." Socrates is silent about the immortal as a
characterization of the psychē and conspicuously refrains from
referring to "the immortal (part) of man" parallel to "the mortal of him." If the mortal that dies when death approaches is
the living being as such, the union of body and psychē, then the
immortal that withdraws "safe and incorruptible" must be
nothing other than the quality of deathlessness that characterizes every ensouled body or embodied psychē, whenever it exists. Cebes transforms his previous exuberant response into the
rather subdued, "It appears so"; for Socrates has finally compelled him, and perhaps the others as well, to realize that it is
the man whom death approaches, the man Socrates, whose
imminent death they pity and fear.

    As if to combat the moderation of the conclusion they have
justifiably reached, Socrates enthusiastically proclaims one last
consequence: "Then above all, Cebes, psychē is immortal and
imperishable, and our psychai will really be in Hades." Socrates'

surprising certainty about this conclusion "above all" (*pantos mallon*) echoes the certainty he expressed at the conclusion of the first argument he conducted with Cebes (cf. 72d). That echo is confirmed by Socrates' sudden reference to the plural of psychē for the first time in this argument and his sudden mention of Hades for the first time in the second half of the dialogue. In fact, however, whereas the first argument was supposed to investigate whether the psychai of the dead are in Hades, it concluded only that they exist. And while the present argument concludes that "our *psychai*" *will* be in Hades really, the first argument affirmed that there really is coming back to life. Socrates does not explain how he can be certain that our psychai will be in Hades if, as he has just demonstrated, the psychē cannot be dead. He expresses his certainty, moreover, at the very moment he recalls, but does not renounce, his previous certainty that the living come to be from the dead. The echo of the first argument's conclusion in that of the last thus serves only as a reminder of the anonymous interlocutor's observation of their apparent contradiction.

In the transition from the first to the last argument, the consideration of one pragma coming to be from its opposite is transformed into the consideration of one pragma coming to be *what* it is, characterized by a quality that necessarily excludes its opposite.[37] The final argument asks no longer about the coming to be or passing away of a living being, but rather, about the cause of the body being, coming to be, or ceasing to be alive; for this question the safe but simple answer, "Participation in the *eidos* of life," can be supplemented by the refined answer, "*Psychē* which always brings forward life to the body it occupies." Yet Socrates' reminder of his first argument at the conclusion of his last does not appear where it does by accident: the move beyond the demonstration of immortality to the issue of imperishability is a return to the question of the necessary existence of the psychē, rather than of its necessary characterization as what it is. Socrates indicates the problematic status of this return when he concludes his last argument, like the first, with the announcement that our psychai will be in Hades "really" (*tō onti*), literally "in being," rather than "in *logos.*"[38]

[107a2–107b10]   Cebes first admitted the "great encouragement and trust" required to show that the psychē of the dead man has some power and phronēsis (70b); he now admits only that he has nothing more to say against the argument, nor can he distrust these logoi. He encourages Simmias and the others, nevertheless, not to be silent, since there may be no other opportunity to speak or hear about these matters: all Socrates' efforts have not removed Cebes' fear that the logos will die with the death of Socrates. Simmias, on the other hand, although he too can think of no further objections, cannot help but distrust these logoi, given, he explains, the magnitude of the subject in contrast with our human weakness.[39] Like the reflections with which Simmias introduced his earlier objection (85c–d), his present ones turn out to be a parody of the principles of Socratic inquiry. For Socrates, too, acknowledges that a clearer investigation is required of their first hypotheses, however trustworthy they may seem. But despite their apparently common recognition of our human weakness, Socrates, unlike Simmias, does not abandon the goal that would motivate continuation of the investigation. Only if one could go through it sufficiently, Socrates adds, would he follow the logos as far as humanly possible. The process of defending a hypothesis on the basis of a higher one, Socrates explained to Cebes, must be carried on until "something sufficient" is reached; at that point, he now promises Simmias, you will seek nothing further.

The first hypothesis that underlies the series of arguments as a whole would seem to be the agreement, which Phaedo only summarized, on the being of the eidē as the cause of the pragmata being what they are. The investigation that Socrates now recommends would have to justify, then, the separation of eidē from pragmata, while clarifying the mediating level that allows for the relation of "participation." This would entail in turn a reconstruction of the unity of the dialogue divided in two halves, the first beginning with the principle of the mutual generation of opposite pragmata, the second with the principle of the mutual exclusion of opposites themselves. But the complementary relation between these principles does not resolve the apparently contradictory content in the two halves of the dialogue based upon them. While the series of arguments in the first half assumes the separability of the psychē from the body after death, when it is in contact with the beings themselves, to which it is akin, it is precisely that assumption that is denied by the final argument. It alone demonstrates the immortality of the psychē; yet that immortality is not eternal existence after death, but rather, the essential relation of psychē—and not a cognitive one[40]—with one eidos only, that of life, which it brings forward to the body it occupies as long as it exists.

Reconstruction of the unity of the dialogue would thus appear to require a resolution of the tension between psychē as a principle of life and psychē as mind; but what the *Phaedo* suggests, rather, is an alternative to the latter. A psychological analysis of thinking and knowing is replaced, that is, by a logical one, and precisely because of the passions shown to lie behind the positing of the pure psychē as nothing but a medium of cognition. In the second half of the dialogue, "mind" appears only when Socrates imagines a claim that all his actions are directed by it,[41] motivated, presumably, in no way whatsoever by desire, fear, hope, anger, or any other passion; such a claim thus implies the absence of psychē, even though mind is impossible without psychē. Socrates indicates in this way the problematic character of the premise of Anaxagorean teleology—that mind is the cause of all, arranging the best for each and the good for all in common. It was the unavailability of such knowledge of the good, Socrates confessed, that compelled him to replace teleology with his own second sailing. Yet when Socrates labels the procedure he adopts in that second sailing a "*technē*," he arouses our suspicions about its status. For Socrates certainly has not solved all the unanswered questions that remain in his elaboration of this art of reasoning; and in fact, just to the extent that it is an art, it could not determine the ends for which it serves as a means. It is, rather, the motivation of the practitioner of the technē of logos that guides the direction in which it is applied. What the technē of logos replaces is not the human psychē as such, but precisely and only the notion of psychē as mind, abstracted from all human pathē.

The final argument of the *Phaedo,* which results from that replacement, ought to be, apparently, a "purification" of the logos from all rhetoric motivated by self-interest; this of course implies some relation between them, at least an understanding of the self-interest from which the logos is supposedly liberated. The purification of the logos is, one might say, an idealization. For not only does the presumably discarded rhetorical element come back with a vengeance to haunt the ensuing mythos, but it is already present in the abrupt conclusion of the final argument. In fact, even before that point, the argument has a persuasive appeal, to Cebes among others, based on the assumption of the ordinary understanding of "immortality." It is, nevertheless, the definitions and principles stipulated in the argument that provide the means to correct its merely persuasive appeal. The interpretation resulting from that correction separates in logos, and for the sake of logos, only the mutually exclusive opposite eidē, while identifying psychē as nothing but the inseparable cause of life in the body. The separability of pure logos exemplified by the final argument may be an idealization; but it is one—unlike the idealized separate psychē—that precludes its illusory identification with the self. It precludes, consequently, the paradoxical combination of resentment of life and the longing for eternal existence.

CHAPTER TWELVE

Mythos

[107c1–107d4]   When asked whether everyone could give a logos of these matters, Simmias betrayed his fear that on the morrow there would no longer be any man able to do so (76b); when warned of the need to sing charms daily to comfort the child in us moved by the fear of death, Cebes betrayed his fear that someone able to do so could nowhere be found, since Socrates was about to leave them (77e–78a). The speeches have grown longer, the day shorter, and however successfully the logos may have been preserved, "this Socrates who is now speaking and arranging what is being said" (115c) will not be present much longer to protect it. That fact is nowhere more striking than in Socrates' acknowledgment of the need for further examination of the first hypotheses of their arguments, which would have to be continued, he insisted, until arriving at "something sufficient." But Socrates now replaces that task, in the short time left before he must drink the poison, with a mythos about the fate of the psychē after death. He knows a "likely story,"[1] it seems, that can take the place of that sufficiency he claimed to have sought in knowledge of the good, showing the work of mind arranging things as is best for each and good for all in common (cf. 98a–b). Relative to that standard of sufficiency, life is always too short; mythos would seem to be necessary in some form, consequently, for any inquiry.

Socrates opened the conversation by remarking on the

strange character of what we call pleasure; he addressed those
remarks, just after sending Xanthippe away in tears, to his interlocutors as "he men" (andres, 60b).[2] He now addresses them in
the same way once again, when he introduces his concluding
mythos with a remark on what we call life. Yet despite that
qualification, he transforms the conclusion of the last argument
into a hypothesis: It is just to consider that, if the psyche is
immortal, it is necessary to care for it not only for this time we
call life, but for all time.[3] In making his exhortation conditional,
Socrates implies that the immortality legitimately demonstrated in the previous argument does not mean the continued
existence of the psyche apart from the body after death. But he
indicates, at the same time, that the necessity of care for the
psyche in what we call life is entirely independent of the question of our future existence. That familiar Socratic care for the
psyche that has emerged only implicitly at fleeting moments
throughout the conversation cannot come to the foreground
until the completion of the last argument, which was intended
to illustrate the turn from concern with the self to concern with
the logos itself. In order to carry out that turn, Socrates transformed the danger of sailing through life, for which Simmias
sought a safe vessel, into the danger of contradictory speech, for
which the techne of logos was to provide a safe defense. He
transforms it once more when he adds that to neglect care for
the psyche would now appear to be a terrible danger; and it is
safety in the face of this danger that is to be provided, presumably, by the mythos Socrates is about to deliver.

Before offering his defense of philosophy as the practice of
dying, Socrates expressed the hope that "there is something for
the dead and, as it is said of old, something better for the good
than for the bad" (63c). It is to such a hope—which has hardly
been confirmed by the preceding series of arguments—that Socrates now returns. Death would be a blessing for the bad if it
were a release from everything,[4] he argues; for in being freed
from the body, they would be freed at the same time from their
own evils and—he admits explicitly for the first time—from the
psyche to which such evils must belong. Death would be a benefit to himself, Socrates conceded earlier, even if there is noth-

ing for the dying man, since he would at least be released from his ignorance or folly, whose continuation would have been an evil (91b). Socrates now confirms the desirability of escaping from the evils that belong to the psychē itself, while denying that the termination of life is the condition for that escape: but now, since it is manifestly immortal, there would be no salvation for it except by becoming best and most prudent (phronimos). Socrates refers, one can assume, to the psychē; but its manifest immortality is only its inability to be dead whenever it exists, and the evil from which it must escape is not life itself— as the genuine philosophers believe—but the opposite of being good and prudent.[5] The phronēsis, therefore, that Socrates identifies as the only salvation cannot be that which the genuine philosophers seek as the automatic result of dying, when the psychē is separated from the contamination of the body.

Death alone is no escape, Socrates argues, because the psychē takes with it into Hades its education and nurture.[6] Just this consideration has been absent from Socrates' attempts to demonstrate, in the first argument that "the *psychai* of the dead are in Hades" (72d), in the second, that "our *psychai* are before we were born" (76e), and in the last, that "our *psychai* will be in Hades" (107a). In the third argument, on the other hand, Socrates admitted that not every human life is conducted in accordance with the true nature of the psychē, and it is the manner of life a man has led that determines what the destiny of his psychē is "like." That the invisible psychē, in any case, departs into Hades as the place most like itself (80d), is the sort of charm we ought to chant to ourselves, Socrates insisted, in order to assuage our childish fear of death. Now the story he is about to tell about the "journey abroad" after death is, Socrates admits at its conclusion, a magic charm designed to work on the experiences of the psychē. As such, it must represent a continuation of the third argument, which brought the first half of the conversation to an end. Only the comic imagery of that speech, which concluded with a description of the hierarchy of classes of human psychai, ranging from the bestial to the divine, foreshadows Socrates' present attempt to lend support to the hope that death brings something better for the good than for the bad.

[107d4–108c5]   Shifting to indirect discourse in the middle of
his sentence about the education and nurture of the psychē—
"which are said to benefit or harm the dying man greatly from
the outset of his journey"—Socrates continues his report, although he begins referring not to the psychē, but to the man
who has died. The *daimōn* allotted to each man leads him after
death to a certain place, where all are gathered together to be
judged;[7] then, after journeying into Hades led by one guide and
experiencing there what is necessary for the requisite time,
another guide brings him back. Socrates recalls the ancient
logos about the cycle of living and dying, which provided the
hypothesis of his first argument. He intended then, apparently,
to guarantee the necessary eternity of the cycle (cf. 77d) by
demonstrating the impossibility of a genesis in the direction of
one of two opposite states without a return genesis in the direction of the other. But it is precisely such an irreversible
linear motion that Socrates is about to describe as the fate of
any human beings who are perfectly impure or perfectly
pure[8]—if there are any. In the present tale, moreover, Hades
represents the place of imprisonment after the judgment of the
dead man; but it represented in the first series of arguments an
at least temporary escape from the punishment of life, which
consists in the imprisonment of the psychē in the body.

Although he claimed to be no mythmaker (61b), Socrates
now competes with Aeschylus, whose Telephus asserts that a
simple road leads into Hades: if there were one simple path,
Socrates reasons, there would be no need of guides, yet there
seem to be many divisions in the path, as the holy rites and
laws here give witness.[9] Socrates does not explicitly offer his
own interpretation of the complexity that characterizes the
road into Hades. But his account of the daimōn who leads the
dying man recalls the role previously assigned to a personified
philosophy, who takes hold of the psychē when it is welded to
the body and encourages it gently, trying, although not necessarily succeeding, to set it free (82e–83a). Socrates proceeds to
distinguish the orderly and prudent psychē, which follows its
guide and is not ignorant of its circumstances, from the psychē

that is desirous of the body and therefore flits about the visible place for a long time until after much struggling it is led away by force. Socrates will try to persuade Crito, at the conclusion of this tale, that he himself, being aware of his circumstances, has no interest in flitting about the Athenian prison any longer, but is prepared to follow, without any struggle, the guidance of the man in charge of administering the poison.

In contrasting the fate that awaits the pure psychai with that of the impure, Socrates recalls the language of the mysteries (cf. 69c): while the psychē that has lived purely and measurably enjoys gods as companions and guides and dwells in its fitting place, the psychē that is impure and responsible for impure acts, like unjust homicides, is shunned by all and left to wander about in perplexity.[10] Now Socrates had originally contrasted the orderly and prudent psychē with one that cannot give up its attachment to the body. But whereas the prudent psychē might reasonably be identified as one having lived purely and measurably, it is far from evident why its opposite, the body-loving psychē, should be represented by the murderer. Perhaps Socrates is thinking of those who committed murders in the belief, based on their love of the body, that the greatest punishment is death—that is, separation from the body. If Socrates exemplifies the orderly and prudent psychē, his contrary might be exemplified by the Athenian dēmos, which condemned him, perhaps unjustly, to the punishment of death, believing it to be the greatest evil.[11]

[108c5–108e3]   Socrates' speech, introduced to show why we must care for our psychē through all time, seems to be completed; his mere mention of the fitting dwelling places of the various kinds of psychai explains the multiplicity of paths and places in the other world as an image for the multiplicity of ways of life, based on the education and nurture by which every psychē is said to be harmed or benefited greatly on its journey. But Socrates suddenly makes the surprising announcement that there are many wonderful places on the earth, and that the earth itself, he is persuaded,[12] is not what it is thought to be, in size or shape or any other way, by those who usually speak about it. When Simmias interrupts to express his interest in this cryptic allusion, Socrates agrees to speak about the earth from hearsay. He was willing to speak from hearsay about the prohibition against suicide, Socrates told his interlocutors at the outset of the conversation, since he found it most fitting to investigate and mythologize, in the time between dawn and sunset, about his imminent journey abroad (61d–e); he could not, therefore, be accused of idle chatter even by the comic poet who portrayed him as an investigator of things above the heavens and beneath the earth (70b–c).[13] Plato portrays Socrates, at the end of the *Phaedo*, carrying out precisely that investigation: he has Socrates take revenge, just before the execution of the penalty assigned by the Athenian dēmos, against the comic poet who is accused of being the original source of his conviction.

Socrates offers to tell Simmias about the *idea* of the earth and its places, but his reference to this idea—which seems rather surprising after the use of the term in the preceding argument—calls for a careful qualification: he needs no art of Glaucus simply to relate what he is persuaded of, but to demonstrate its truth would be too difficult for the art of Glaucus.[14] Even if there were a sufficient art, he himself might not be adequate to practice it, Socrates humbly admits, recalling his ironic judgment not on the impossibility of investigation of nature, but on his own natural unfitness for it (96c). And in any case, he adds, his own life would not last long enough for completion of the logos; with this last painful reminder Socrates brings to mind the incomplete investigation of the first hypotheses of their arguments, for which the present speech must serve as a replacement.

[108e4–109a8]   Socrates identifies the premise of his account, before and after stating it, as "the first of which I am persuaded": *if* the earth is in the center of the heavens and is round, then it needs neither air nor anything else to prevent it from falling, but the homogeneity of the surrounding heavens and its own equipoise suffice to hold it. The shape and position of the earth, and why it is necessarily best for it to be as it is, is precisely the knowledge Socrates claimed to have sought so eagerly in the teaching of Anaxagoras (97d–e), which turned out to be no less disappointing than all the other theories that neglected the causality of the good. Yet the explanation Socrates now offers for the hypothetical position of the earth in the center of the cosmos seems to satisfy the principle of sufficient reason, without being a teleological explanation based on knowledge of the good: it simply assumes that there is no reason why something completely balanced would ever incline in one direction rather than another.[15]

Socrates implicitly criticized Anaxagoras for trying to construct a theory of the cosmos governed by mind in accordance with the good, while neglecting all consideration of the human good. He chose, therefore, to illustrate the failure of the Anaxagorean project—its inability to distinguish between a cause and that without which it could not operate as a cause—by considering the cause of his present situation: it would be as if someone were to claim that Socrates does all that he does through mind, then go on to assign as the cause of his sitting in the Athenian prison the mechanical operation of his bones and sinews, rather than his opinion of what is best. But while Socrates could thus explain his disappointment in Anaxagoras, he was not himself able to carry out the intention of demonstrating how the arrangement of the cosmos reflects the power of the good. He seems prepared finally to confront that challenge. Yet the knowledge Socrates now claims to possess is not of the good as a cosmological principle, but only that the psychē must become as good and as prudent as possible: his present speech is only a magic charm designed to make a man courageous in living or dying (114d). The account Socrates has just offered of the earth at rest in the center of the heavens may be his answer to Anaxagoras; but rather than provide a cosmological theory demonstrating the best arrangement for each and the good for all in common, it seems in fact to be only an image of his own action, or nonaction, of remaining at rest in the Athenian prison.

Socrates has found an appropriate subject of investigation for the short time left before he will be transformed by the poison into a corpse devoid of all self-motion. For the earth that is characterized by the absence of motion would seem to represent pure body separate from psyche; Socrates' account, as will soon become evident, is in fact an autopsy that renders visible the hidden insides of this gigantic corpse. Socrates' cosmological geography is an image of the body "writ large"[16]—a paradoxical choice, it would seem, to illuminate the fate of the psyche after death, in light of the purity or impurity of its way of life. But purification was first identified as the effort of the psyche to separate itself from the body, accustoming itself to collect and gather itself together from "everywhere" (67c–d). And if the psyche is imprisoned in the body, as Socrates affirmed in concluding his argument on its likeness to the invisible, by means of its own desires, nailed in by every pleasure or pain it experiences, then its character should be revealed in and through the nature of its attachment to the body. That is precisely what Socrates is about to illustrate by describing the places of the earth in which various kinds of psychai belong.

[109a9–110a8]   The earth is so gigantic, Socrates is persuaded, that those who dwell between the pillars of Heracles and the river Phasis—the inhabitants of the Mediterranean region— could be likened to ants or frogs around a pond, unaware of the other inhabitants of other regions. But the earth is in fact covered by many hollows of all different forms (*ideai*) and sizes, filled with water, mist, and air that are the sediment of what is called by the physicists "ether," the pure heaven in which the earth itself (*aute he ge*) lies in its purity. The pure psyche itself by itself, released at death from the contamination of the body, has as its counterpart in Socrates' tale the pure earth itself, beyond its briny hollows.[17] Like the genuine philosophers who claim to have knowledge of the pure psychē while alive and imprisoned in the body, Socrates claims to have knowledge of the earth itself while remaining sunk in one of its hollows. To account, consequently, for our systematic deception, Socrates must rely on analogy: like creatures dwelling on the bottom of the sea, believing it to be the heaven and never rising above the surface to see how much more pure and beautiful the region beyond is, we dwell in one hollow of the earth but believe we live on its upper surface, and we call the air *ouranos*, as if it were the heaven in which the stars move. But just as the things in the sea are covered with mud and brine, so those here on earth are corrupted and corroded, while the things beyond are as superior to those of our region as ours are to those in the sea. Only if one of us could fly up on wings and lift up his head, just as a fish could lift up his head from the water, would he see what is beyond;[18] and if his nature were sufficient to bear the sight, he would know that it is the true ouranos and the true light and the true earth.

Looking down on the inhabited world from the viewpoint of the true heavens, Socrates offers an image of the cave; but now the walls of the polis within which we are chained prisoners are replaced by the boundaries of the known world, the shadows cast on the wall by artificial objects reflected in the light of man-made fire replaced by the natural phenomena of our environment systematically misperceived through our murky depths.[19] Socrates thus prepares to elaborate his earlier description of the imprisonment of the psychē in the human body, chained by its attachment to pleasure and pain and compelled to view the beings through the prison bars of the senses (82e). The winged flight of that rare inhabitant able to lift his head out of this region should represent the philosopher's longed-for flight from the body, as the condition for direct contact of the pure psychē with the pure beings; yet, like the pursuit of pleasure that always brings in its wake its opposite, the pursuit of the purified region beyond our own leads to the vision of the earth itself—an image of pure body separate from psychē.

[110b1–111c3]   Socrates uses the word *mythos* for the first time when he offers to tell Simmias something worth hearing about the things on the earth beneath the heavens. Socrates begins this mythos as he did his account of the idea of the earth, with "what is said first": if the earth itself could be observed from above, it would appear like those twelve-sided leather balls, divided into a patchwork of colors.[20] These are brighter and purer, more and more beautiful, than any we have seen here, and from that perspective even these hollows filled with water and air furnish some kind of eidos of color, so that the whole produces the glistening illusion of one continuous multicolored eidos. Correspondingly beautiful are the trees and flowers and fruits that grow on the true earth. And while our precious stones are corroded by the vapors and liquids that run together here, the earth itself is adorned by jewels that are pure and smooth and transparent; gold and silver, moreover, are not hidden as here but lie in open view, a blessed sight for the observer.[21] The pure earth offers not the noetic vision by the psychē of invisible ideas, but purified aesthetic vision by purified body. *Eidos*, which in the last argument meant a determination in logos, is now only an embroidered phantasm of color, and the earth "patched up" by those hues replaces the psychē "patched up" by its contamination with the somatoeidetic (81c).

On this true earth, Socrates continues, live many animals and men, some dwelling inland, others on coasts about the air, just as we dwell about the sea, and others on islands surrounded by air. The seasons there are so tempered that its inhabitants have no diseases and live much longer than we do here—although they will soon be identified as one class of the dead![22] In sight and hearing and phronēsis and all such, they are as superior to us as air is superior in purity to water, and ether to air. This ratio of elements, with the highest unknown to us, presumably accounts for our state of systematic delusion;[23] but to rise above the indented surface of the earth on which we dwell is only to reach the same element, in its purest form. Phronēsis, moreover, which the genuine philosophers claim to

seek through the separation of psychē from body, seems to
have become nothing but one more faculty of perception and to
belong apparently to men and animals alike. The inhabitants
of this paradise of the body, with their intensified sensation to
which all cognition has been reduced, need not imagine or
fabricate images of absent gods: they enjoy communion face to
face in sacred groves or temples where the gods dwell really (tō
onti).[24] And since, furthermore, the sun and moon and stars can
be seen just as they really are, there is no need to rely on
observation through images:[25] given this direct contact with
the pragmata themselves, no second sailing is required (cf.
99d–e). In all other ways, Socrates concludes, their blessed-
ness is in accordance with this.[26]

[111c4–113c8]   From his account of the true earth, Socrates
turns to the hollows (koila)—the bellies or bowels of the
earth[27]—sunk under its outer surface. Of these, some are
deeper and wider in comparison with our own, some deeper
but narrower, and some less deep but broader: the one in which
we live is at least not the most inaccessible to the region beyond. The hollows are connected, Socrates continues, by subterranean channels through which water flows from one into
another, as in mixing bowls.[28] And in the depths of the earth
are "everlasting rivers of incalculable magnitude," which fill
the various regions through which they run, moving up and
down as if by some kind of oscillation. Preparing to explain the
nature of this oscillation itself (hautē hē aiōra),[29] Socrates refers for the first time to phusis and drops the preceding indirect
discourse that was prefaced by "It is said." While he appeals to
Homer and the many other poets who gave the name "Tartarus" to the greatest of the chasms bored right through the
whole earth,[30] Socrates does not need the poets to explain the
cause of all the rivers flowing into, and back out of, this chasm:
since the liquid there has no foundation, it oscillates up and
down, running toward one side of the earth and then the other.
The earth itself, according to Socrates' explanation, requires no
foundation as the cause of its motionlessness, since there is

simply no reason for it to move in one direction rather than another. Socrates now offers a correlative explanation for the motion of the rivers within the earth, whose oscillation from one direction to its opposite is caused simply by the absence of any foundation. This mechanical oscillation, which provides the source of motion for the circulatory system of the earth body, has taken over the function of psychē as the source of motion for any living body.

When the liquid is set in motion, Socrates continues, the wind and air follow, and their oscillation produces terrible and irresistible blasts rushing in and out: just as the water flowing through the channels within the earth operates like blood flowing through the veins of the body, the wind rushing through the inner earth operates like the inspiration and expiration—or any other release of air!—in a living animal.[31] When the water flows out of Tartarus and withdraws to the so-called lower regions,[32] it runs through the earth, filling the streams there as if pumped into them, and when it is set in motion toward this side, it fills the streams here, just as the blood circulating through the veins fills the places in the body that have been emptied.[33] These streams produce seas and rivers and springs at various places and then pass back under the earth again. And each river gains its particular quality and color from its mixture with the parts of the earth through which it flows, just as the colors of the streams of nutriment are produced as they flow through various parts of the body.[34] Finally, all flow back into Tartarus, on either the opposite side from which they flowed out or the same side. And some empty at the lowest possible point into Tartarus, after circling like serpents around or within the earth once or many times, just as the intestines coil through the lower belly.[35] Yet all must descend below the point at which they flowed out, closer to the center of the earth, but not beyond it.[36]

As the locus of origin and return for all the great subterranean rivers, Tartarus takes the place of the heart, the source of circulation for the blood that flows to the limbs and back again in the body of a living animal. The heart is set in the body,

according to one "likely story," like a guard chamber in the
acropolis of the city, which allows for the rule of the best:[37] for
while the wrath of thumos boils up whenever logos announces
some unjust action, either from without or from the desires
within, the circulation impelled by the heart delivers to the
organs of sensation the commands and threats that are to be
obeyed by all in all ways. A political metaphor thus allows for a
teleological account in which the structure of the body is determined in accordance with the passions of the psyche. Socrates is about to accomplish the same purpose now that he has
described the circulatory, respiratory, and alimentary systems
of the great earth body as a metaphor for those of a living
animal. In place, however, of the food particles digested by the
inner fire and transported through the blood stream, nourish-
ment for the earth body is provided, as Socrates will shortly
indicate, by the ingestion, digestion, and excretion of human
psychai!

Appealing once more to the authority of the poets, Socrates attributes a particular significance to four—two pairs of
opposites—of the many great streams circulating through the
body of the earth.[38] The greatest and outermost, which winds
in a circle, is called Okeanus,[39] and opposite to it, pouring
through many desolate places in the opposite direction, is the
Acheron. The Acherusian lake, at which this river finally ar-
rives, is the gathering place of most of the psychai of the dead,
who must remain there for some appointed time before coming
back to life again. The third river, which is called Pyriphlegethon, pours out between the first two, comes to a place burning
with fire, produces a lake boiling with water and mud, and
then winds many times around the earth before flowing back
into Tartarus. And the fourth river, which issues opposite to it,
comes first to a terrible place the color of lapis lazuli, takes
"terrible powers" into its waters as it passes under the earth,[40]
then circles in the opposite direction of the third river, before
emptying on the opposite side into Tartarus. The lake produced by this river is the Styx, the river itself the Stygian, but
called by the poets Cocytus.[41] As the name-givers of the great

and terrible rivers of the underworld, the poets appeal to our
fear and guilt by fabricating images of human pathē[42]—Pyriphlegethon, burning fire of passion; Styx, icy frost of hatred;
Cocytus, sorrow of shrieking and wailing:[43] they justify Socrates' transformation of the mechanistic circulatory system of
the earth body into the fitting context for a story about the
destiny of the human psychē.

[113d1–114c6]   After completing his account, then, of the
outer surface of the true earth and its inner circulatory system—both invisible, to human eyes at least (cf. 79b)—Socrates
returns to his description of the journey of the dead into Hades.
Arriving at the region to which each is led by his daimōn, each
is judged as to whether he has lived beautifully and piously or
not: Socrates does not yet raise the question of whether a noble
or beautiful life is identical with a pious one. He implicitly
admits the possibility of deception in this judgment, furthermore, by repeatedly affirming, in the following account, that
the dead—who are not simply psychai—only *appear* to belong
to one class or another.[44] To link this division of classes with
the system of four great rivers, Socrates begins, not acciden-
tally, with the only one for which he acknowledged such a
purpose: the Acherusian lake is the destination of all who are
found to have lived in the middle state, neither a beautiful or
pious life nor the opposite. But while Socrates first assigned to
this place most of the psychai of the dead, it must in fact be the
source of all living men, since it is the only region from which
psychai were said to be sent back to be born again into living
beings. Yet when he now announces that those who dwell for
the appointed time in the Acherusian lake are there purified,
Socrates no longer speaks of a return to life, and he is as silent
about the nature of this purification as he is about the deeds
that render it necessary.

Why Socrates begins his account with the middle condition
of those sent to the Acherusian lake, while remaining silent
about their eventual departure, is revealed by the role they play
in the fate of the others. At one extreme from this mean are

those who seem to be incurable, having committed many great acts of sacrilege or many unjust and lawless homicides or other such deeds;[45] it is a fitting fate that these should be thrown into Tartarus and should never emerge, for their interminable punishment is nothing but an image of their incurable evils. Those, on the other hand, who committed an act of violence out of anger against father or mother, then lived the rest of their lives in repentance, or those who committed any homicide in the same way, appear to belong in Tartarus as well; but since to repent is, by definition, to be released from that region, they are cast out after one year by the wave pulsing through Tartarus, the homicides through Cocytus, those who attacked father or mother through the Pyriphlegethon. Carried by the current to the Acherusian lake, the repentant call out to those they have slain or attacked, begging to be allowed to come into the lake; if they persuade their victims, they come out and leave behind their sufferings, but if not, they are carried back into Tartarus and then into the rivers, and this is repeated until they are able to persuade those they have wronged.

This is the penalty, Socrates adds, imposed by their judges. But it is the purely mechanical operation of the circulatory system of the earth body that accomplishes the purpose of the homicide law that requires an involuntary slayer to absent himself for a year from the region inhabited by his victim, in order to allow the dead man's wrath to abate.[46] The goal of the recycling of sullied psychai in the invisible rivers of the underworld is purification, and the deeds thought to induce pollution—sacrilege, murder, violence against parents—are those that form the material of tragic drama.[47] Like the legal code for the treatment of pollution laid down by the Athenian Stranger in Plato's *Laws*, the system of purification in Socrates' Hades is based not on punishment, assuming responsibility, but on the psychological phenomena of guilt and absolution, anger and forgiveness; in Socrates' Hades, however, where the dead can speak for themselves, the victims have complete power to decide whether or not to pardon those who have wronged them.[48] The fate of the impure who repent is determined, therefore, not

by evidence of moral improvement, but rather by skill in the art
of rhetoric: the necessary condition for release is successful
persuasion, by which the guilty man transforms his victim's
anger into forgiveness. But Socrates has concealed a crucial
problem: there is no guarantee that the victim was or still is, an
inhabitant of the Acherusian lake. A crime committed against
either one who has been purified and released or one doomed to
Tartarus forever could never be forgiven: justice can be carried
out only if there are no extremes, with all men remaining in
purgatory. Otherwise, the repentant murderer is automatically
doomed to exile in the rivers of the underworld:[49] Socrates, who
may never have to pay a penalty for injustice in the Acherusian
lake, would thus condemn to eternal punishment in Hades the
Athenian dēmos, who condemned him to death in one day and
then lived to repent it.[50]

Socrates supports this possibility in the account he now
offers of the fate of the pure, to balance that of the incurably
impure—for otherwise nature would be lame (71e): those who
are found to have excelled in pious living, liberated by their
own weightlessness from the regions of the earth as from pris-
ons, rise upward into their pure abode on the outer surface of
the earth (cf. 82e–83a).[51] The pious, who sought throughout
their lives separation from the body construed as a prison of
the psychē, are rewarded at death by release from imprisonment within the body of the earth; but their pure dwelling
place is only the surface of the earth itself, which has been
described as an intensified realm of the body and the senses.
Those, like the genuine philosophers, who desire nothing but
"noetic vision," contact of the pure psychē with the pure beings, Socrates now condemns to the abode of aesthetic vision—
forever! The inhabitants of the Acherusian lake who lived a life
in the middle, as well as those who paid the penalty in Tartarus
for their great sins but then obtained forgiveness from their
victims, all receive another chance, another life on earth; only
those who have lived a pious life, together with the incurably
evil, are precluded forever from release from the body, banned
eternally from contemplation of the "ideas."

Socrates confirms this terrible condemnation in the conclusion through which he finally brings to light a division
within the class of the purified: whereas those who are found
to have devoted themselves to the holy mount upward to dwell
on the surface of the earth, only those "sufficiently purified by
philosophy"—for the first time, Socrates does not say they
merely appear so—live altogether without bodies, passing to
even more beautiful abodes. Socrates removes, through this
explicit distinction, the mask behind which he has, for certain
purposes, provisionally hidden himself: release from the body
is a reward not for those who pursued it as a goal—the initiates
who will dwell with the gods (69c, 111b–c)—but only for those
whose separation from the body is simultaneously separation
from the self, from the inseparable union of psychē with body.
That this "sufficient purification by philosophy" consists in
the turn to investigation through logoi Socrates suggests by
admitting his inability to describe, in the context of this mythos, the abodes beyond the surface of the earth in which the
bodiless philosopher belongs. In any case, Socrates concedes,
his remaining time on earth would not suffice for the task—the
very reason he gave for his inability to demonstrate the truth of
the mythos, to which this account must be equivalent, and
which was itself in turn equivalent to a continued examination
of the first hypotheses of their arguments.

[114c6–115a2]   But Socrates does not need to reach this point
of sufficiency in order to afirm, in closing his address to Simmias, that it is necessary to participate in virtue and phronēsis
"for the sake of these things"—namely, the "beautiful prize
and great hope" of Tartarus for the evil, and paradise for the
pure. Of course it would not be fitting for a man with sense,
Socrates acknowledges, to insist that everything is just as he
has narrated. But it would be fitting to admit that something
like it is true—since the psychē is manifestly immortal—of our
psychai and their dwelling places: the paradoxical truth revealed by the mythos is that attachment to the psychē entails
attachment to the body.[52] It is worthwhile to risk accepting

this, Socrates adds, for the danger is beautiful. Against the terrible danger of neglecting care for the psychē (107c), one must risk the beautiful danger of chanting such a story to oneself, as if it were a magic charm—which is the reason, Socrates claims, that he has expanded the mythos for so long, given the brevity of the time left to him.

After reflecting in this way on the status of the mythos, and no longer addressing Simmias alone, Socrates announces, once again, what is required "for the sake of these things";[53] only now the motivation of hope for the beautiful prize has been replaced by acceptance of a beautiful danger, and what is necessary is only confidence about one's own psychē, based on the way one has lived one's life. One would exhibit a very foolish confidence in dying, Cebes insisted, unless one possessed a complete demonstration of the immortality and imperishability of the psychē (88b; cf. 95d). Socrates now concludes his mythos—as he did his initial defense (69c), as well as the first series of arguments (84a–b)—with his third and final affirmation of the alternative grounds for such confidence.[54] Socrates announced his wish, at the beginning of his initial defense, to explain why it appeared likely to him that a man who really spent his life in philosophy would be confident when about to die and of good hope for attaining great blessings there when he has died (63e–64a); like the mixture of mythos and logos introduced by that defense, which has been separated in the second half of the dialogue, the hope for reward after death and the confidence in dying that Socrates first combined have now been properly separated from each other.

He is confident about his own psychē, Socrates concludes, who in his life "bid farewell" to the pleasures and adornments of the body as being alien, but was serious about those of learning. Socrates recalls the speech concluding the first half of the conversation, in which he described the "lovers of learning" who do not care for the body but for their own psychē, who bid farewell to the lovers of the body while turning to follow philosophy wherever it leads (82c–d). But whereas the psychē was then said to be enslaved to the body by submission to pleasure in general—since its source, Cebes agreed, is "mostly the visible things"—Socrates now, for the first time, admits the possibility of pleasures that belong properly to learning. To pursue these, Socrates adds, is to adorn the psychē with no alien adornments, but with those that belong to it—moderation and justice and courage and freedom and truth. In his account of true virtue at the conclusion of his initial defense, Socrates added to moderation and justice and courage "*phronēsis* itself" (69b); he now replaces the latter, in his final description of the proper "cosmos" of the psychē, with freedom and truth. He indicates the perhaps surprising distinction between, on the one hand, participation in phronēsis based on hope for the beautiful reward of a particular fate after death and, on the other, pursuit of the pleasures of learning and adornment of the psychē with freedom and truth based on the need to be confident about one's own psychē in living and dying. But the distinction Socrates presents in reflecting on the status of his mythos, addressed to a man with sense, should be no more surprising than his separation of the pious, whose reward has been described most beautifully, from the philosopher, whose fate after death has been shrouded in silence.

CHAPTER THIRTEEN

Pharmakon

[115a3–116a3]   Socrates concludes his mythos with a description of the man who is confident about his own psychē and is therefore prepared for his journey into Hades when fate calls him. Indeed, his own time has now arrived, Socrates announces to his companions, "as a tragic man would say." Having described the journey of the psychai of the dead into Hades and their cleansing in the rivers of the earth body, Socrates declares his intention, before departing on that journey, of cleansing his own body.[1] He betrays the corporeal root of the notion of purification and the metaphorical status of its interpretation as a separation of psychē from body.[2] Despite his allusion to the call of fate, Socrates—who appears to have taken responsibility for attending the trial, for provoking the conviction, or at least the death sentence, and for having it carried out[3]—is determined now to bathe himself. For to do so is better, he believes—though perhaps a violation of established ritual—than to give the women the trouble (*pragmata parechein*) of bathing the corpse. Socrates' concern for the women seems to be his way of expressing the shame he feels at the thought of becoming, after death, a mere pragma. Yet Socrates attempts, precisely by speaking of the corpse, to separate "himself" from his body and to identify the latter as the alien pragma that is about to "admit death." The problematic character of this attempt is immediately indicated, however, by

Phaedo's continuation of the narrative; for his reference to Socrates "himself" (autos) recalls the first word of the dialogue, which designated the living being as an inseparable whole consisting of body and psychē. Just this question of the identity of the self becomes the explicit theme of the exchange Socrates shares with Crito in a brief interlude between announcing his intention of bathing himself and actually getting up to do so.

Crito, who has been silent ever since his initial interruption to report the warning concerning the effects of the poison, now returns to offer his aid to Socrates in carrying out any last wishes. Appearing only in the outer frame of the logos, Crito is the necessary support for Socrates' deeds. Asking Socrates for instructions regarding his children or anything else, Crito displays the same concern he showed in their private conversation.[4] And Socrates answers Crito, as he did throughout that conversation, that he has nothing new to request but only the same old demands:[5] if they take care of themselves—not only their psychai!—they will serve Socrates and what is his, as well as themselves; but if they neglect themselves and the traces of the speeches uttered just now and long ago, no matter how intensely they might make promises at the moment, they would accomplish nothing. Just when Crito promises to strive eagerly to do as Socrates asks, however, he betrays the limitations of his eagerness;[6] for his very question—in what way Socrates wishes to be buried—violates just what Socrates claims to have been trying to establish throughout the conversation.

Bury me however you wish, Socrates responds, "if you can catch me and I don't escape." With that remark he laughed gently, Phaedo reports, while looking up at the others. Socrates displays the same painful pleasure as he did when he laughed gently at Simmias' hesitation to disturb him with an objection, wondering how he could persuade others that he was facing no misfortune, when he could not make even those present believe it (84e). Socrates cannot now persuade Crito, let alone others, that "I am just this Socrates who is now conversing and arranging each of the things spoken," for Crito could hardly be convinced that Socrates, his lifelong friend, is nothing but the logos. He seems to think, Socrates reproaches him, that all these speeches about his departure to the joys of the blessed have been uttered only to encourage his companions as well as himself. But this is precisely the warning Socrates himself issued to his companions (91a): Socrates' attempted persuasion of Crito, who represents the human perspective as such, is, as always, an attempted persuasion of himself.[7]

Continuing his bittersweet playfulness, Socrates requests that the young men give security to Crito, only the opposite of that which Crito offered the judges at the trial; for Crito gave security that Socrates would remain in the Athenian prison,[8] whereas the young men must give security that Socrates will not remain when he dies, but will go away and withdraw. Crito offered security that Socrates would remain in prison, while devoting all his efforts to persuading him to run away; Socrates asks the young men to give security that he will withdraw at death, with full recognition of their desire that he remain at their side.[9] If Socrates were to withdraw, rather than remain behind and be destroyed at the approach of death, he would confirm in his own deed the logos concerning opposites themselves, or that which is essentially characterized by an opposite. Socrates thus recalls his description of the immortal that withdraws, in contrast with "the mortal of us" that dies when death approaches the man (106e). But to ascribe withdrawal at death to himself, Socrates must identify the psychē with the self as a whole, while at the same time assuming its separation from the body.

Socrates indicates his awareness of this difficulty by emphasizing the way it is necessary to speak: in order that Crito may bear it more easily when he sees the body of Socrates being burned or buried and may not be troubled by the belief that Socrates himself will be suffering something terrible, he must not say that he is laying out "Socrates" or carrying away "Socrates." Such speeches, which are not beautifully spoken, implant some kind of evil in psychai: the very name "Socrates," which presupposes the identity of him who is now conversing with that which will soon be laid out, borne to the tomb, and buried, produces that monster, the fear of death, which they have striven manfully to overcome. The separation that may be unintelligible in deed must be preserved in speech, for Crito must be confident—like the man who must be confident about his own psychē (114d)—and say that it is only the body of Socrates that will be buried. It can be buried, therefore, in whatever way he finds most dear and lawful. While the characteristics of being dear and being lawful may not be identical for Crito—as his private conversation with Socrates indicates—Socrates tries, just as he did in that conversation, to satisfy simultaneously his own principle, the wishes of his friend Crito, and the demands of the law.[10]

Phaedo introduced this exchange by reporting that Socrates autos announced his intention of going to bathe; he concludes it by reporting, "that one spoke these things, and then went inside to bathe and Crito followed him (autos)." Phaedo's narrative frame belies the theme of the exhange it surrounds: it reveals the limitations of mere speech in establishing the separation Socrates demands between himself and the silent, motionless corpse he will soon become. But "this Socrates now conversing and arranging each of the speeches" is in fact only a representation in Phaedo's narrative report: the reality behind the separation of Socrates from Socrates, of which he cannot persuade his companions or perhaps himself, is the separation of the living Socrates, whose life is about to come to an end, from the written image, created by the Platonic art of writing.

[116a4–116b8]   Phaedo began his report with a description of the young men commanded by the jailer to wait outside the prison while the eleven were releasing Socrates from his chains (59e); he now describes the young men commanded by Crito to wait outside the inner chamber of the prison cell while Socrates bathed himself. In this interval, Socrates performs an experiment, as it were, testing the young men's response to his absence. They began by conversing with each other about what had been spoken, Phaedo reports, but then turned to discuss in detail the misfortune that had befallen them. The speeches that may have convinced them that Socrates suffers nothing terrible in dying have only confirmed their own sense of being abandoned. The pathos they suffer is not pity but self-pity: Socrates' test run of his own absence testifies to his greater success in defending the prudence of his willingness to die than in defending his justice in running away from friends and masters (cf. 63b).

"We felt simply as if we were being deprived of a father and would spend the rest of our lives as orphans,"[11] Phaedo admits and then immediately reports that Socrates completed his bath and prepared for the visit of his own children, who were about to become real orphans.[12] The outer frame preceding the logos, when Crito helped carry out Socrates' wish of having Xanthippe taken home, is now complemented by the outer frame following the logos, when Crito remains with Socrates in the inner chamber to help carry out his directions to the women of the family. Socrates returned to them, Phaedo continues, only after spending a long time within—perhaps part of it alone[13]— for it was nearly sunset. Despite his promise to try to narrate everything, Phaedo's bodily absence from the inner chamber has the same effect, paradoxically, as his nonbodily absence from the philosophic peak of the discussion, which he could only report in the same summary outline. Phaedo's narration has progressed, in any case, almost completely from speech to deed, for when Socrates returned and sat down, "not much more was said."

[116b8–116d7]   This closing of the frame around the logos is indicated by the entrance of the servant of the eleven, the same man, presumably, who released Socrates from his chains at the outset of the day and gave directions about how he would die.[14] Despite, or perhaps because, he has taken no part in the discussion, only the servant of the eleven acknowledges its suppressed political context. Just because he has not heard Socrates defend his belief that death is not an evil, he alone grasps Socrates' invisible anger and the knowledge on which it is based:[15]

> Oh Socrates, I will not blame you as I do the others for being angry and cursing me when I, compelled by the

rulers, pass on the order to drink the poison; but you I have known in all this time to be the noblest and gentlest and best man of all who ever arrived here, and now especially, I know that you are not angry with me but with those others, for you know who are to blame (*tous aitious*) (116c).

It is no accident that the man most concerned with the question of responsibility should bring to light the practical reflection of Socrates' theoretical analysis of cause (*to aition*): he hits upon the truth of Socrates' charge against those who are groping in the dark when they name as cause those subordinate conditions necessary for carrying out the intention that constitutes the true cause. As if he had heard Socrates acknowledge that the true causes of his situation were the Athenians' belief that it was best to condemn him and his own subsequent belief that it was best and most just to undergo the penalty they commanded (98c–99b), the servant of the eleven expresses gratitude for Socrates' recognition of his subordinate status. He suggests, however inadvertently, that Socrates' anger might be directed justifiably even beyond the Athenian dēmos, insofar as it, too, is only a subordinate instrument for carrying out the intention of superiors: "It is perhaps not irrational," Socrates admitted, "that a man must not put himself to death before a god sends some necessity," as he judges to have now come to himself (62c).

The servant of the eleven bids farewell to Socrates with words that Socrates might well address to himself: "Now, for you know what I have come to announce, farewell, and try to bear as easily as you can the necessities." As the man burst into tears with these words, Socrates looked straight up at him (*anablepsas*): Phaedo reports one more gesture, in a series of increasing intensity, that betrays the pathē concealed by speeches alone.[16] "Goodbye (*chaire*) to you too," Socrates responds, while promising to do what he advised. Socrates addresses to the servant of the eleven the ambiguous farewell that he offered to none of his interlocuters but only asked Crito to deliver to the man in charge of administering the poison, when he issued the warning that Socrates should try to converse as little as possible (63d–e). But while dismissing the servant of the eleven with the expression that has indicated delight in being rid of something troublesome, Socrates remarks to the others how "urbane" the man is; he has, after all, just praised Socrates as the best among the criminals he has known in the Athenian prison! Throughout the imprisonment, in fact, the man has been coming to visit and converse, Socrates mentions, and then praises him as the best of men. For while the others, moved by resentment concealed as pity, construe Socrates' death as evidently self-willed and have therefore put him on trial for injustice and imprudence, only the servant of the eleven recognizes Socrates' noble and gentle anger, which is based on a true understanding of responsibility. As if foreseeing that the others are about to weep at their own misfortune, Socrates marvels at how nobly the servant of the eleven weeps not for himself, but for Socrates.

[116d7–117e3]   Having promised to try to bear as easily as possible "the necessities," Socrates asks Crito to have the poison brought out, or at least prepared. But Crito is as eager as ever to postpone these necessities: the sun has not yet set, he argues, and others have drunk the poison very late after the order was issued, meanwhile feasting and drinking and having intercourse with those they desired. Socrates does not repeat his account of the philosopher's disdain for the pleasures of the body; he acknowledges only that they would act suitably if they believed that they would profit from such actions, but he believes there is no profit in drinking the poison a little later. Just this realization that life no longer had any profit must have moved Socrates to embrace, rather than struggle against, the "call of fate," not simply at this final moment with the sun still upon the mountains, but from his first recognition of the intention of the Athenian dēmos to force him to give up the practice of philosophy.

Socrates is as successful in persuading Crito as he was, apparently, in persuading the Athenians that there was no point in continuing a life no longer worth living.[17] But, against his wishes, Socrates had to wait a long time, Phaedo remarks, after Crito signaled to the boy standing near that it was time to bring the man who was to administer the poison, to whose authority Socrates at last submits, after a daylong delay. When he asks, however, what he must do (*poiein*), he is told he must do nothing, only walk until his legs become heavy, then lie down, and the pharmakon will act of itself (*auto poiēsei*). Despite Socrates' will to maintain control over the act of dying, his transformation from an agent carrying out his own intentions to a motionless corpse will be fittingly accomplished as a mechanical result of the self-acting poison.

Socrates' painful recognition of this fact is both concealed and revealed by Phaedo's account of his response when handed the cup of poison. Interrupting his narrative to address himself to Echecrates—as if to relive as closely as possible the intense pathē of that moment—Phaedo describes how Socrates took the cup gently, without trembling or changing color or expression. But Phaedo's careful observation, which is in conflict with his own interpretation of it, betrays the truth of Socrates' experience: at the moment he took the cup so steadily, Phaedo adds, Socrates looked up at the man from under his brows, bull-like (*taurēdon hupoblepsas*). Socrates suddenly turns into an image of the Minotaur, the mythical monster symbolizing the fear of death. Socrates/Theseus has been victorious over that monster, thanks to his discovery of the safety of taking refuge in logoi. But the salvation of the logos is not, or is only in a sense, the salvation of Socrates himself:[18] with the cup of poison in his hands, Socrates betrays his realization that "this Socrates now conversing" is not identical with the logos itself. For this brief moment, perhaps, Socrates succumbs to the fear of death, or at least he presents that appearance to his audience.

Socrates asks, at the same moment, whether he might pour a libation from the drink to someone.[19] His request seems to be an accusation against the gods for imposing on him the present necessity;[20] that claim, after all, furnished Socrates' only defense against the charge of injustice in running away from life, and the implicit charge of impiety underlying it. But Socrates is prevented from expressing his ironic gratitude to the gods, for he is told that the authorities have prepared only as much poison as they believe measurable—enough, presumably, to end a man's life. When Socrates was warned originally, however, not to get heated up by conversing all day, or a greater quantity of poison would be required to produce its effect, he had boldly responded, "Let him prepare to give it twice, or if necessary thrice" (63e); that response calls to mind, in the present context, the formula of the libation, "Thrice to Zeus the savior."[21] Had Socrates remained silent all day, perhaps the cup of poison would have held enough to accomplish its primary purpose, with some to spare. The daylong conversation has replaced, it seems, a ritual libation to the gods: Socrates could not devote himself to the logos and at the same time display his piety, even in its most ironic form.

He must, nevertheless, offer to the gods at least a prayer, Socrates insists, that his change of abode from here to there be a fortunate one. With the simple wish, "May it come to be so,"[22] Socrates raised the cup to his lips and drank the draught, according to Phaedo, very readily and calmly. But the others, at the sight of this act, could no longer contain themselves; while Crito had been compelled to leave even earlier in tears, and Apollodorus had burst into wailing, making everyone but Socrates lose control, Phaedo wrapped his face up in his cloak,[23] he confesses, and wept for himself. Socrates reproaches the men—"Oh wondrous ones"—for behavior he expected from the women he sent away, having heard that "it is necessary to die in silence" (en euphēmia).[24] Yet, since Socrates might have chosen, presumably, to remain in the inner chamber and die alone, he seems to have gone out of his way to compel his companions to watch him die.[25] He makes the occasion of his own death an experiment, intended to test the power of logos over the pathē;[26] but it is a test that none of his companions passes, for they check their tears finally only out of shame at Socrates' command—"Keep quiet and overcome."

[117e4–118a8]   After walking about until his legs were heavy, Socrates lay down, Phaedo recounts, and the man administering the poison touched him, examining his feet and legs, until when he pinched his foot hard, Socrates felt nothing. After being released from his chains at dawn, Socrates sat up and rubbed his own leg, remarking on the paradoxical experience caused by release from the pain of being fettered, which was itself recognized only in retrospect as the condition for the subsequent feeling of pleasure. Now at dusk, Socrates can no longer actively rub his own leg, which has been rendered motionless and numb by the poison: Socrates is being released from the self-imposed chains of attachment to pleasure and pain.[27]

As the poison extended its effect, the attendant continued his examination upward, demonstrating to the others—apparently having them, too, feel Socrates' body—that he was growing cold and rigid. A war of opposites—heat and cold, life and death—is being played out on the battlefield of the body of Socrates. As soon as the cold reached the heart, the attendant explained, he would depart:[28] just as the servant of the eleven unwittingly confirmed Socrates' theoretical analysis of cause, the man who administers the poison unwittingly confirms his account of that which must withdraw, if it is not to be destroyed, at the approach of an opposite. When the numbness reached the area of the groin, Phaedo continues, Socrates uncovered his head, for it had been covered some time, apparently, after he lay down on his back and the attendant began to examine his body growing cold. Was Socrates, then, like Phaedo, compelled by shame at his fear or self-pity to cover his head? Or did Socrates, who just identified himself in relation to others, as "the Socrates who is now conversing," cover himself solely for the sake of his companions? Actually, we are not told that it was Socrates himself who performed the deed. The very fact that his head was covered is revealed, in any case, only in retrospect, when Socrates uncovers himself—like the pain that is revealed as pain only when release from it is experienced as pleasure.

Socrates manifests this recovery when the numbness reaches the organ of generation. He addresses to Crito at this moment his last words: "To Asclepius we owe a cock;[29] but pay it and do not neglect it." Socrates marks his success in the practice of dying by remembering the god of healing; he believes it necessary, apparently, to supplement the hymn to Apollo he claims to have produced as a rite of purification.[30] Asclepius should be a model for the best physician, Socrates argues on one occasion,[31] since he was willing to heal those who could recover and lead a normal life, but not those who would go on living only with suffering or with constant pampering. Socrates contrasts his own view, however, with that of Pindar and the tragedians, who affirm that Asclepius, though a son of Apollo, was bribed by gold to heal a man already at the point of death. Asclepius, whom Socrates now thinks of in his last words, seems, then, to have a double significance. Does Socrates express his gratitude to the healing god, who knows when it is no longer worth living, for his own recovery from the disease of life?[32] Or does Socrates, who announced his call of fate "as a tragic man would say," offer at the last moment a bribe to the healing god to fight off the approach of death—one last affirmation of the goodness of life?[33]

Whatever union of opposites Socrates is portrayed as experiencing at his release from life, Plato has him express appreciation for another recovery that is concurrent with the portrayal of that release. From Phaedo's narrative we know of one case of illness—the cause of Plato's absence from the scene of Socrates' death (59b); and the sign of recovery from that illness is nothing but the Platonic dialogue itself, which has provided this image of the dying Socrates. The pharmakon that Socrates drinks is simultaneously a poison that brings his life to an end and a remedy that cures a disease. But it is a different pharmakon—that of the written word[34]—that truly fulfills the practice of dying, as a separation of logos from the living self. The Platonic Socrates thus invests his dying words with an appropriate implication of gratitude—Thank god for Plato!

[118a9–118a17]   Crito agreed to carry out Socrates' wish and
was ready for any further requests; but Socrates made no reply,
and after a little while, Phaedo remarks, he moved. Socrates'
original formulation of what death is revealed it to be two
things—the body becoming separate from the psychē and the
psychē being separate from the body (64c). Socrates now enacts
in deed this double determination in speech. If his last words
mark the withdrawal of the psychē, his last movement must be
an involuntary reflex of the body; or rather, as the course of the
dialogue has taught, what seem to be separate signs of psychē
and body are in fact the signs of psychē as agent of thought or
speech and psychē as source of motion or life, with the former
dependent on the latter. That Socrates' final intentional action
must have been to re-cover his face after uttering his request to
Crito is revealed, once again, only retrospectively: after that
last unwilled movement, Phaedo reports, Socrates was uncovered by the attendant. But the final deeds are performed, of
course, by Crito: without disclosing whether he remembered
the speeches Socrates recommended to inspire confidence,
Crito covered the eyes and mouth of the corpse.[35]

Having completed his account of everything said and done,
Phaedo closes the frame around his narration: "Such was the
end of our friend, of all those of his time the best and most
prudent (phronimos) and most just." He pays tribute to Socrates only as the best of his contemporaries: Socrates is no
longer. The true "cause" of his death, Socrates insisted, was his
belief that it was more just and noble to endure the penalty
imposed by the Athenians, who found him guilty of injustice
and impiety. But it is with regard to the charges of injustice and
imprudence, for which Socrates was put on trial on the last day
of his life, that Phaedo pronounces the final judgment of exon-
eration. He is silent about Socrates' piety;[36] or, one could say,
he replaces that question with the judgment about his superlative goodness.

Notes

INTRODUCTION

1. The variety of approaches to the dialogues might be divided into three kinds—subject to all the usual qualifications of any typification: (a) The tradition predominant in English language scholarship is interested primarily in analyzing the arguments, abstracted from their literary presentation; as a result, fallacies in the arguments are generally assumed to be due to Plato's failure to carry out his intention, while credit for our recognition of these fallacies is often given to contemporary tools of analysis. (b) The tradition represented primarily by the Tübingen school (see the works of Hans Joachim Krämer and Konrad Gaiser referred to in the bibliography) takes its bearings from the reports of Plato's "unwritten teachings" in Aristotle and later doxographic sources; it seeks, on that basis, to reconstruct the systematic character of Platonic philosophy, in contrast to which the dialogues are thought to have merely a protreptic function. (c) According to the tradition that can be traced back at least to Friedrich Schleiermacher (see also note 11 below), the Platonic dialogue is a unified whole, whose philosophic content cannot be separated from its dramatic form, since the latter is no mere compromise but in fact the only proper mode for philosophic communication through the written word.

2. See Francis M. Cornford, *The Republic of Plato* (London: Oxford University Press, 1941), p. xxvii.

3. See Hans Wagner, "Platon und der Beginn der Metaphysik also Wissenschaft," in *Kritik und Metaphysik: Festschrift für Heinz Heimsoeth*, pp. 363–82.

4. See R. Hackforth, *Plato's* Phaedo, p. 3; see also A. E. Taylor, *Plato, the Man and his Work*, p. 176.

5. See Hackforth, p. 3.

6. For a review of the controversy, see Hackforth, pp. 127–31. See also note 24 below, and note 1, chapter 10.

7. See G. M. A. Grube, *Plato's Thought*, p. 129.

8. See Leo Strauss, "Plato," in *History of Political Philosophy*, p. 7.

9. See *Phaedrus* 274d–278b, and Ronna Burger, *Plato's* Phaedrus: *A Defense of a Philosophic Art of Writing*, particularly the introduction and the chapter entitled "The Art of Writing."

10. *Phaedrus* 264b–c.

11. On the approach to the reading of the dialogues advocated here, see especially Leo Strauss, *The City and Man*, pp. 50–63; Jacob Klein, *A Commentary on Plato's* Meno, introductory remarks; Stanley Rosen, *Plato's* Symposium, introduction.

12. This qualification was inspired by the recent appearance of two books on the *Phaedo* that claim to be guided by the same hermeneutic principle. That this common claim leads to very different results, which distinguish the two works from each other and from the present study, is instructive. In *The Deathday of Socrates*, Jerome Eckstein's concern with how "psycho-dramatic reality pervades and tempers the dialogue's logic" (p. 51) leads him to see the arguments as "one prolonged blast of Platonic irony" (p. 11), motivated by Plato's primary intent to discredit the rationality of Socrates' "heroic suicide." Of course it is not clear that this thesis could account for the specific ways in which each argument is ironic, nor for the structure that relates them to one another. That Socrates presents fallacious arguments for immortality, in any case, does not necessarily mean that he is portrayed as believing them, or even wanting to believe them; in fact he repeatedly indicates his awareness of their deficiency, and when he acknowledges the true motivation for his acceptance of his death, it is not a belief in immortality to which he refers.

In *Plato's* Phaedo: *An Interpretation*, Kenneth Dorter seeks to synthesize the analytic with the dramatic approach, which he takes to be influenced in part by Schopenhauer's and Husserl's views of the superiority of direct to indirect evidence. But since Platonic dramaturgy surely requires for its interpretation "inferring," not merely "intuiting," it hardly seems to be a direct means of conveying insights, in contrast to the "indirect and often tendentious technique of argument"

(p. ix). By attending to Socrates' rhetorical purpose, Dorter recognizes that his attempt to demonstrate the personal immortality of the soul is only an appeal to "popular religious imagination"; yet Socrates does demonstrate, Dorter thinks, a meaningful sense of immortality, whose subject is the "world-soul" of which all individual souls are portions (pp. 44, 157). It is not at all evident, however, that a demonstration of such "impersonal immortality," any more than one of "personal immortality," could avoid the fundamental misconceptions that Socrates warns against when he insists on the necessity of replacing "investigation of the beings themselves" by his own "second sailing" and illustrates that replacement in the final argument of the dialogue.

13. Because of the possibly inappropriate connotations of the word "soul," psyche will hereafter remain untranslated. The traditional understanding of psyche relevant to the *Phaedo* and other Platonic dialogues is brought to light in Aristotle's account of the views handed down by his predecessors: the distinguishing characteristics of psyche are thought to be its functions as source of movement or life and of sensation or cognition (see especially *De anima* 1.2).

14. This is emphasized by Schleiermacher in the introduction to his translation of the *Phaedo* (see *Platon Werke*, vol. 2.3, p. 9). "Wir treffen heir," Hegel remarks on the *Phaedo*, "am wenigsten geschieden die Weise des Vorstellens und des Begriffes" (*Vorlesungen über die Geschichte der Philosophie*, Theorie Werkausgabe, vol. 19, p. 52).

15. The Greek word will be used rather than translated, because the multiplicity of associations with *logos*—particularly the broad sense of speech as opposed to deed, which includes the precise sense of argument as opposed to myth—is preserved and exploited throughout the dialogue.

16. See Aristotle *Metaphysics* 987b10–14, 29–32.

17. See Aristotle's critique of this doctrine (*De anima* 407b20–24).

18. "Music" might seem, consequently, to be too restrictive a translation of *mousike;* but it is intended to capture Socrates' reconstruction—as well as its possible Pythagorean source (see John Burnet, *Plato's* Phaedo, note on 61a3)—in labeling philosophy "the greatest music," and thus indicating its continuity with, as well as difference from, poetry as "demotic music." On the translation of *mousike*, see Alan Bloom, *The Republic of Plato*, p. xiii. The command of Socrates' dream—*poiei kai ergazou*—might be translated "do" or "practice" music, but it seems here to have the connotation "produce" and "fabricate works."

19. See *Apology* 28d–29a.

20. See *Crito* 48b–e and the entire speech Socrates delivers in the name of the laws of Athens.

21. In the ordinary sense, which appears frequently in the Platonic dialogues (see for example *Symposium* 209a), phronēsis means practical wisdom, a capacity for sound judgment, especially in political affairs. When Cebes first raises the question of whether the *phronimos* man would not be most fearful of death (62d), he seems to understand phronēsis as the prudential pursuit of one's true self-interest. Yet this would seem to be a very odd capacity to ascribe to the disembodied psychē, as the "genuine philosophers" do, and as Cebes asks Socrates to prove. The tension between the two demonstrations Cebes demands—of Socrates' prudence in accepting his death and of the possession of phronēsis by the psychē after death—makes the meaning of phronēsis a thematic question of the dialogue.

22. *Pragma*, which is most often translated simply "thing," is related to the word *praxis* and often has the connotation of being a matter of importance or concern. Socrates clarifies its particular usage in the *Phaedo* when he distinguishes "opposites themselves," which are always mutually exclusive, from "opposite *pragmata*," the things characterized by those opposites that come to be from each other (103b). A pragma in this particular sense is a subject characterized by a quality, like "Socrates greater" or "Socrates smaller"; while it is contrasted with the qualities "greatness" or "smallness," which remain what they are through all changes, it denies the possibility of an identical subject, "Socrates," which remains the same through all changes.

23. *Technē* is here translated "art" in the sense of a set of rules or method of making or doing. Socrates distinguishes it, in the *Gorgias* (465a), from mere practice based on experience (*empeiria*), which cannot give a logos of its subject and therefore lacks knowledge of cause.

24. Socrates' pre-Socratic starting point therefore illustrates the necessity of beginning in error. If his intellectual autobiography were simply an account of an accidental development, rather than a necessary one, it would be hard to explain, as Michael Davis argues, why the *Phaedo* should reproduce that development in its own structure. See "Socrates' Pre-Socratism: Some Remarks on the Structure of Plato's *Phaedo*," *Review of Metaphysics* (1980):574.

25. See *Phaedrus* 274e–275a; Cf. Jacques Derrida, "La Pharmacie de Platon."

CHAPTER ONE

1. Within the Platonic corpus, four dialogues present a Socratic conversation through the perspective of a narrator other than Socrates himself: the *Phaedo* and *Theaetetus*, in which Socrates seems to choose the reporter who will reconstruct the conversation after his death, are complemented by the *Parmenides*, and the *Symposium*, in which a young Socrates and Socrates' own report of himself when young, respectively, are represented through the recollection of multiple reporters. The *Theaetetus*, whose narrator and auditor appear among those present at Socrates' death, is the first, according to dramatic chronology, and apparently most aporetic, of the dialogues centering on Socrates' trial and death, the *Phaedo* the last and apparently most dogmatic. Socrates' account, in this last conversation, of his way of investigation through logoi recalls the lesson he learns in the *Parmenides* when criticized for his inadequate defense of the ideas and asked to follow Parmenides' model of a "hypothetical method." The most emotional of those present at the conversation on the day of Socrates' death, which begins at dawn and ends at dusk, is the narrator of the *Symposium*, which begins at dusk and ends at dawn, when Socrates compels two poets to admit the possibility of the same man writing by art both tragedy and comedy. The dialogue on *erōs* and the dialogue on the "practice of dying" seem to form together one whole (see note 29, chapter 13); they represent, Friedrich Schleiermacher suggests, "two aspects of the philosopher as such" (see the introduction to his translation of the *Phaedo* in *Platon Werke*, vol. 2.3, pp. 5–8).

2. Compare *"Platōn de oimai ēsthenai"* (59b) with Phaedo's introduction, *"hōs men egō oimai"* (102a) to his summary of what seems to be the philosophic peak of the dialogue.

3. The first word points ahead, at the same time, to the formula for the separate *eidos*, *"auto kath' auto"* (100b; Cf. 65d, 66a, 74a, 75c–d, 78d, 103b,e, 106d).

4. The only other occasion is in the *Apology*, where Socrates mentions that Plato is present (34a), and that he, along with Crito, Crito's son, and Apollodorus, commanded Socrates to propose a fine, for which they would give security, large enough to satisfy the jury (38b). Jerome Eckstein interprets Plato's absence from the *Phaedo* as a sign of his disapproval of Socrates' decision to accept the death sentence (see *The Deathday of Socrates*, pp. 28, 30).

5. In no other dialogue, Schleiermacher remarks in his intro-

duction to the *Phaedo,* is the mimetic element so completely determined by, and unified with, its subject matter, and nowhere does it have a greater right to be so (p. 9).

6. Cf. *Phaedo* 117d; *Symposium* 173d–e; *Apology* 34a.

7. Phlius, home of Echecrates and the last of the Pythagoreans (see Diogenes Laertius *Lives of Eminent Philosophers* 8.46), where, according to legend, Pythagoras first used the word *philosophos* (see Cicero *Tusculan Disputations* 5.3), provides the fitting context for Phaedo's reconstruction of the conversation Socrates is about to begin with an appeal to the "genuine philosophers."

8. Phaedo does not specify the length of time that passed between Socrates' trial and death, but Xenophon tells us that it was thirty days (see *Memorabilia* 4.8.2).

9. See Plutarch *Lives,* "Theseus," chapter 23.

10. While pity is distress at our neighbor's misfortune and envy at his prosperity, a man who comes to feel one, Cicero maintains, is always susceptible to the other (*Tusculan Disputations* 3.20–21).

11. On these individuals, and the other Platonic dialogues in which some appear, see John Burnet, *Plato's* Phaedo, pp. 7–11; see also W. D. Geddes, *The* Phaedo *of Plato, pp. 195–202.*

12. Consider the characterization of Menexenus in the *Lysis* (especially 211b–c) and of Ctesippus in the *Euthydemus* (especially 283e, 288b, 300d).

13. On the correspondence that makes the *Phaedo* a mythological account of Socrates' death, in which the "new and true Theseus" is Socrates, and the "old and true Minotaur is the monster called Fear of Death," see Jacob Klein, "Plato's *Phaedo,"* in *Journal of St. John's College* (January 1975):1–2.

14. Referring to the absent Aristippus, Cleombrotus, and Plato, Phaedo brings his list to seventeen. Five of those he names appear in the list of seventeen young men, together with their fathers or brothers, whom Socrates mentions at his public trial as those with whom he conversed (*Apology* 33d–34a). This list happens to be parallel, Leo Strauss observes, to the list of seventeen named or unnamed individuals—including the poets and their fictional characters!—with whom Socrates claims he would like to converse in Hades (*Apology* 41a–c). See Leo Strauss, "On Plato's Apology of Socrates and Crito," in *Essays in Honor of Jacob Klein,* pp. 160–63.

15. See *Phaedrus* 264b–c, and the discussion of logographic necessity in the introduction.

16. See *Apology* 30e–31a.

17. The phrase that literally means "for the sake of the holy" (*hosias heneka*) comes to mean "for form's sake" (see Seth Benardete, "A Reading of Sophocles' *Antigone*," *Interpretation* (1975):193).

18. The first of the cases mentioned in Plato's *Laws* in which suicide is not to be punished—followed by the stress of cruel and inevitable calamity or desparate and intolerable disgrace—is the sentence of the city requiring self-slaughter (873c).

19. Cf. *Crito* 45e–46a.

20. See *Republic* 514a–520d.

21. See *Apology* 37e–38a.

22. See *Crito* 52e, 53d–e.

23. See *Crito* 53b–c.

24. Socrates does not tell Crito why he could not travel to far away well-governed cities like Sparta or Crete, which the laws mention (52e)—precisely the journey undertaken by the Athenian Stranger of Plato's *Laws*, whom Aristotle calls "Socrates" (*Politics* 2.6), as Leo Strauss observes (*The Action and the Argument of Plato's* Laws, p. 2).

25. See *Theaetetus* 143a–c.

26. See W. K. C. Guthrie, *A History of Greek Philosophy*, vol. 1, p. 179.

CHAPTER TWO

1. The dream speaks in the words of Achilles, who stubbornly rejects Odysseus' entreaty to return to the war, by threatening to set sail for his homeland Phthia (*Iliad* 9.363); Achilles' homeland is in lawless Thessaly, where Crito proposes Socrates should escape (*Crito* 53d). But the beautiful woman in Socrates' dream must be the goddess Thetis, who warns her son Achilles that, if he avenges the death of Patroclus, "immediately after Hector, death is appointed unto thee" (*Iliad* 18.96). Achilles' rejection of a long but disgraceful life is the response Socrates cites in his public trial when he insists that he must remain at his appointed station of practicing philosophy (*Apology* 28d). By combining the two Homeric passages in the dream he relates to Crito, Socrates can affirm the journey to death as his true homeland, without abandoning responsibility to Athens. See the analysis of this passage by Leo Strauss, "On Plato's *Apology of Socrates* and *Crito*", in *Essays in Honor of Jacob Klein*, pp. 164–65.

2. See *Crito* 43a.

3. On the function of the eleven and their connection with public execution, see Aristotle *Athenian Constitution* 52. The jailer's reference to "the eleven" in general anticipates the question of responsibility, which is appropriately brought up at the conclusion of the dialogue by the "servant of the eleven" (cf. 116c).

4. Plato seems to go out of his way to let us know that Socrates, who is about to speak of the philosopher's desire to escape from the body, is the father of a child young enough to be held in his wife's arms (cf. *Apology* 34d).

5. In the *Crito*, for example, we are never told that Socrates rose from his reclining position for a conversation in which he conspicuously avoids the words *psychē* or *philosophy* (see 47d–48a).

6. What Xanthippe is reproached for, it seems, is the fact that she cried out (*aneuphēmēse*); yet when the men can no longer hold back their tears at the sight of Socrates drinking the poison, he reproaches them for acting like women, reminding them that "it is necessary to die in *euphēmia*" (117e; cf. note 24, chapter 13).

7. Lamentation (*threnon*) stands at the center of Socrates' list of seven *pathē*, in which the psychē itself suffers from a mixture of pleasure and pain (*Philebus* 47d–e).

8. Socrates expresses the same wonder each time he confronts a problem of the relation of opposites (cf. 60b, 62a, 97a).

9. The "wishing" of pleasure and pain not to come to be present together is like the "wishing" of greatness or smallness in us not to admit the other, which may require the destruction of one at the approach of its opposite (see 102d–e).

10. Perhaps no one would ever claim that pain is simply the cessation of pleasure; but the more persuasive claim that pleasure is simply the cessation of pain can be denied only by establishing the possibility of an autonomous intermediate state that is neither pleasure nor pain (see *Philebus* 43d–44d; *Republic* 583c–585a).

11. On the command of Socrates' dream—to "make music"—see note 18, introduction. The identity of Socrates' dream, despite its multiple variants, (cf. *Apology* 33c) poses another version of the problem implicitly raised by the identity of the Athenian ship (see note 9, chapter 1) and finally by the identity of an individual whose body is constantly being worn away and replaced within one lifetime (87d–e).

12. See *Apology* 23a–b.

13. On the possible Pythagorean source of the identification of

philosophy as "the greatest music," see W. D. Geddes, *The Phaedo of Plato*, p. 209.

14. Cf. *Apology* 20b–c; *Phaedrus* 267a.

15. The misunderstanding against which Socrates issues this warning is illustrated by the anecdote Cicero reports: according to Callimachus, Cleombrotus of Ambracia was so convinced that death is no misfortune that he flung himself from the city wall into the sea after reading Plato's book (*Tusculan Disputations* 1.84).

16. Philolaus, said to be the first to put Pythagorean teaching into writing, taught at Thebes, to which he escaped after the expulsion of the sect from southern Italy (see W. K. C. Guthrie, *A History of Greek Philosophy*, vol. 1, p. 179). Clement of Alexandria claims to quote Philolaus on the source of his Pythagorean teaching: "The ancient theological writers and prophets also bear witness that the psychē is yoked to the body as a punishment and buried in it as in a tomb" (*Stromata* 3.17). Among other echoes in the *Phaedo* of doctrines ascribed to Philolaus is Simmias' image, supported by Echecrates (88d), of the psychē as a harmony (see Guthrie, p. 312). For a critique of the authenticity of the fragments assigned to Philolaus and a defense of their post-Platonic source, see Erich Frank, *Platon und die sogennanten Pythagoreer*, especially pp. 291–302.

17. Compare Diotima's warning that Socrates must be eager to follow her initiation into the mysteries of erōs (*Symposium* 210a), Socrates' acknowledgment of his eagerness to initiate Meno into the mysteries of the proper way to give a unified definition of virtue (*Meno* 77a), and Socrates' admission to Glaucon that his eagerness to reveal the idea of the good could make him look ridiculous (*Republic* 506d). Cf. the analysis of the latter passages by Konrad Gaiser, "Platons *Menon* und die Akademie," p. 348, and Hans Joachim Krämer, "Über den Zusammenhang von Prinzipienlehre und Dialektik bei Platon," in *Das Problem der ungeschriebenen Lehre Platons*, ed. Jürgen Wippern, pp. 431–32.

18. For an analysis of proposed translations and interpretations of this passage, see David Gallop, *Plato Phaedo*, pp. 79–83; Kenneth Dorter, *Plato's Phaedo*, pp. 12–16; Geddes, pp. 213–17.

19. This would seem to be the Platonic reversal of the "tragic" understanding of "divine jealousy," according to which the gods would claim that death is better for man than life (cf. Cicero *Tusculan Disputations* 1.113–115). Consider Herodotus' report of the story Solon tells Croesus, which presents two contrasting responses to the

question of human happiness: the point of view of the sacred is represented by the fate of Cleobus and Biton, through whom "the god showed it was better for a man to die than to live" (*Histories* 1.31.3; see the analysis by Seth Benardete, *Herodotean Inquiries*, pp. 185, 212).

20. As Nietzsche puts it: "Man muß durchaus seine Finger danach ausstrecken und den Versuch machen, diese erstaunliche finesse zu fassen, daß der Wert des Lebens nicht abgeschätzt werden kann. Von einem Lebenden nicht, weil ein solcher Partei, ja sogar Streitobjekt ist und nicht Richter; von einem Toten nicht, aus einem anderen Grunde." (Das Problem des Sokrates, p. 2). Cf. Michael Davis, "Plato and Nietzsche on Death: An Introduction to Plato's *Phaedo*," *Ancient Philosophy* (1980):78.

21. The "simplicity" of the divine prohibition against suicide will inspire wonder, Geddes argues (pp. 215–17), precisely because it is valid even for those and on those occasions when death is indeed superior. Or, as Hans Reynen argues, the dubiousness of the claim that life is always superior is meant to put into question the unconditional status of the divine prohibition against suicide ("*Phaidon* Interpretationen: zu Plat. *Phaed*. 62a und 69a–b, *Hermes* (1968):42–46).

22. Olympiodorus interprets Socrates' cryptic formulation to mean that suicide is forbidden with regard to the body that it harms but justified because of a greater good to the psychē (*Commentary on the Phaedo* 1.9).

23. Once this ambiguity is taken into account, it is no longer as easy to find in this passage, as Jerome Eckstein does, as an indication of Plato's accusation of Socrates for the decision to take his own life (see *The Deathday of Socrates*, pp. 13, 45).

24. Cf. the etymology of "Zeus," which Socrates derives from his two names (*Zēna* and *Dia*): together they signify the nature of "the god through whom all the living always have life" (*Cratylus* 396a–b).

25. See *Crito* 51b–c.

26. See *Apology* 28d–e.

27. The word *phroura*, which appears in a fragment assigned to Philolaus (DK 32B15), could mean either prison (see *Gorgias* 525a) or guard house (see *Critias* 117d; *Laws* 760a, c, 762c). Cf. Socrates' etymology of "body" (*sōma*) in connection with "to keep safe" (*sōzetai*, *Cratylus* 400c), which is juxtaposed with an etymology connecting "body" and "grave" (*sēma*), in which the psychē is said to be buried (cf. *Gorgias* 493a).

28. Cf. *Laws* 902b, 906a; *Critias* 109b.

29. Cf. Phaedo's final judgment on Socrates as "the most *phronimos*" man of his time (118a). Cebes unwittingly puts into question the relation between the understanding of phronēsis as a state of the pure psychē after death, which Socrates ascribes to the genuine philosophers, and Socrates' own understanding and exemplification of phronēsis (cf. 69a, b, c, 94b, 107d, 108a, 114c).

30. See *Apology* 26b-28a.

31. Cf. *Cratylus* 403a-404b.

32. See 100d; cf. 114d; *Meno* 86b.

33. Appropriately, Simmias brings to mind the Pythagorean maxim—"Friends have all in common" (see Iamblichus *Vita Pythagorae* 81, 87; cf. *Phaedrus* 279c; *Lysis* 207c; *Republic* 449c; *Laws* 739c). But just to the extent that Simmias does not share with Socrates the need he expresses, he puts into question the possibility of their "friendship."

34. See 60b-c and 103a-c.

35. Cf. 63e, 64c, 65c, 82d, 83d, 100d, 101c, d, 114e, 116d.

36. See *Apology* 29c-d.

37. Cf. *Gorgias* 498e; *Philebus* 59e-60a; *Laws* 957a; and the remarks of Paul Friedländer, in *Platon*, vol. 3, p. 61.

CHAPTER THREE

1. Contrast *Apology* 40a and 38c.

2. Paul Friedländer (*Platon*, vol. 3, p. 473) appropriately refers to Heidegger's description of *sein zum Tode* as a condition of which *Dasein* would be deprived by death itself (see especially *Sein und Zeit*, p. 261).

3. The word *philosophountes*—which Simmias introduces and Socrates uses throughout his defense, along with "true philosophizers" and "correct philosophizers," and apparently interchangeably with "true philosophers," "genuine philosophers," and "correct lovers of learning"—often seems to have a derogatory sense, indicating particularly the disdainful conception of the philosopher on the part of the many (cf. *Apology* 23d; or Callicles' speech in the *Gorgias* 485b, c, d).

4. Socrates, who won't profess knowledge when conscious of his own ignorance, can hardly have the attitude toward life that he

ascribes to the "true philosophers," R. Hackforth argues, (*Plato's Phaedo*, p. 16).

5. Cf. 65d, 74a, 100b, 102a–b. On the status of the agreement *that* something is, which seems to be the necessary premise for determining *what* it is, see Hans Wagner, "Die Eigenart der Ideenlehre in Platons *Phaedo*," *Kant-Studien* (1966):6.

6. At the conclusion of his public trial, Socrates defends the possibility that the death sentence he has received may be something good, on the basis of the presumably exhaustive alternative that death is either a continuation of his own life on earth, or that it is a "wondrous gain" simply in being virtually nothing, like the most unconscious dreamless sleep (see *Apology* 40c–e).

7. Cf. *Philebus* 47b.

8. Olympiodorus finds it puzzling that the attainment of phronēsis, ordinarily understood as the statesman's practical judgment (cf. *Symposium* 209a), should be designated as the goal of the philosopher's purification after death (*Commentary on the Phaedo* 3.6).

9. See note 35, chapter 2.

10. Continuing, however ironically, his attempted unification of demotic music with the greatest music, Socrates appeals to the poets who are constantly "drumming into our ears" that the sight and hearing of men have no contact with the truth (65b); Socrates will characterize in the same way the ousia he is always "drumming into our ears" (cf. 76d–e, 100b). Olympiodorus (4.13), surprised perhaps by Socrates' reference to the poets, suggests that they are Parmenides, Empedocles, and Epicharmus, as well as Homer, from whom he quotes *Iliad* 5.127–128.

11. Consider Socrates' etymology of "Phersephone" (*Cratylus* 404c–d), or of sophia (412b). Cf. Aristotle *De anima* 424a17–24, 429a13–18, 432a1–3; and the analysis by Stanley Rosen, in "Thought and Touch: A Note on Aristotle's *De anima*," *Phronesis* (1961):127–37, especially p. 132.

12. Cf. *Meno* 72d–e; *Philebus* 26b.

13. Cf. 78d, 92d, 101c; and David Gallop's note on this phrase (*Plato Phaedo*, pp. 227, 230). See also Hans Wagner's account of ousia as the general title for the determination of the object, "that which each happens to be" ("Die Eigenart der Ideenlehre in Platons *Phaedon*," *Kant-Studien* (1966): 8). The connection between the philo-

sophic sense of *ousia* and its ordinary meaning as "property" is preserved in our use of the word "substance."

14. Cf. 67c, 79a; cf. also *Sophist* 227c.

15. When Theaetetus is puzzled by the Eleatic Stranger's division of hunting into that of living and lifeless prey, the Stranger affirms that both exist, although no special name belongs to the latter (*Sophist* 220a); he brings to light Theaetetus' ignorance of their own effort. See also *Euthydemus* 290b–d, or the legislation about hunting with which the Athenian Stranger completes his regulation of education (*Laws* 823b–824c).

16. Either they are led themselves "together with the *logos*" to this conclusion (see Gallop, pp. 11, 227), or, assuming Schleiermacher's transposition, they are led to recognize the hindrance of having "the body together with the *logos* in the investigation," echoing Socrates' prior description (66a) of investigating without dragging the senses along with *logismos* (see John Burnet, *Plato's* Phaedo, p. 36). In either case, the genuine philosophers are far more preoccupied with their resentment of the contamination of the psychē by the body than they are with considering what the role of logos is.

17. It is on the basis of the principle, "Like knows like," Aristotle asserts, that his predecessors established their various accounts of psychē (*De anima* 405b14–16). But consider Socrates' description of the fate of the pure in his concluding myth (114b–c and 111a–c).

18. Cf. 82c, 83e. Socrates attempts to establish the combination of philosophic and "thumoeidetic" traits in the nature of the guardians of his best city by obtaining Glaucon's agreement, without examination, on the identity of love of wisdom and love of learning; the latter is supposed to be exemplified by the dog, who is friendly to the familiar and hostile to the unknown, regardless of benefit or harm (*Republic* 376a–c)!

19. Socrates will recall this passage in his mythological description of the purified psychē being released from the regions within the earth as from a prison (114b). Cf. *Timaeus* 69c–70a.

20. Cf. *Phaedrus* 265d–e, 266b; *Sophist* 253d; *Statesman* 282b, 287c.

21. See *Sophist* 226d.

22. But laughter, or even a gentle smile, may be a sign of fear, as the deeds reported by Phaedo suggest: see 59a, 62a, 64a, 77e, 84d, 86d, 115c. On laughter as a mixture of pleasure and pain, see *Philebus* 50a.

23. Cf. 80d, 81a; *Gorgias* 493b; *Cratylus* 403a.

24. Cf. *Phaedrus* 227c, 257a–b; *Symposium* 177d–e; *Theages* 128b; *Lysis* 204b–e. In the conversation he conducts with Theaetetus after hearing of his indictment and before his trial, Socrates ascribes to himself an art not of erotics, but of midwifery, modeled on that of women who are barren or too old to conceive and bear children of their own (*Theaetetus* 149b–150d).

25. The sign Socrates interprets as a "divine necessity" sanctioning this release may be the disappearance of his *daimonion*; for he attributes to its noninterference his decision to face the trial while aware of its likely outcome (*Apology* 40c). The daimonion does seem to provide or protect Socrates' life impulse: it kept him not only from unpromising associations (see *Theages* 128d–130e), but also from participation in politics, which might have meant an early death (see *Republic* 496c–d; *Apology* 31d).

26. That the love of pleasure is omitted here as a sign of love of the body (see Olympiodorus 7.5, Damascius 1.137) suggests that, while the genuine philosophers identify all love of the body with love of pleasure, Socrates silently rejects the identification of all pleasure as corporeal (cf. 114e).

27. Cf. *Republic* 580d–581c.

28. Cf. *Apology* 37c; *Gorgias* 512e; *Laws* 944e.

29. Socrates seems to adopt—as he did in his nonsymmetrical analysis of the so-called pleasant and the painful (60b)—the assumption of the severe men he describes to Protarchus, who claim that all pleasure is nothing but release from pain (see *Philebus* 43c–44d).

30. Cf. *Protagoras* 355b–356c. Aristotle begins his account of the specific moral virtues with courage followed by moderation, "for these seem to be the virtues of the irrational parts" (*Nichomachean Ethics* 1117b23–24).

31. If courageous action can be produced not only by courage itself, but also by cowardice, moderate action not only by moderation itself, but also by incontinence, not only would opposite causes produce the same result (97a–b), but also one cause would produce a result opposite to its own nature (101b); and if fear of pain could produce courage as well as cowardice, while fear of deprivation of pleasure could produce moderation as well as incontinence, one cause would in each case produce opposite results (101a).

32. If Socrates does face death courageously, is it not because he fears as a worse evil the way he would otherwise have to go on living (cf. 99a; *Apology* 29a–c, 37b–e; *Crito* 47d–48d)? Of course, Socrates'

claims may be, as he himself admits, the sign of his love of victory on this occasion (cf. 91a–b, 115d), so that his courage and/or moderation would be displayed only in spite of those claims. Cf. Aristotle *Nichomachean Ethics* 1117b10–13.

33. Cf. *Meno* 88a–d; *Protagoras* 332a–333b, 349e–350c, 360b–e; *Laches* 194d–195a, 199c; *Charmides* 165c–167b; *Laws* 688a–b, 963a–965e; Aristotle *Nichomachean Ethics* 1103a4–10, 1144b1–1145a.

34. Pains and fears should correspond, it seems, to pleasures and desires, but Socrates is silent about the last; he has, after all, just described demotic moderation coming into being not from desire for pleasures, but from fear of their deprivation.

35. The Eleatic Stranger contrasts the mathematical measure, concerned always with greater and lesser in relation to each other, and the measure of the mean (*Statesman* 283d–285e); see Seth Benardete's discussion of their relation in the chapter entitled "Metrics" in his commentary on the *Statesman* (*The Being of the Beautiful* III. 113–19).

36. See the analysis of various translations and interpretations of this passage by Hans Reynen, "*Phaidon* Interpretationen: zu Plat. *Phaed.* 62a und 69a–b," *Hermes* (1968):46–60.

37. Cf. *Republic* 583b, 586b–c; cf. also *Philebus* 42a–c; *Protagoras* 356a–357b.

38. It is unclear at 69c1–3—perhaps intentionally so—whether moderation and justice and courage are linked to "the true", which is some kind of purification, or to phronēsis, which is some kind of purgation. Cf. Aristotle's distinction between virtue, which makes us aim at the right mark, and phronēsis, which makes us take the right means (*Nichomachean Ethics* 1144a6–8).

39. Condemning the way the poets praise justice and condemn injustice, Adeimantus refers to their description of the impious and unjust buried in the mud in Hades (*Republic* 363d); but Socrates takes up the same description as an image of "the eye of the psychē sunk in barbaric mud," from which dialectics leads it upward to the *archē* (533c–d).

CHAPTER FOUR

1. Cf. Homer *Iliad* 23.100, and Socrates' criticism of such fear-inspiring poetry (*Republic* 387b).

2. The claim that what is must necessarily be in some place and

occupy space, but what is neither in heaven nor on earth has no being, is, according to Plato's Timaeus, what "we say as if seeing in a dream" (*Timaeus* 52b–c). The physicist must have knowledge of place, Aristotle argues, for it is generally assumed that things that are, are in some place, while that which is not is nowhere (*Physics* 208a27–33).

3. Cf. the double determination of psychē suggested by *Phaedrus* 245e and 249b–c, or by *Sophist* 248d–249b; cf. also Aristotle *De anima* 403b25–27.

4. Socrates rebukes Polus for praising rhetoric as the most beautiful art before answering what it is (*Gorgias* 448d–e); he disapproves of his conversation with Thrasymachus, trying to consider whether justice is virtue or vice, ignorance or wisdom, and whether or not it brings happiness, before knowing what it is (*Republic* 354b–c); he criticizes his procedure with Protagoras, trying to determine whether virtue is teachable before asking whether it is knowledge (*Protagoras* 360e–361c); but although he first tells Meno that they cannot know whether virtue is teachable before knowing what it is (*Meno* 71a–b), Socrates then suggests that, like geometers who assume the nature of something as known and then argue from that as a hypothesis, they ought to assume that virtue is knowledge in order to deduce its teachability (86d–87c).

5. It is only to those who voted for acquittal at his public trial that Socrates suggests telling stories to each other (*diamuthologēsai*) as well as conversing (dialegesthai) about whether death is something good or not (*Apology* 39e).

6. See *Apology* 19b–c, and Socrates' protest that Meletus must think he is prosecuting Anaxagoras when he charges Socrates with inventing theories about the sun being a stone or the moon earth (26d).

7. See *Apology* 19d.

8. See Aristophanes *Clouds* 1480; cf. *Republic* 488e, and Socrates' apparent praise of Anaxagoras in the *Phaedrus* (270a).

9. On Aristophanes' critique of Socrates, which could be understood as an attack against his indifference to "demotic music," see Leo Strauss, *Socrates and Aristophanes*, pp. 1–3. See also Stanley Rosen, *Plato's* Symposium, pp. 121–23.

10. Although the subject psychai is not mentioned, it is implied by the participles in the feminine plural. On the ambiguity of *gignesthai*, which could mean "to be born," "to come into being," or, with a complement, "to become something," see David Gallop, *Plato* Phaedo,

pp. 105–06. If the subject is "psychē," the verb should be translated "to be born," since the argument denies that it comes to be in the strict sense; if the subject is "the living," being born and coming to be would be identical.

11. Socrates uses only the last part of the ancient logos when he repeats as the antecedent of the argument that the living are born again from those who have died; otherwise the claim that the psychai "are there arriving from here" would include in the premise that which is to be derived from it (see R. Hackforth, *Plato's* Phaedo, p. 59, n. 2).

12. Cf. Aristotle's reference to the psychē as "the place of the *eidē" (De anima* 429a27).

13. See Aristotle *Metaphysics* 987b1–4.

14. The beautiful and the ugly, furthermore, seem to exemplify the opposites themselves that are "unwilling" to coexist in something at the same time, whereas that which comes to be more beautiful in relation to one thing would still be less beautiful, that is, more ugly, in relation to something else (cf. *Hippias Major* 289a–d).

15. Cf. the characterization by Plato's Timaeus of the aesthetic, in contrast to the noetic, as that which comes to be in some place and passes away out of it (*Timaeus* 52a).

16. Cf. also *Theaetetus* 159b–c.

17. By means of these opposite geneseis, the pre-Socratics could account for a plurality of phenomena, without having to admit coming into being out of nothing and passing away into nothing (see Aristotle *Physics* 187a12–b1, 188a19–32, b21–30, 191a23–34). On the processes of cooling and heating, see Anaximander *DK* 12A10; Anaximenes *DK* 13B1; Philolaus *DK* A27; Anaxagoras *DK* 59B8; Heraclitus *DK* 22B126. On separation and combination, see Anaximander *DK* 12A9; Empedocles *DK* 31B17; Anaxagoras *DK* 59B17; Cf. Aristotle *On Generation and Corruption* 322b6–8, 329b25–30.

18. When Theaetetus admits that he is made dizzy by these puzzling cases in which something comes to be greater without increasing, smaller without decreasing, Socrates assures him that this sense of wonder is the beginning of philosophy (see *Theaetetus* 154c–155d). Cf. Seth Benardete, *The Being of the Beautiful*, I. 105–07.

19. Those who postulate one underlying substratum must identify coming to be and passing away as alteration, Aristotle reasons, while those who postulate more than one underlying substratum must identify coming to be and passing away with combination and

separation (*On Generation and Corruption* 314b1-6, 315b16-24). Cf. Damascius *Commentary on the Phaedo* 1.190.

20. The comparatives illustrate opposites that are contradictories, with no intermediary, so that a logical inference is possible from one to the other. Living and dead, on the other hand—like just and unjust or beautiful and ugly (see *Symposium* 202a-b)—are not contradictory but contrary opposites; since something may be neither dead nor alive, no logical inference is possible from the denial of one to the affirmation of the other. On this distinction, see Aristotle *Metaphysics* 1055a38-63. On its role in the present argument, see P. W. Gooch, "Plato's *Antapodosis* Argument for the Soul's Immortality: *Phaedo* 70-72," in *Proceedings of the Seventh Inter-American Congress of Philosophy*, vol. 2, p. 243.

21. Insofar as all things that come into being do not proceed from their opposite form but from their own privation (see Damascius 1.246; Aristotle *Physics* 191b13-17), Socrates could infer only that, if something comes to be alive, it must have been previously not alive.

22. Cf. Heraclitus DK 22B88. In accordance with the model on which the argument has been based, "being asleep" should only mean being less awake, and by implication "being dead" should mean being less alive. If, Socrates claims at his public trial, being most awake, and by implication most alive, is to engage most constantly in the activity of examination, then most men are indeed more or less asleep—that is, throughout their lives, more or less dead. If death is not simply a continuation of his own way of life, Socrates surmises at the end of the trial, then it is like the deepest sleep with no awareness (*Apology* 40c-e); the Athenian dēmos, whom Socrates describes as a slumbering horse unwilling to be awakened by his gadfly activity (30e-31a), illustrates the truth of his claim that the unexamined life is not worth living.

23. But even if one could infer that something that now awakens must have been previously asleep, or that something that falls asleep must have been previously awake, it does not follow that something that now awakens must have previously fallen asleep after first being awake. Socrates could argue, then, according to Julian Wolfe, that if the psychē comes to be alive, it must previously have been not alive, but not that it must previously have died ("Plato's Cyclical Argument for Immortality," in *Proceedings of the Seventh Inter-American Congress of Philosophy*, vol. 2, p. 253). Of course Wolfe assumes that being alive, as a characteristic of the

psychē , is to animate a body, being not alive, to exist apart from a body, and dying, to cease animating a body, but these definitions are to be found nowhere in the argument.

24. Cf. *Symposium* 207c–e; *Laws* 721c, 773e, 776b. In the context of criticizing the ideas as useless in accounting for genesis, Aristotle describes the coming to be of natural things, where the generator is of the same kind as that which is generated: man generates man (*Metaphysics* 1033b30–33).

25. Cf. Socrates' appeal to the general principle of *antapodosis* in *Republic* 563e, or Timaeus' account of the antapodosis of inspiration and expiration (*Timaeus* 79e).

26. Cf. 81b–e, 83d–e, 113a; cf. also Anaximander *DK* 12A9, or Heraclitus *DK* 22B94. But Socrates' present argument, as the ancient commentators recognize (see Olympiodorus 10.14), would preclude the possibility of that eternal condemnation of the incurably wicked or eternal reward of the purified that Socrates describes in his concluding myth (see 113e, 114c).

27. See Kenneth Dorter, *Plato's* Phaedo, p. 45.

28. Socrates here introduces "always" for the first time, Hackforth argues (p. 64), since it is only at this point that he attempts to demonstrate the everlastingness of the cycle from one opposite to the other.

29. Cf. Aristotle's interpretation of the position of Heraclitus (*Eudemian Ethics* 1235a25–27).

30. The consequence that would result from the denial of opposite geneseis, as Socrates' ambiguous use of gignesthai may suggest, is that everything would cease coming to be anything at all (see Gallop, p. 112). Is the cycle of genesis ceaseless, Aristotle asks, because the passing away of a this is the coming to be of something else, and the coming to be of a this the passing away of something else? (*On Generation and Corruption* 318a24–26).

31. Socrates presents the equivalent in logos to Anaxagoras' cosmological chaos when he uses the same allusion to describe the confusion of the disputatious, who do not separate the positing of hypotheses from the derivation of their consequences but mix everything together (101e).

32. Given the indeterminacy of the Anaxagorean mixture, as Aristotle interprets it, nothing could be truly predicated of the underlying substance (see *Metaphysics* 989b6–20).

33. Cf. Aristotle *Metaphysics* 989a33–b4.

34. Cf. Damascius 1.228 and Strato's criticism of the argument (in Hackforth, p. 195). After asking whether the cyclical structure of becoming is accomplished in the same way by all things, Aristotle answers that only for those things whose substance is imperishable is the recurrence numerically the same, while in all others it is the same only in species (On Generation and Corruption 338b12–19).

35. The premise that nothing comes from nothing, Aristotle claims, is a principle held in common by all the pre-Socratics (see Physics 187a27–30).

36. Cf. Aristotle On Generation and Corruption 318a13–24.

37. See Melissus DK 30B8; cf. Walter Bröcker, Platos Gespräche, p. 128.

38. The consequence of such a reduction, Aristotle argues, is the impossibility of explaining change—which requires that there be an "out of which" and a "to which"—as well as the denial of the law of noncontradiction (see Metaphysics 1009a22–38, 1010a1–38).

39. Compare Socrates' silence about any nonmoving beings in his attempt to demonstrate that the indestructibility of "the whole heaven and all genesis" depends upon the ungenerated and indestructible arché constituted by self-moving motion, which could be "not shamefully" identified as the ousia and logos of psyché (Phaedrus 245d–e); cf. Laws 895a–896a.

40. The disturbance of modern editors who bracket the manuscript reading of the final phrase of this conclusion—"And it is better for the good but worse for the evil"—is hardly surprising; if authentic, it would be Plato's acknowledgement of the inappropriateness of the argument to respond to Cebes' demand for a demonstration to justify the "great and beautiful" hope promised by Socrates' defense (70a–b). See H. G. Gadamer, "The Proofs of Immortality in Plato's Phaedo," in Dialogue and Dialectic, pp. 25–26.

41. The expression tō onti appears seventeen times in the Phaedo, fourteen times in the first half of the dialogue, prior to Socrates' account of his turn from investigation of the beings to investigation through logoi. In the second half of the dialogue, which illustrates that turn, the first occurrence distinguishes what is truly a cause "in being" from a mere co-cause, that is, teleology from mechanism (99b), both of which are contrasted, however, with the eidē; the last occurrence, in Socrates' myth, refers to the real presence of the gods with the purified (111b); the central occurrence is in the conclusion of the final argument, affirming that our psychai will "really" be

in Hades (107a). Compare the seventeen cases of false opinion that Socrates outlines for Theaetetus, the first fourteen of which are impossible, and only the last three possible (*Theaetetus* 192a–c).

CHAPTER FIVE

1. Cebes introduces the word *athanaton,* whereas Socrates ascribes the quality "deathless" to the psychē at no point prior to the final argument (105e ff.); he uses it in the third argument only as the principle to which the psychē is akin (79d, 80b, 81a), and once as the characteristic, "so to speak," of the bones and sinews (80d).

2. Cebes also introduces the term *eidos,* in its prephilosophic sense of "body" or "figure," especially the living human body. On the relation between this colloquial sense and the technical use of the term in the arts of rhetoric, medicine, and mathematics, see A. E. Taylor, "The Words *Eidos, Idea* in pre-Platonic Literature," in *Varia Socratica,* 1st series, especially pp. 182, 251. See also Jacob Klein's discussion of how, from the ordinary meaning of *eidos* as "looks" or "appearance," "Plato derives—by way of contrast, paradox, and pun— his understanding of the *eidos* as *aeides,"* the invisible object of thought (*A Commentary on Plato's* Meno, p. 50).

3. Cf. *Meno* 82b–86b. In the account Socrates first offers to Meno (81c–d), the identification of learning as recollection follows from the premise of immortality, whereas in Socrates' own reflections after his exhibition on the slave boy (86a–b), the immortality of the psychē follows from agreement on the possibility of learning (see Klein, p. 180). In the argument Socrates now conducts, the preexistence of the psychē should follow from the account of recollection, but Simmias will affirm his acceptance of recollection on the basis of the preexistence of the psychē (92d; see Klein, p. 132).

4. Cf. *Phaedrus* 249d–251a.

5. And yet the image example provides the model for the rest of the argument, as J. L. Ackrill observes ("Anamnesis in the *Phaedo:* Remarks on 73c–75c," in *Exegesis and Argument, Phronesis,* supplementary vol. 1 (1973):185). The example of Simmias and his picture seems, moreover, to make anamnēsis indistinguishable from *eikasia,* that capacity to perceive an image as an image that Socrates assigns to the lowest section in his image of the divided line (see *Republic* 509e–510a).

6. Cf. *Cratylus* 432b–d.

7. Cf. *Republic* 472d–e.

8. It is, perhaps, for this reason that Socrates illustrates the possibility of pure pleasure by referring to the sight of images, not of living beings, but only of geometric figures (see *Philebus* 51c).

9. Do we know it, what it is (*auto ho estin*)?, Socrates asks, where *auto*, referring to the equal itself, is simultaneously the direct object of "know" and the subject of "what is" (cf. 75b6, d1; see David Gallop, *Plato* Phaedo, pp. 119–20, 229). Cf. note 5, chapter 3.

10. On the controversy over whether this refers to different observers or to different relations in which the phenomena stand, and for this translation, which is intended to preserve that ambiguity, see Gallop, pp. 122–23, 220. See also the analysis of different interpretations by K. W. Mills, "Plato's *Phaedo* 74b7–c6," *Phronesis* (1957):128–33.

11. For sticks and stones may be equal in length, for example, but not weight (see Richard Haynes, "The form equality, as a set of equals: *Phaedo* 74b–c," *Phronesis* (1964):20. The problem, then, with which Socrates is concerned is not one constituted by and correctable by perception itself, as in a dispute among different observers. He is concerned, rather, as his later discussion of opposites suggests, with the apparently contradictory claim that phenomena, while remaining the same, are both equal and unequal—a claim that would be corrected by specifying the different relations in which these opposite qualities are ascribed (cf. *Parmenides* 129c–e).

12. "The equals themselves" seems, then, to refer to the properties themselves that are equal and never seem unequal to anyone (see Michael Wedin, "*Auta ta Isa* and the Argument at *Phaedo* 74b7–c5," *Phronesis* (1977): 198–99). Cf. Socrates' account of the monads under consideration in the arithmetic of the philosophers in contrast with the unequal units counted in the arithmetic of the many (*Philebus* 56d–e).

13. The formula suggests those "mathematicals" to which Plato, according to Aristotle, assigned an intermediary status: insofar as they are eternal and unchangeable, the mathematicals are unlike the phenomena, but insofar as they are a plurality of many alike, they are unlike the eidē (see *Metaphysics* 987b14–18). Against this interpretation, J. M. Rist argues that *hē isotēs, auto to ison,* and *auta ta isa* are simply three phrases Plato uses to describe the form of equal because he felt no one of them to be entirely satisfactory (see "Equals and Intermediaries in Plato," *Phronesis* (1964):31). To support this claim, Rist contends that *hē trias, hē idea tōn triōn,* and *ta tria* at *Phaedo*

104a–e are three different ways of referring to the form threeness (p. 29). But three must be related to the triad just as whatever is to be two must participate in the dyad and whatever is to be one in the monad (101c). If the equals themselves "bring forward" the *idea* of equality to any equal phenomena, like the dyad that "brings forward" the *idea* of the even to any collection of two (105a), they would indeed seem to be intermediary between "opposites in nature" and the things characterized by them (cf. 102d–103b).

14. Self-predication would be entailed, then, as J. M. Rist observes (p. 32), only by the equals themselves; cf. R. E. Allen, "Participation and Predication in Plato's Middle Dialogues," *Philosophical Review* (1960):150. It would be difficult to account for why Plato introduced these various terms if one were to argue, as K. W. Mills does, for example, that he failed to distinguish between them ("Plato's *Phaedo* 74b7–c6," *Phronesis* (1958):49).

15. Cf. Socrates' account in the *Cratylus* of the name-givers who, while whirling around and dizzy with confusion themselves, mistakenly projected their own state onto the phenomena and laid down names in accordance with their belief that all things are in motion (439c).

16. Yet, if knowledge of the equal itself implied knowledge of its opposite (cf. Gallop, p. 130), why would it be necessary to have acquired knowledge before birth of the greater and the smaller as well? And since one thing can certainly be greater or smaller than another, what would it mean to say that it falls short of the greater or the smaller (see John Burnet, *Plato's* Phaedo, p. 58)? Cf. Socrates' attempt, in the *Philebus*, to identify "the *genos* of the unlimited" by including within it "the things that appear to us to become more and less," in contrast to "the limit," to which the equal and equality belong (24e–25b; but contrast 25d–e).

17. "The holy" takes the place here of health and strength in the list Socrates presented to Simmias in his initial defense to illustrate "the being, what each happens to be" (65d); cf. Socrates' description in the myth of the fate after death of those found to have lived a holy life (113d, 114b). The holy appears only one more time in the dialogue, in conflict with the good: despite the fact that it may be better for the philosopher to be dead, it is not holy to benefit himself (62a).

18. On the metaphor of stamping with a seal, see *Philebus* 26d; *Statesman* 258c.

19. Cf. for example, *Crito* 50c; *Republic* 534d; *Protagoras* 329a; *Gorgias* 449b.

20. Cf. for example, *Euthyphro* 5d; *Charmides* 159a; *Laches* 190e; *Hippias Major* 286d; *Theaetetus* 146c; *Minos* 313a.

21. For if we already possessed the answer, why would we engage in inquiry at all (cf. *Meno* 80e)? Socrates identifies the dialectician, in the *Cratylus*, as he who knows how to ask and answer (390c), but he suggests the etymological derivation of *hēros* not only from *erōs*, but also from *erōtan* ("questioning"), so that the heroes must have been rhetoricians and dialecticians who knew not how to answer, but only how to question (398d).

22. Cf., for example, *Meno* 97e–98a; *Gorgias* 465a; *Republic* 534b; *Theaetetus* 202c; *Statesman* 286a.

23. Cf. *Phaedrus* 249b–c.

24. Cf. Aristotle *Posterior Analytics* 71b6–8, 99b26–34.

25. See note 13, chapter 3.

26. Just as the first argument proves that the psychē continues to exist after death in Hades, but not that it is imperishable, Olympiodorus argues, the second argument proves that it exists for some time before birth, but not that it is ungenerated (*Commentary on the Phaedo* 11.2).

27. Simmias' fear that when the psychē is released from the body, it will suffer corruption (*diaphtheiresthai*, 77b) echoes Cebes' fear that when a man dies, his psychē suffers corruption and is destroyed (*diaphtheirētai te kai apolluētai*, 70a); both interlocutors conclude their later objections to the argument by expressing their fear that, at death, the psychē is destroyed (*apollusthai*, 86d, and *apolētai*, 88b).

28. See 71d10–13 and 72a4–6, in contrast with 70c8–9, d3–4, 71d14–15, 71e14–72a2, d1–3, d8–9.

29. On the various traditional enumerations and divisions of the arguments, see W. D. Geddes, *The* Phaedo *of Plato*, introduction, pp. xviii–xix. See also note 1, chapter 8.

30. See Kenneth Dorter's analysis of the relation between the first and second arguments, which show different sides of the separated soul as motive and wise; while the third argument makes this disparity explicit, Dorter finds its reconciliation in the final argument, which defines soul as the bearer of the form "life" to the body (*Plato's* Phaedo, pp. 44–46). But to take this as a reconciliation ignores

the radical consequences of the transition from the first to the second half of the dialogue: the relation of psychē to life in the final argument in no way suggests the cognitive relation between the psychē and the forms that is assumed in the first series of arguments.

CHAPTER SIX

1. See note 22, chapter 3.

2. Cf. *Charmides* 155e–157c, 175e–176b. Just before presenting a comic description of the reincarnation of the psychē in other species, Socrates recommends that Cebes pay money to be enchanted by the Pythagoreans, perhaps, or the legendary Thracian orphics (see John Burnet, *Plato's* Phaedo, p. 64), as if they were sophists; Socrates certainly gives Cebes a double-edged message in advising him to be charmed by himself, if not by another, while simultaneously disenchanting him about enchantment.

3. Compare the final stage of the last argument, where Cebes agrees that the immortal must escape destruction, *if* anything can (106d).

4. To give a logos of the being of the ousia would be, Hans Wagner argues, to seek a definition of a determination as such ("Die Eigenart der Ideenlehre in Platons *Phaedo,*" *Kant-Studien* (1966):13–14).

5. For an analysis of the monoeidetic form as the Platonic transformation of the conditions of Parmenidean being to each among a plurality of ideas, see Gerold Prauss, *Platon und der logische Eleatismus,* pp. 36–40. This "early theory of ideas" becomes subject to criticism, Prauss argues (pp. 174–83) in the *Theaetetus* and *Sophist,* whereas one, if not the, primary exposition of it is in the *Phaedo,* and particularly in this passage (p. 36). But given the manner in which it is introduced and employed here, one can hardly assume that it is meant to be uncritically accepted.

6. Socrates foreshadows the examples in his final argument, in which the even is opposed to the odd as well as to the uneven, the hot and cold opposed to each other as well as to the "unhot" and "uncoolable," on the basis of which the psychē is said to be "not dead" (105d–e).

7. Cf. 80d, 81a; *Cratylus* 403a; *Gorgias* 493b.

8. For the insides of the living body are as invisible, Socrates implies in his concluding myth, as the psychē is said to be (see chapter 12).

9. The ancient commentators find it necessary to explain why Plato should call phronēsis a pathēma of the psychē (see the *Commentary on the Phaedo* of Olympiodorus, 13.19, and of Damascius, 1.334, 2.39).

10. Damascius distinguishes the three parts of the argument as concerned with being as sensible and intelligible, with cognitive power and activity, and finally with practical power and activity (1.325).

11. The six terms seem to correspond in pairs to the three parts of the argument, beginning with the last. The center is marked by the reverse order, in which noetic and monoeidetic are opposed to polyeidetic and "anoetic." While *anoēton* could mean "incapable of thinking" (cf. 88b4, 95c4, d7; see also Hackforth, *Plato's Phaedo*, p. 64), its opposite, *noēton*, means "accessible to thought." The ancient commentators, however, attempt to assimilate the positive term to the negative, in order to deduce the characterization of psychē as "capable of thought" (see Olympiodorus 13.2, Damascius 1.315).

12. The art of embalming is one sign of Egypt as *the* symbol of the fixed and permanent (cf. *Phaedrus* 274c–275b; *Timaeus* 21e–23c; *Laws* 656d–657b; cf. also Herodotus *Histories*, book 2).

13. It is precisely the bones and sinews that Socrates will describe in great detail as the mechanical cause of his sitting in prison— the necessary condition for, but not to be identified with, the intention that is truly a cause of his situation (98c–d). But Socrates' playful attribution of "deathlessness" to them points ahead to the connection he will bring to light between mechanism and teleology, body and psychē: his bones and sinews, Socrates will admit, would have been carried off long ago by an opinion of the best, had he not considered it more just to remain behind (99a).

14. After he has seen a perfect likeness of the dead Patroclus, Achilles discovers, "So even in the house of Hades soul and image are, after all, something" (*Iliad* 23.103–104). Hades, Seth Benardete comments, "is the locus of the reality of the image; it is the natural home of the poet." See "On Greek Tragedy," in *The Great Ideas Today*, pp. 135, 140.

15. Cf. *Apology* 41a–c; *Crito* 54b–c; *Gorgias* 523a–527a; *Republic* 363c–e; but contrast *Republic* 386a–387c.

16. Cf. *Cratylus* 403b–404b.

17. Cf. *Laws* 959b.

18. Cf. Socrates' etymology, for which he credits the Orphic po-

ets, of the "body" (sōma) as the "grave" (sēma) of the psychē (Cratylus 400c).

19. Cf. Republic 500d, 619c–d; Protagoras 323a–b; Meno 73a–c; Gorgias 504d–e, 507d–e.

20. See note 35, chapter 2.

21. See Republic 514a–518b. See also Alan Bloom, The Republic of Plato, pp. 404–05; Leo Strauss, "Plato," in History of Political Philosophy, p. 31.

22. See Republic 515c–e.

23. Compare Republic 517a with 521b and 540b.

24. Philosophy persuades the psychē to "withdraw" (anachō-rein) intact from the senses, just as an opposite or anything essentially characterized by an opposite must withdraw (hupekchōrein) from the approach of the other opposite, unless it is to be destroyed (cf. 102d, 103d, 104c, 106e).

25. Cf. Timaeus 73b–d, 91a–d.

26. This double motivation—refraining from bodily pleasures for the sake of (toutōn heneka, 82c) entering the genos of the gods and following the guidance of philosophy for the sake of (toutōn toinun heneka, 83e) communion with the divine and moneidetic—is echoed in the double motivation Socrates affirms at the end of his myth—participating in virtue and phronēsis for the sake of (toutōn dē heneka, 114c) the rewards described in the mythos and being confident about one's own psychē, for the sake of (toutōn dē heneka, 114d) being prepared for the call of fate.

27. See Robert Loriaux, Le Phédon de Platon, vol. 1, pp. 186–87.

28. Cf. Léon Robin, Platon Phédon, notice, p. 35.

CHAPTER SEVEN

1. Socrates alone falls into silent reflection once more in the conversation, just after restating Cebes' objection to the argument (95e), which he subsequently interprets as a question about the cause of coming into being and passing away in general and offers his "intellectual autobiography" in response.

2. Cf. Theaetetus 189e, and Sophist 263e.

3. See note 22, chapter 3.

4. Cf. Paul Friedländer, Platon, vol. 3, pp. 32–33. Given the controversy over the historical accuracy of the portrait of Socrates in

the *Phaedo*, it is of interest to consider the description that the ancient "biographies" ascribe to Plato. He was an Apollonian man, according to certain dreams and his own words, for he called himself a "fellow servant of the swans." Socrates is said to have dreamed, before Plato became his pupil, that an unfledged swan sat in his lap, then grew wings and flew away with a cry that made all who heard it spell-bound. And Plato is said to have dreamed, before he died, of a swan darting from tree to tree, unable to be caught by the fowlers; this dream, according to the interpretation of Simmias the Socratic, meant that all men would try to grasp Plato's meaning but none would succeed, and each would understand him according to his own views. (See L. G. Westerink, trans. and ed., *Anonymous Prolegomena to Platonic Philosophy*, p. 2; see also Diogenes Laertius, "Plato," in *Lives of Eminent Philosophers* 3.5).

    5. See *Apology* 20e–21a.

    6. See *Apology* 29a.

    7. See *Apology* 37c.

    8. On the meaning of *harmonia* as "attunement," from which the meanings of "scale" and "octave" are derived, see W. K. C. Guthrie, *A History of Greek Philosophy*, vol. 1, p. 223. When Simmias later refers to harmonia in the works of the craftsmen, he points to its original sense as a "fitting together," from the verb *harmottein* (see David Gallop, *Plato* Phaedo, p. 147).

    9. On the Pythagorean conception of the heavens as harmonia and number, which may constitute the basis for this account of psychē, see Aristotle *Metaphysics* 985b31–986a6; cf. *Timaeus* 37a. On the controversy over the Pythagorean origin of the doctrine, see John Burnet, *Plato's* Phaedo, p. 82; F. M. Cornford, "Mysticism and Science in the Pythagorean Tradition," *Classical Quarterly* (1922):145–50. On Philolaus as Simmias' authority for the notion of psychē as harmonia, see Guthrie, pp. 312–17.

    10. Cf. the speech of the physician Eryximachus in the *Symposium* (187a–188b), where harmonia reveals the relation between music and medicine, for health is identified as the result of the opposites hot, cold, wet, and dry being brought together in ordered harmony through "heavenly Eros"; see also Alcmaeon DK 24B4. The understanding of harmony as a balance of contrary elements of the body is a more appropriate definition of health, Aristotle argues, than of the psychē (*De anima* 408a2–4). He raises the question of whether the

supporters of the theory understand harmony as the logos of the combination or rather as the actual mixture of contraries and then argues that the psychē can be neither (407b33–35).

11. Cf. *Timaeus* 36e–37c, 47d, 90d; *Protagoras* 326b; *Laws* 653e–654a, 664e–665a, 689d; *Republic* 430e, 591c–d; Aristotle *Politics* 1340b17–19.

12. Cf. *Republic* 530d–531c.

13. Cf. Aristotle *Metaphysics* 1083b8–19, 1090a30–35.

14. Consider the use of *sumphōnein* in Socrates' account of his art of hypothetical reasoning (100a and 101d).

15. The last word of Simmias' speech is apollusthai (86d5), just as the last word of Cebes' speech is apolētai (88b10). See Konrad Gaiser, *Protreptik und Paränese bei Platon*, p. 151.

16. Cf. 60a, 63a, 116d, 117b. Burnet (p. 84) notes that the verb *diablepō* occurs nowhere else before *On Dreams* (462a12), where Aristotle, explaining dream images as movements in the sense organs, refers to children who, staring with wide open eyes (*diablepousin*) in the dark, see multitudes of phantoms before them and cover their heads in terror.

17. The conjunction of Simmias' persuasive, and therefore misleading, image with Cebes' image, which could not be mistaken as such, calls to mind the conjunction of the two images of the psychē that Socrates presents in the *Theaetetus:* in contrast with the laughable image of an aviary (197d–200c), the image of a wax block containing the impressions of memory (191c–e, 194c–195a) is so intuitively persuasive—as its predominance in the philosophic tradition might suggest—that it conceals its status as an image. See Seth Benardete's discussion of the images in his commentary on the *Theaetetus* (*The Being of the Beautiful* I.154–69).

18. On the notion of the psychē wrapping itself in the garment of the body, see Empedocles *DK* 31B126.

19. This problem was introduced by Phaedo's original reference to the ship of Theseus (see note 9, chapter 1) and was then implied by Socrates' image of Penelope's web (84a). Cf. Diotima's teaching on erōs as the principle through which the mortal participates in immortality, according to which not only the body but also the psychē and even knowledge possess no permanent identity, but only a constant perishing and coming to be (*Symposium* 207d–208b).

20. By implicitly showing Socrates' acceptance of Cebes' challenge, Schleiermacher argues, Plato presents a critique of the Pythago-

reans, who assume reincarnation to be a proof of immortality (*Platons Werke*, vol. 2.3. p. 12).

21. Cebes, like Simmias, believes he has proven the mortality of the psychē against Socrates' attempt to deny it; but Socrates has announced twice, before and after his third argument, that the psychē dies (77d, 84b).

CHAPTER EIGHT

1. Although Socrates' discussion with Phaedo on the subject of misology is the center of the dialogue both quantitatively and thematically, it is displaced from the center by the relation among the arguments, as the following outline of the structure of the dialogue shows:

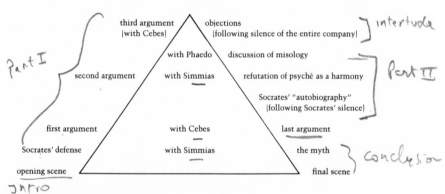

2. This has been taken as evidence for the identification of Echecrates as a member of the Pythagorean community in Phlius (see Diogenes Laertius *Lives of Eminent Philosophers* 9.46). If Philolaus maintained the notion of the psychē as a harmony of corporeal elements together with a belief in its immortality, Socrates' refutation of Simmias would indicate Plato's charge against the self-contradictory presuppositions of the Pythagorean teaching (see W. K. C. Guthrie, *A History of Greek Philosophy*, vol. 1, pp. 312–19).

3. Phaedo anticipates the metaphoric language through which Socrates will describe the war of opposites on the battlefield of the pragmata (cf. 102d–106e) when he compares Socrates to a general who

calls his men back from flight. Socrates prepares for that image when he encourages his ally Phaedo, if the logos escapes him, to take an oath like the Argives not to let his hair grow until winning a victory over the Thebans (89c; see Herodotus *Histories* 1.82).

4. Whereas the first argument concluded with the claim that "there is really (*tō onti*) coming back to life" (*to anabiōskesthai*, 72d), Socrates marks the new direction of the discussion by expressing his hope only that the logos will be brought to life again (*anabiōsasthai*, 89b).

5. Cf. the use of this image in the *Euthydemus* (297c).

6. Cf. *Apology* 20e–22e.

7. The generation of opposite pragmata is exemplified in the first argument, therefore, by comparatives, the greater and the smaller (70e), whereas the mutual exclusion of opposites themselves is exemplified in the last argument by the great and the small, distinguished from the pragma that shares in both, being greater in one relation and smaller in another (102b–e).

8. When Glaucon describes the perfectly just and the perfectly unjust man, each of whom appears in perfect opposition to what he truly is, Socrates commends the way he polishes up his two statues (*Republic* 361d, cf. 540c).

9. See *Apology* 23a–b.

10. See Konrad Gaiser, *Protreptik und Paränese bei Platon*, pp. 153–57.

11. The beautiful persuasiveness of the first series of arguments seems to have the same status as the "beautiful danger" of accepting Socrates' final myth as a magic charm (114d). When an interlocutor in a Platonic dialogue gives approval to an argument by responding "beautifully" (*kalōs*), Seth Benardete observes, it is often a sign that some difficulty has been avoided, thus allowing the argument to proceed ("The Right, the True, and the Beautiful," *Glotta* 41 (1963):55–58).

12. Cf. *Apology* 40c.

13. Although most editors follow Stephanus in reading *agnoia* (ignorance), John Burnet notes (*Plato's* Phaedo, p. 92), the manuscript authority supports the reading *anoia* (folly).

14. Socrates would have to persuade himself that erōs is not itself a blessing (cf. *Phaedrus* 245b–c).

15. Cf. 62c; *Apology* 38c; *Crito* 45c–46a; *Theaetetus* 149b–151d.

16. But when Socrates likens himself before the Athenian jury to a gadfly stinging a sluggish horse, he defends this activity as a gift of

the god to the city (*Apology* 30e–31a). Compare the warning, however, that Socrates issues to his interlocutors before entering into his radical proposals for the communization of his "best city in speech" (*Republic* 450d–451b).

CHAPTER NINE

1. The reason why Simmias and Cebes show such enthusiasm for the recollection argument may be that it seems to them a perfect combination of the Pythagorean belief in reincarnation and the Socratic method of inquiry (cf. John Burnet, *Plato's* Phaedo, pp. 51–52); yet they don't seem to be at all disturbed by the question of why Socratic inquiry is necessary if, according to the argument, recollection is awakened by perception alone.

2. Plato's Timaeus describes the cosmic psychē as a harmony not of corporeal elements, but of mathematical ratios (*Timaeus* 35a–37d). Philolaus, according to one late report (Claudianus Mamertus), described the psychē as "set in the body by means of number and an immortal and incorporeal harmony" (*DK* 44B22); F. M. Cornford defends the authenticity of this ascription in "Science and Mysticism in the Pythagorean Tradition," *Classical Quarterly* (1922):146. The way in which Plato has Simmias interpret his own image may constitute his criticism of the ambiguity of the Pythagorean doctrine, with its lack of separation between numbers, physical elements, and psychic qualities (W. K. C. Guthrie, *A History of Greek Philosophy*, vol. 1, pp. 312–17).

3. Socrates' use of the image might reflect the notion that rhythm and harmony not only affect, but may be construed as imitations of, the pathē of the human psychē (see *Republic* 398e–399c, 401c–e; *Timaeus* 47d–e, 90d; *Laws* 812c–d, cf. 653d–654a, 665a, 672c–d; cf. also Aristotle *Poetics* 1448b20–24, together with 1449b27–28).

4. Consider Aristotle's remarks on the inseparability of the pathē of the psychē from the body (*De anima* 403a4–b19).

5. Simmias refers here to the procedures of the geometers, and thus points to the link between reliance on images and the use of hypotheses for deducing consistent consequences (cf. *Republic* 510b–511a, *Meno* 86e–87b).

6. For an analysis of the complex structure of the following section and its various interpretations, see W. F. Hicken, "*Phaedo*

93a11–94b3," *Classical Quarterly* (1954):16–22. David Gallop (*Plato Phaedo*, pp. 158–67) offers the following outline of the chiastic structure of the set of arguments:

(a) premises for argument A (92e4–93a10)
(b) premises for argument B (93a11–c10)
(B) argument B (93d1–94b3)
(A) argument A (94b4–95a3)

7. Socrates recalls the original premise of his third argument (78c) and with it, the undefended assumption of the noncomposite nature of the psychē.

8. Cf. Aristotle *On Interpretation* 16a10–18. The perplexities that result from not taking into account the distinctive status of a whole as a unity of its parts are exhibited in the final discussion of the *Theaetetus* (201e–206b; cf. *Sophist* 261d–263d; *Statesman* 278a–d). See also Gerold Prauss, *Platon und der logische Eleatismus*, pp. 140–82.

9. "More and more fully," according to Damascius (*Commentary on the Phaedo* 1.368), means either in quantity (the intervals and their combination) or in degree (our perception of higher and lower pitches); he takes Socrates' statement as a denial that a harmony can be more or less in quantity—though it might be so in degree—since there are only different harmonies based on different musical ratios.

10. What, Damascius asks, does Socrates mean by saying that the harmony is itself harmonized? For what is really harmonized is the substratum, insofar as it is a harmony that has its cause elsewhere (1.381).

11. Socrates and Glaucon discuss the various harmonies, which have different effects on, because they are themselves imitations of, states of the psychē; but they do not suggest that one is more or less of a harmony than another (see *Republic* 398e–399c). According, however, to Damascius' report on the view of the followers of Aristoxenus, shared by some Pythagoreans, the octave was called "the fullest," being most of all a harmony, the fourth considered least of all a harmony (1.368).

12. Cf. Aristotle *Categories* 3b33–4a9, together with *De anima* 402a23–26.

13. Socrates attempts to establish, according to Hicken (pp. 16–21), only that the specific character of an attunement must reflect and be reflected by the character of the process of attunement with which it is associated; but this does not seem to account for Socrates' implicit distinction between the psychē as a kind, which exists when the

body as substratum is correctly attuned, and its qualification as more or less virtuous, insofar as the psychē itself is the substratum correctly attuned or not.

14. Cf. Socrates' first oath by Zeus, which contrasts the philosopher with the lover of money or honor (82d). His oath, *pros Dios*, might be literally translated, "with regard to Zeus," that is, *the* standard for the psychē with nous and *aretē* (cf. *Philebus* 30d; *Phaedrus* 252c).

15. On the controversial reading of this passage, see R. Hackforth, *Plato's* Phaedo, pp. 115–16; see also Gallop, pp. 162, 233.

16. Cf. note 16, chapter 5. Socrates foreshadows here his account of the cause of anything coming to be what it is by "participating in the proper ousia of each in which it participates" (101c, cf. 100c).

17. Cf. *Republic* 439a–e; *Philebus* 34e–35d.

18. Homer *Odyssey* 20.17–18.

19. See *Republic* 439e–441c. But the interpretation through which Socrates is able to separate *thumos*, as a third part of the psychē, between *epithumetikon* and *logistikon*, is problematic, as he himself admits (441c), for the intermediary seems always to join forces with one pole in opposition to the other. Leontius' desire to see corpses of enemies of the city would seem to represent thumos as much as it would desire, so that his self-reproach, like that of Odysseus, would exhibit an inseparable reason and anger against an inseparable anger and desire, or anger against itself.

20. This self-alienation suggests that thumos, unlike desire, has no natural object but can transfer itself from one object to another without awareness (see Seth Benardete, "On Plato's *Timaeus* and Timaeus' Science Fiction," *Interpretation* (1971):55–56). Describing topics useful for the rhetorician wishing to appease his audience, Aristotle notes that men cease to be angry with the dead (*Rhetoric* 1380b25–29); his quotation from Homer, however, describing Achilles' wrath against the dead Hector, in fact points to the nature of this easily misdirected passion: "For behold in his fury he doth despite to the senseless clay" (*Iliad* 24.54).

21. See *Republic* 436b–c, cf. 603c–d; *Gorgias* 482b–c. Cf. also Aristotle *Metaphysics* 1005b12–34.

22. The goddess Harmonia, according to Damascius (1.377), represents the noetic and separate harmony, and Socrates' "propitiation" is his detachment of that true harmony from its phantom. Cf. *Philebus* 22c.

23. See Pindar *Pythian* 3.88–99; cf. Pausanius *Description of Greece* 9.12.3.

24. Cf. Friedrich Schleiermacher, *Platons Werke*, vol. 2.3, p. 12 and note 20, chapter 7.

CHAPTER TEN

1. Contrast the defense by John Burnet (*Plato's* Phaedo, pp. xxxviii–xviii) of the autobiography as a portrait of the historical Socrates with, for example, R. D. Archer-Hind's contention that "such inquiries must have always been alien to the strongly practical genius of Socrates" (*The* Phaedo *of Plato*, p. 86). See also R. Hackforth's discussion, in *Plato's* Phaedo, pp. 127–31. But in accordance with the theme of the dialogue—and perhaps of every Platonic dialogue—the importance of Plato's presentation of Socrates' autobiography lies in the fact that it is, as Paul Friedländer puts it, "the way philosophy discovers itself" (*Platon*, vol. 3, p. 56). Cf. note 24, introduction.

2. Since the primary meaning of *aitia* is charge or accusation, based on the notion of human responsibility, it is hardly accidental that Socrates chooses his own condemnation and acceptance of it to illustrate what is "truly an *aitia.*" Gregory Vlastos argues that, given the range covered by Socrates' use of the term, the proper translation of *aitia* would be "reason" (see "Reasons and Causes in the *Phaedo,*" *Philosophical Review* (1969):291–325). If Socrates is concerned with an *aitia* useful for "conceptual clarification," and "cause" refers only to a temporal antecedent that is the sufficient condition for a subsequent event, the latter is indeed a misleading word for the former. It is precisely by using the word *aitia*, however, that Socrates draws attention to the limitations, as well as the virtues, of his reconstruction of its meaning: the eidē cannot replace mechanistic or teleological causality, but they are the "causes" of the determinacy of the pragmata, hence of their intelligibility.

3. Whereas Socrates tossed himself *anō katō* investigating these questions, that is precisely how the disputatious describe the tide in the Euripus, as an image for the instability of logos and all the beings (90c).

4. On the hot and the cold, see Archelaos *DK* 60A17 and Empedocles *DK* 31B68; on the blood, see Empedocles *DK* 31B105; on air, see Anaximenes *DK* 13B2 and Diogenes of Apollonia *DK* 64B4, 5; on fire, see Heraclitus *DK* 22B64; on the brain, see Alcmaeon *DK* 24A5.

5. Michael Davis sees the questions about life and thinking as amounting to the Socratic question, "What is man?" ("Socrates' Pre-Socratism: Some Remarks on the Structure of Plato's *Phaedo*," *Review of Metaphysics* (1980):560).

6. See 82d, 93b; cf. note 37, chapter 2 and note 21, chapter 13.

7. Cf. *Parmenides* 143c–d; *Hippias Major* 302a–b.

8. Cf. *Hippias Major* 300a–303d.

9. See *Theaetetus* 155d; Aristotle *Metaphysics* 982b12–19; cf. 60b, 62a.

10. Cf. *Parmenides* 142d–e; *Sophist* 237d; Aristotle *Metaphysics* 1054a13–19.

11. Cf. Aristotle *Metaphysics* 984a18–21, b8–11.

12. Aeschylus *Prometheus Bound* 450. This allusion would be especially appropriate if, as Seth Benardete shows, Prometheus' gift of the arts would have been useless had he not coupled it with "blind hopes" to replace the pre-Promethean situation of man, characterized by the constant awareness of death ("On Greek Tragedy," pp. 116–22).

13. Socrates separates his report of Anaxagoras' claim that mind is the cause of all (see *DK* 59B12, 13) from his own interpretation of it in terms of the good (cf. Aristotle *Metaphysics* 984b14–18, 985a18–21).

14. Cf. *Ion* 531d–532b; *Republic* 333e–334a. Socrates stresses that the epistēmē of what is best and what is worse is the same: if the good were known by nature rather than by "science," it might not entail knowledge of what is worse (cf. *Republic* 409a–e).

15. Plato's Timaeus delivers the same critique, reproaching those who mistake co-causes for the cause operating as far as possible in accordance with the idea of the best (*Timaeus* 46c–d). But he must make a new beginning in turning from the causality of mind to that of necessity as the "wandering cause," for mind could persuade necessity to bring only "the greater part" of the cosmos to perfection (47e–48a).

16. Consider Socrates' image for the problem of the good of his best city in speech: although it may be best for the eyes of a statue to be painted a brilliant purple, it may not be good for the whole statue, of which those eyes are only a part (*Republic* 420c–d).

17. Cf. *Republic* 505a–b; *Lysis* 219c–220b; cf. also Aristotle *Metaphysics* 994b9–16.

18. Aristotle considers Anaxagoras' *nous* a *"deus ex machina"* (*Metaphysics* 985a18–22).

19. Socrates recalls not only the action accompanying his open-

ing remarks on pleasure and pain (60b), but also the conclusion of the third argument, with its detailed description of the preservation of the corpse and its characterization of the bones and sinews as "so to speak, deathless" (80d).

20. See *Apology* 30d.

21. For by rejecting an earlier flight from the Athenian prison, Socrates can flee from the approach of the metaphoric "opposite" to his own essential determination, namely the command of the dēmos to cease the practice of philosophy: he thus exemplifies in his own conduct the battle of opposites he is about to analyze (cf. 104b–c).

22. Cf. *Timaeus* 46d–e; Aristotle *Physics* 199b34–200a5.

23. The vortex theory that Socrates describes is ascribed by Aristotle to Empedocles (*De caelo* 295a17–18), and the theory of the flat earth supported by a foundation of air to Anaximenes, Anaxagoras, and Democritus (*De caelo* 294b14–15).

24. Socrates begins his concluding myth, however, with a hypothesis about the position of the earth that leads to consequences that seem to satisfy the principle of sufficient reason, without depending on knowledge of the good (see 108e–109a and note 15, chapter 12).

25. Cf. *Cratylus* 418e–419b.

26. Socrates' image implies either the necessity of taking to the oars when the wind has failed (see Menander frag. 241) or, as the scholiast on this passage suggests, making a second, safer journey. The Socratic second sailing not only proves to be safer, but can also be understood as a laborious human effort that must be undertaken in the absence of a more direct route. Its apparent inferiority, in any case, must be put into question in light of the danger or unreliability of the first way. Compare the uses of the image in *Statesman* 300c; *Philebus* 19c; cf. Aristotle *Nichomachean Ethics* 1109a34–35; *Politics* 1284b19.

27. On Socrates' second sailing as a means of overcoming misology, see K. M. W. Shipton, "A good second-best: *Phaedo* 99bff.," *Phronesis* (1979):33–54. But the second way pursued by Socrates cannot be distinguished from the first as probability is to the ideal of certain knowledge, as Shipton argues, for Socrates' hypothesis of the causality of the ideas is intended to provide absolute certainty, at the price, of course, of abandoning probable knowledge of coming to be. His technē of logos would thus seem necessarily to alter the goal that he claimed to have sought in Anaxagorean teleology, rather than to be distinguished merely as a different means (see Shipton, p. 40; Kenneth Dorter, *Plato's* Phaedo, p. 120).

28. Socrates' specification of the sun being eclipsed cannot, therefore, be a "mere illustration" (Burnet, p. 108) or "mentioned merely as the occasion when people are most inclined to look at it" (David Gallop, *Plato* Phaedo, p. 177).

29. Consider Socrates' use of the verb *pragmateuomai*, "to be concerned with" (99d, 100b, cf. *diapragmateuomai*, 95e), or the noun *pragmateia*, "a matter of concern," or "occupation" (64e, 67b), or the expression *pragmata parechein tini*, "to cause someone trouble" (115a). Cf. Socrates' account of the first name-givers who, becoming dizzy in their search for the beings, did not "accuse" their own pathos, but believed that *auta ta pragmata* are by nature turning and always in motion (*Cratylus* 411b–c).

30. On the allusion to the divided line and the cave, see René Schaerer, "La Composition du *Phédon*," *Revue des Etudes Grècques* (1940):38–40. For a discussion of dianoetic eikasia, through which an image fulfills its function as an image by pointing beyond itself, see Jacob Klein, *A Commentary on Plato's* Meno, pp. 112–25 (on the divided line and cave in particular, p. 125).

31. On *erga* as the result of human action, in contrast with "mere speeches," see particularly *Apology* 32a–e. After reminding Glaucon that their purpose in constructing a model of the best city was not to demonstrate the possibility of bringing it into being, Socrates asks whether it is possible for anything to be realized in deed as it is in speech, or rather whether action is by nature less able to attain to truth that speech (*Republic* 473a). But contrast Xenophon *Memorabilia* 4.4.10.

32. Cf. *Republic* 507d–509b.

33. For a discussion of the difficulties involved in the meaning of *sumphōnein*, see Richard Robinson, *Plato's Earlier Dialectic*, pp. 126–29. If it means "to be consistent with," that would seem to be an inadequate ground for positing as true whatever is consistent with the initial hypothesis, but if it means "to be deducible from," it would seem equally inadequate to posit as not true whatever cannot be deduced from the hypothesis. Robinson concludes that propositions deduced from the hypothesis are to be considered true, whereas those whose contradictory follows from the hypothesis are to be considered untrue; for a similar interpretation, see Hackforth, p. 139. It should be noted, however, that Socrates claims to posit not as false, but only as "not true" whatever does not harmonize with the hypothesis: he means, perhaps, only that it is impossible to establish, on the ground

of a given hypothesis, the truth of something that cannot be deduced from it.

34. Among others, Robinson (pp. 143–44) and Norman Gulley (*Plato's Theory of Knowledge*, pp. 40–41) argue that there is no necessary connection between the hypothetical method and the ideas as cause.

35. To create an image, for example, that represents the combination of the great and the beautiful would require the special art of "phantastics"—knowledge, that is, of how to adjust the proportions of the great in order for it to appear beautiful from the perspective of the perceiver; see *Sophist* 235d–236c and Seth Benardete's commentary in the chapter entitled "Appearing" (*The Being of the Beautiful* II. 109–12).

36. That Socrates proceeds to illustrate his hypothesis with regard to the beautiful and the great but not the good indicates, Kenneth Dorter argues, a deficiency Plato may have recognized in the "theory of forms," which must posit something it cannot clarify; it involves the circularity, he suggests, that knowledge of the forms both presupposes knowledge of the good and is presupposed by knowledge of the good (*Plato's* Phaedo, p. 139).

37. The interlacing of words, in that case, is not merely "curious and characteristic" (Burnet, p. 110).

38. Consider the sequence of questions Socrates poses to Hippias—beginning with the agreement that all the beautiful are beautiful by the beautiful, then inferring that the beautiful is something, and finally asking what it is (*Hippias Major* 287c–d). While the *auto* points to the being in itself of the idea, its being is precisely for the other, as Nicolai Hartmann puts it, since it is the hypothesized ground through which anything in the world of becoming can and should be judged as being (*Platons Logik des Seins*, p. 244).

39. This allusion to the ritual address to the gods (see *Cratylus* 400d–e; cf. *Philebus* 12c; *Timaeus* 28b) depends on the reading *hopos prosagoreumenē*, "however it may be called," rather than *hopos prosgenomenē*, "however it is added to it" (see Burnet, p. 111; Gallop, pp. 234–35); if the latter reading were correct, Socrates might be implying one more version of the problem of addition lurking behind the notion of "participation." On either reading, Socrates clarifies the grounds for the unwillingness he expressed to insist on his thoughts about the afterlife (63c) or the unwillingness he will express to insist on the truth of his concluding myth (114d).

40. Cf. Aristotle's critique of Platonic "participation" (*Metaphysics* 987b10–14); Socrates' analysis in the *Phaedo,* according to Aristotle's interpretation, should be criticized for presenting the eidē as sufficient to account for genesis, as well as being (see *Metaphysics* 991b3–9; *On Generation and Corruption* 335b8–17).

41. Socrates says goodbye to these wise causes, while the psychē of the philosopher, according to his earlier description, says goodbye to the body (65c), or those who care for their own psychē say goodbye to those who live in service to their bodies (82d); cf. 63e, 116d.

42. Even the most beautiful maiden, Socrates gets Hippias to agree, is ugly when compared with the race of gods (see *Hippias Major* 289a–d). When Plato speaks of things which have their character *pros ti* ("in relation to something"), he is focusing, John Brentlinger argues, on "incomplete" predicates—those which do not make a complete statement when joined to a subject term unless a completing substantive is understood from the context; he is not concerned to distinguish between attributives (which are completed by general terms) and comparatives and relations (which are completed by singular terms). See "Incomplete Predicates and the Two-World Theory of the *Phaedo,*" *Phronesis* (1972):70–71. On the wide range of *pros ti* predicates, which include concealed comparatives ("large" or even "beautiful"), more overtly relational terms ("equal"), and some which are neither ("one"), see G. E. L. Owen, "A Proof in the 'Peri Ideon'," in *Studies in Plato's Metaphysics,* p. 306.

43. See note 31, chapter 3.

44. In contrast with the answer, "By number," where the dative *plethei* is supplemented by the accusative *dia to plethos,* the answer "by magnitude" (*megethei*) is not supplemented by the neuter substantive; Socrates suggests perhaps, by this lack of parallel, the impossibility of reducing measure to number, pointing to the problem of incommensurability (see Jacob Klein, *Greek Mathematical Thought and the Origin of Algebra,* pp. 67–68).

45. Reading *ephoito,* "would attack," rather than *echoito,* "would hold on to" (see Gallop, p. 235; Burnet, p. 113), although in either case Socrates' warning seems to be directed against a challenger who demands a defense of the hypothesis before examining its consequences. That "safety of the hypothesis" that Cebes is told to "hold on to" must be the causality of participation in the eidē, in accordance with which all further consequences are to be examined. Since Socrates now specifies the harmony or discord of the consequences with

each other, *sumphōnein* would seem to mean here consistency; but the fact that Socrates is now considering the *hormēthenta* of the hypothesis—that is, that which follows from it—would seem to confirm the meaning of *sumphōnein* at 100a as entailment (see Kenneth Sayre, *Plato's Analytic Method*, pp. 9–11).

46. The status of any particular hypothesis as a measure of the truth of its consistent consequences can itself be justified, Hans Wagner argues, only insofar as it is based on the safe hypothesis of the causality of the ideas (see "Platos *Phaedo* und der Beginn der Metaphysik als Wissenschaft," in *Kritik und Metaphysik: Festschrift für Heinz Heimsoeth*, pp. 367–71). That the "*logos* judged strongest" at 100a is not necessarily identical with the safe hypothesis of the causality of the ideas at 101d does not itself justify R. S. Bluck's identification of the former with Socratic definitions and the latter with Platonic separated eidē (see *Plato's* Phaedo, pp. 160–65).

47. It has been suggested that, since no single proposition could logically entail contradictory consequences, either some of the consequences may contradict other standing assumptions—illustrated by Socrates' refutation of Simmias' image of the psychē as a harmony—or the hypothesis itself must be a whole made up of parts, some of which are latently inconsistent with each other; see the analysis by Robinson (pp. 131–33), who finds here the general assumption of the elenchic procedure, in which a hypothesis may by itself entail the contradiction of itself. Paul Plass suggests the existence of the ideas as an illustration of the fundamental hypothesis, and the causality of participation in the ideas as a concordant consequence, in contrast with all other kinds of cause (see "Socrates' Method of Hypothesis in the *Phaedo*," *Phronesis* (1960):103–12). But Socrates seems to be intentionally obscure about whether the being of the ideas and their causality are both parts of one hypothesis, or one a consequence of the other.

48. This procedure may explain the fact that ancient writers, including Proclus and Diogenes Laertius, credit Plato with the invention of the mathematical method of "analysis" (see Jacob Klein, *Greek Mathematical Thought*, p. 260; see also Sayre, p. 25). The mathematical analytic method, Klein explains, begins with the assumption of what is sought, as if it were given, then proceeds through its consequences to a truth already granted (see pp. 155, 260–61). If the analysis generates consequences convertible with the original hypothesis, that hypothesis can be proved through the method of "synthesis," by re-

versing the order of propositions arrived at during the analysis (see Sayre, pp. 20–28). The difficulties that Sayre finds in applying this analogy (see pp. 37–38) seem to be reflected in this fact: the analytic process as typically represented in the Platonic dialogues shows a given hypothesis to be refuted by leading to contradictory consequences rather than vindicated by leading to something incontrovertibly true (see Klein, A Commentary on Plato's Meno, pp. 83–84).

49. "The best among the higher hypotheses," Hartmann argues, cannot be one more hypothesis among others, and must therefore be the principle of hypothesizing itself (p. 253); cf. Paul Natorp, Platos Ideenlehre, p. 155. But Socrates has never identified the hypothetical procedure of reasoning as itself a hypothesis, and it is not clear what it would mean to do so.

50. The Eleatic Stranger, remarking on the criteria for determining the fitting length of a discourse intended to make its hearers "more dialectical" (Statesman 286d–287a; cf. 302b), suggests the necessity of a compromise between the primary goal of discovering the beings and whatever discovery constitutes the ostensible goal of the discussion (see Seth Benardete, "On Plato's Timaeus and Timaeus' Science Fiction," Interpretation (1971):50).

51. Cf. Aristotle Nichomachean Ethics 1095a30–35.

52. Cf. Republic 454a–b, or the Athenian Stranger's classification of the sophist as antilogikos, where Socrates seems to show up in the money-wasting, private part of the class (Sophist 225c–e).

53. Cf. Republic 393b.

54. Cf. Socrates' warning to Theaetetus of an antilogikos attack against the "impurity" of their dialegesthai (Theaetetus 196d–197a), together with Socrates' admission on the following day of his fear of being "worthless in logoi," for which he suspects the Eleatic Stranger may have come to refute them (Sophist 216a–b).

CHAPTER ELEVEN

1. See Gerold Prauss's discussion of the contrast between the Platonic notion of the individual thing as a mere aggregate dunameis and the Aristotelian notion of substance and attribute, in Platon und der logische Eleatismus, especially pp. 99–101; cf. note 5, chapter 6. Plato is committed to the view, as Hector-Neri Castañeda puts it, that ordinary individuals are bundles of microindividuals; at least what he says about the soul in the Phaedo suggests

that Plato rejected the notion of an indeterminate, quality-less substrate as the core of ordinary individuals (see "Leibniz and Plato's *Phaedo* Theory of Relations and Predication," in *Leibniz: Critical and Interpretative Essays*, pp. 132–33). Castañeda goes on to suggest that the identification of the self with the soul, as a self-identical substrate regardless of its properties, is an idea too advanced for the author of the *Phaedo* at the time he wrote it; yet that idea is precisely the target of Plato's critique.

2. Simmias is just like the middle finger between a larger and smaller one, which Socrates chooses to illustrate the nature of those perceptions whose contradictory report awakens thought. When perception of the middle finger as at once great and small puts the psychē into a state of perplexity, it summons logismos and *noēsis* to investigate whether these are one or two; whereas for sight great and small are simply mixed together, noēsis must clarify how each can be one and both together two; it is compelled, consequently, to see them as separated, and finally to raise the question, "Whatever is the great and again the small?"; in this way, Socrates concludes, we are led to distinguish the noetic from the visible (see *Republic* 523b–524d). Cf. note 19 below.

3. "The great and the small," Aristotle reports, as a replacement for the Pythagorean infinite, constitutes, together with "the one," the first principles of Platonic philosophy (see for example *Physics* 187a17–19; *Metaphysics* 987b21–27). For an analysis of these principles, see Hans Joachim Krämer, *Arete bei Platon und Aristoteles*, especially pp. 250–59; on the Aristotelian and doxographic sources, see Konrad Gaiser, *Platons ungeschriebene Lehre*, pp. 522–33. On their role in the *Sophist, Parmenides*, and *Philebus*, see Jacob Klein, *Plato's Trilogy*, pp. 61–63.

4. For an analysis of the similar use of this metaphor to account for the transformation of the elements of the cosmos (*Timaeus* 57a–c), see David O'Brien, "A Metaphor in Plato: 'Running Away' and 'Staying Behind' in the *Phaedo* and *Timaeus*," *Classical Quarterly* (1977):297–99.

5. Cf. *Theaetetus* 159b–c.

6. See John Burnet, *Plato's* Phaedo, pp. 116, 117, 119, 121.

7. No one present except Socrates, Hans Georg Gadamer argues, could have raised this objection ("The Proofs of Immortality in Plato's *Phaedo*," in *Dialogue and Dialectic*, p. 35). Plato seems to offer a different clue, however, by connecting Phaedo's uncertain re-

port of Plato's absence (59b) with his inability to name the challenger of Socrates' argument.

8. See especially *Statesman* 262d–e. Cf. Jacob Klein's analysis of these most comprehensive eidē of number, in *Greek Mathematical Thought and the Origin of Algebra*, p. 57.

9. Socrates refers to each number that is odd "by nature" as a singular entity (*hē trias, hē pemptas*), while he refers to each number in "the other (*heteros*) series" as a collection (*ta dua, ta tettara*) and says nothing about their being even "by nature." This is unlikely to reflect "no systematic distinction" (David Gallop, *Plato* Phaedo, p. 201); for if evenness is defined as division into two equal parts, and oddness as division yielding a remainder of one indivisible unit, evenness would be common to numbers as well as to infinitely divisible magnitudes, while oddness alone would be characteristic of discrete and indivisible units that can be counted (see Klein, pp. 57–58). The priority of the odd over the even is suggested as well by the Pythagorean identification of the even with the infinite and the odd with the limit (see Aristotle *Physics* 203a10–15). Aristotle refers to the Platonic notion of the dyad as *hē hetera phusis* through which numbers other than "the first" can be generated as from a matrix (see *Metaphysics* 987b33–988a1; cf. W. D. Ross, *Plato's Theory of Ideas*, pp. 188–89). The Platonists claim, Aristotle reports, that there is no generation of odd numbers, implying that there is a generation of even ones; he proceeds with an analysis of the construction of the first even from the unequal, the great and small, when equalized (*Metaphysics* 1091a23–26).

10. Socrates introduces the word *idea* as a synonym, apparently, for eidos; but the idea is always spoken of as being "in" something or excluded by something that has the opposite idea in it, although not every idea is an opposite. Each reference to "idea" in this argument is exemplified, furthermore, by mathematicals, either the odd or the even, or the idea of three (104b9, d2, d6, d9, e1, 105d13). But contrast the occurrences of "idea" in Socrates' myth (108d9, 109b5).

11. But cf. *Hippias Major* 302a–b.

12. On the distinction between mathematical number, as a collection of "associable and undifferentiated" units, and eidetic number, as an indivisible unit or a set of "inassociable and differentiated" units, see especially *Metaphysics* 1080b11–14, 1080b37–1083a20, 1090b32–36. See the interpretation of eidetic number by Anders Wedberg, in *Plato's Philosophy of Mathematics*, pp. 80–84, 116–22.

13. Along with other evidence that David O'Brien offers to support the identity of *hē trias* with the idea of three is the fact that it seems to be parallel to *hē duas* and *hē monas*, in which anything that is to be two or one must participate (101c); see "The Last Argument of Plato's *Phaedo*," *Classical Quarterly* (1967):217–19. The only evidence O'Brien considers to be against this interpretation is that *hē trias* is first introduced parallel to *ta dua*, etc.; but see note 9 above.

14. On the controversial readings resulting from the complicated grammar of this passage, see Gallop, pp. 202–03, 235–36.

15. The term *morphē*, which is not used again in the dialogue, was introduced in a consistent way at 103e5 to describe the opposite *eidos* insofar as it represents the character of something that always possesses it—for example, the heat in fire or the cold in snow.

16. Unlike the triad, R. D. Archer-Hind asserts, "the soul which quickens the body is not the idea of soul, but a particular soul, just as the fever is a particular fever" (*The Phaedo of Plato*, pp. 115–16). The psychē, Aristotle maintains (*De anima* 403b14–19), or at least its pathē (cf. 431b25–33), being inseparable from the body, does not have the status of the mathematicals that are inseparable in being but separable in thought.

17. But Socrates has conspicuously omitted snow, which would seem incapable not only of defending itself against the approach of the hot, but also of approaching something else to impose on it its own character.

18. Just as five will not admit the idea of the even, Socrates adds, its double, ten—will not admit the idea of the odd. But in stressing the mathematical operation by which an even number is produced as the double of some odd number, Socrates suggests its simultaneous participation in the even and the odd. See the fragment assigned to Philolaus (*DK* 44B5), in which the even-odd appears as a third, derivative form of number. Cf. also *Parmenides* 143e–144a and the analysis by Wedberg, p. 140; on its relation to Euclid's *Elements* (9.21–34), see Thomas Heath, *A History of Greek Mathematics*, vol. 1, pp. 71–72, 292. The idea of the whole, Socrates continues, would not be admitted by the one-and-a-half and all such, or by the one-third and all such (105b). As a mixed fraction, however, the former would seem to be characterized, once again, by two opposites at once. Since, moreover, the opposite of the whole should be the part, it is not surprising that Socrates suddenly changes the pattern and does not add the complementary claim that no whole number could admit the idea of the part.

If mathematical operations, as Socrates implies, present a threat to the principle of exclusion of opposites, only the eidetic number could guarantee the safety of logos.

19. Given this progression, it is not surprising to find a debate as to whether Plato recognized the distinctive character of relations. That this is precisely the purpose of *Phaedo* 102b–d is the contention of Hector-Neri Castañeda (see "Plato's *Phaedo* Theory of Relations," *Journal of Philosophical Logic* [1972]:467–80). But while Plato does seem to be dealing with genuine puzzles about relational facts, this passage cannot be isolated and, as Castañeda insists, "be understood from what it says" and "not interpreted in view of the final argument for immortality" (see "Plato's Relations, Not Essences or Accidents, at *Phaedo* 102b2–d2," *Canadian Journal of Philosophy* [1978]:52). It is just that context, David Gallop maintains, that shows the contrast between essential and accidental attributes to be Plato's primary concern (see "Castañeda on *Phaedo* 102b–d," *Canadian Journal of Philosophy* [1978]:55). For that purpose Plato seems to have treated relational terms in the modern sense as a subclass of the larger group of incomplete predicates (see David Gallop, "Relations in the *Phaedo*," *Canadian Journal of Philosophy*, supplementary volume 2, p. 162). The question, as Christopher Kirwan understands it, is whether the exceptions Plato admits to the principle forbidding compresence of opposites include all nonessential contraries, all relative contraries, or, as Kirwan maintains, only comparative contraries: Simmias can be greater and smaller, but not simultaneously great and small (see "Plato and Relativity," *Phronesis* [1974]:123–27). But what exactly is contributed to the conclusion of the argument by that admission? Can a man, who cannot be simultaneously alive and dead, nevertheless be more alive in one relation, more dead in another? Is it only the comparison with dying, and in particular with Socrates' dying, that reveals what it means to have been alive?

20. The monad could be the cause of anything being one or of any number being odd without itself being construed as a number. Socrates just listed the even numbers, beginning with two, and the odd, beginning with three (104a–b); he asks, in one discussion, about "number and the one" as if they were not the same (see *Republic* 524d). One is not itself a number, Aristotle argues, but a principle of numbers (*Metaphysics* 1087b34–1088a8).

21. Cf. Jacob Klein, *A Commentary on Plato's* Meno, pp. 142–44.

22. The Pythagoreans, according to Aristotle, identify one as both, since it consists of the limit, which is odd, as well as the unlimited, which is even (*Metaphysics* 986a17–21). Since the fragment assigned to Philolaus refers to the even-odd in the singular (*DK* 44B5), M. E. Hager argues that this characterizes only the one ("Philolaus on the Even-Odd," *Classical Review* (1962):1–2). For an analysis of how the monad could function as a cause of oddness in number without itself being odd, see Wedberg, pp. 137–38; cf. Klein, *Plato's* Meno, pp. 142–44.

23. Cf. Nietzsche, *Die Fröhliche Wissenschaft*, book4, 340 (see note 32, chapter 13).

24. Socrates' list of refined causes, consequently, does not replace his original list of safe ones: he offers no noncontradictory refined cause of something being beautiful, greater or smaller, two or one.

25. Socrates must now demonstrate, David O'Brien argues, that soul excludes death in the new sense—that is, its own destruction (*olethros*)—whereas he has already demonstrated that it can survive the passage from life to death in the old sense—that is, separation from the body ("The Last Argument of Plato's *Phaedo*," *Classical Quarterly* (1968):98). But the first part of the last argument has demonstrated that psychē cannot admit death insofar as it is that which animates a living body; it has not and could not have shown, consequently, the ability of psychē to exist apart from the body.

26. This is just one example of a passage that fell into place thanks to an insight of Seth Benardete.

27. A dead living being, Strato objects, is as impossible as dead psychē (see Damascius *Commentary on the Phaedo* 1.431). To overcome this objection, Damascius postulates a distinction between the life "brought forward," which is the opposite of death and exists in a substratum—that is, the body—and the life "bringing forward," which exists by itself and is identified with psychē (1.458–460). But the distinction seems to be sufficiently accounted for by the difference between body as a neutral subject that can be bonded to either of two opposites and psychē as a "refined cause" inseparably bonded to one opposite.

28. Socrates should not be accused of unjustifiably transferring the ascription of deathlessness from that which has psychē to psychē itself, as David Keyt argues ("The Fallacies in Plato's *Phaedo* 102a–

107b," *Phronesis* (1963):171); for he can, on the basis of the preceding argument, ascribe deathlessness to that which is always the cause of life, even if it is itself not necessarily characterized as living.

29. Only in the case of psychē, O'Brien argues, is it unnecessary to add the qualification "whenever it is," since in being always or essentially athanatos, psychē cannot be or become dead ("The Last Argument of Plato's *Phaedo*," pp. 229–31). But the impossibility of psychē remaining what it is and being dead is not identical with the impossibility of its ceasing to exist, hence the necessity of the supplementary argument to establish the premise that the immortal is imperishable (cf. Gallop, p. 216; Keyt, p. 171). Cebes' cursory agreement to that premise, O'Brien contends, is based on his assumption that *anōlethros* means "always *athanatos*" ("The Last Argument of Plato's *Phaedo*," p. 103); but if he does make that assumption, he illustrates the error of ignoring the distinction between "what" something is and "that" it is.

30. Since the alternative now at stake is that of withdrawal or destruction, it is a demonstration of the indestructibility of psychē that would seem to be required. The formulation of Socrates' question calls attention, therefore, to the first appearance in the argument of the term *anōlethros*, which Cebes introduced with his demand for a demonstration that the psychē is completely deathless and imperishable (88b; cf. 95b–c).

31. But the fact that the two cases are not formulated in precisely the same way—snow, for example, is unhot (*athermon*), but fire is uncoolable (*apsukton*), as Burnet remarks (pp. 123–24)—may be significant insofar as the pair constitute a model for the conclusion of the argument.

32. Cf. especially *Parmenides* 156a–b where becoming (gignesthai) is defined as receiving an ousia, and being destroyed (appolusthai) as losing an ousia: in becoming one, being many is destroyed, and vice versa.

33. *To athanaton* must mean, O'Brien argues, that which is deathless, not deathlessness itself ("The Last Argument of Plato's *Phaedo*," p. 207); for Socrates asks if it is *also* imperishable, although he did not establish the imperishability of the essential qualities in the previous examples. If, however, Socrates means that whatever is deathless is also imperishable, it is odd that he concludes not that the psychē is imperishable, but rather, that it cannot be destroyed.

34. The word *aïdion* has not been mentioned before and will not be mentioned again. Cf. *Timaeus* 29a, 37c–d, 40b; *Philebus* 66a; *Republic* 611b.

35. But Cebes gives no argument to defend the inference from the assumption that there must always be something existing to the required claim that there must be something that always exists (see Gallop, pp. 219–20).

36. The argument would have to demonstrate that psychē is essentially characterized by existence, so that it would necessarily exclude nonexistence. It would thus be shown to be a necessary being, of the kind required as the object of the ontological argument for the existence of God (cf. O'Brien, "The Last Argument of Plato's *Phaedo*," pp. 103–06). That Socrates does not succeed in this demonstration seems to be Plato's indication of the impossibility of treating existence as a predicate that, if denied, would contradict the necessary characterization of a subject (cf. Kant's criticism of the ontological argument, *Critique of Pure Reason*, B621–629).

37. The model for this transformation is the problem of the "cause" of two:

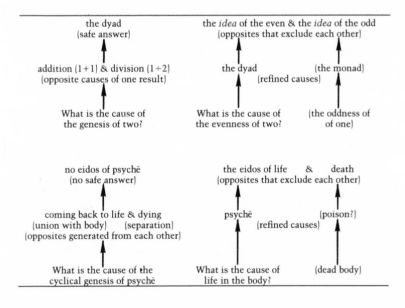

38. See note 41, chapter 4.

39. Compare the claim defending skepticism about our knowledge of the gods attributed to Protagoras (*DK* 80B4).

40. The final argument cannot, therefore, reconcile the conflicting functions of psychē in its relation to the body, on the one hand, and to the forms, on the other, as Kenneth Dorter contends (see note 30, chapter 5). That there is no reference in the last argument to other forms besides life, Dorter argues, is simply because it would have complicated the argument without furthering it (*Plato's* Phaedo, p. 151). But this is one, if not the, crucial issue of the dialogue, and Plato has hardly refrained from complications in this final argument.

41. Apart from its appearances in the discussion of Anaxagoras (97c,d; 98a,b,c; 99a), all other occurrences of *nous* in the dialogue seem to be an informal usage: a man "with sense' " (62e, 102a, 114d), a thought "in mind" (63c), "mindless" demotic virtues (82b), a "sensible" psychē that is virtuous and good (93b).

CHAPTER TWELVE

1. Cf. *Timaeus* 29c.

2. Socrates will use this address on one last occasion (115c), when it is least appropriate as a description but most necessary as an exhortation.

3. Cf. *Republic* 608c.

4. Cf. *Republic* 610d. See also Leo Strauss's analysis of the theme and tone of Moses Mendelssohn's *Phädon*, in contrast to the Platonic dialogue (in the introduction to his edition of Mendelssohn's *Schriften zur Philosophie*, vol. 2, pp. xiii–xxxiii). When Socrates remarks that, if death were the end it would be a benefit to the wicked (*Phaedo* 107c), he does not imply that the belief in immortality is a prerequisite for being good. Mendelssohn's Socrates, on the other hand, is made to claim that, if the soul were mortal, it would make no difference whether my life has been a credit or a shame to creation (*Phädon* 79.30–31). Whereas the comforting character of the belief in immortality is a ground for suspicion in the eyes of the Platonic Socrates, it is, for Mendelssohn's Socrates, a ground for accepting its truth or at least its high probability (88.16–25).

5. Cf. *Republic* 608e–611a.

6. Cf. *Republic* 423d–424a; *Laws* 874d.

7. Cf. *Republic* 617e.

8. Cf. Damascius *Commentary on the Phaedo* 1.492.

9. Cf. *Gorgias* 524a. A tripartite path, Damascius suggests, could be inferred from the cult of Hecate, at places where three roads meet (1.495–496).

10. The Athenian Stranger distinguishes murders committed involuntarily, or in thumos, from those that are voluntary and unjust, resulting from submission to pleasure, lust, or envy (*Laws* 869e ff.). He seems to include among the latter "he who slays the nearest and dearest, himself," and his prescription for the isolation of the tomb of the suicide (873c–d) recalls Socrates' present description of the fate of the unjust murderer in Hades.

11. Cf. *Apology* 30d, 41d.

12. Of the earth's spherical shape, at least, Socrates may be persuaded by the Pythagorean Archytas (see Erich Frank, *Platon und die sogennanten Pythagoreer*, p. 185). On the influence of Democritus or Archelaos on Socrates' account of the hollows of the earth's surface, see Frank, p. 189; cf. Paul Friedländer, *Platon*, vol. 1, p. 287.

13. Cf. *Apology* 18b–c.

14. Cf. John Burnet, *Plato's* Phaedo, p. 150; cf. also note 17 below.

15. Aristotle criticizes the argument, which he attributes to Anaximander, that the earth must remain at rest in the center of the heavens, since it cannot move in opposite directions at once (*De caelo* 295b11–25).

16. Cf. Socrates' construction of the best city in speech as a model writ large, in order to discover the nature of justice in the individual, or as it turns out, in the individual psychē (*Republic* 368d–369a, 434e–435d).

17. Socrates' description of the true earth echoes the description he presents to Glaucon, at the conclusion of an argument on the immortality of the psychē, of the sea god Glaucus (to whom he may allude at *Phaedo* 108d): the difficulty of apprehending the true nature of the sea god, concealed by the earthy accretions clinging to him, illustrates the difficulty of apprehending the true nature of psychē itself, whether polyeidetic or monoeidetic or whatever it is like, as long as it is not cleansed of the earthy accretions clinging to it (*Republic* 611b–612a).

18. Cf. *Phaedrus* 248a–b.

19. Cf. *Republic* 514a–517b.

20. Socrates alludes, Burnet suggests (p. 131), to the Pythagorean

theory of the dodecahedron, with twelve sides, each of which is a regular pentagon. This seems to be the fifth regular solid, most nearly approaching the sphere, to which Plato's Timaeus refers, as that which the demiurge used for the construction of the whole (see *Timaeus* 55c).

21. Like the direct vision of the heavenly bodies and the gods, the precious metals require no technē to be brought into the open (cf. Aeschylus *Prometheus Bound* 501–504, and the analysis by Seth Benardete, in "The Crimes and Arts of Prometheus," *Rheinisches Museum für Philologie* (1964):130–31).

22. Cf. *Apology* 41c.

23. Since Socrates has replaced the image of the cave representing the polis with his account of the hollows of the earth, one might speculate that the epistemological equivalent to this ratio of elements is the ratio represented by the "divided line" (see *Republic* 509d–511e). *Aither*, the highest element that is inaccessible to us, would fittingly correspond to noēsis, while earth would correspond to the domain of *pistis;* and just as eikasia and dianoia, the lower levels of each half of the divided line, are connected by virtue of the doubleness that allows for the recognition of an image as an image, our water, in which images are reflected, is said to be equivalent, as the lowest element here, to the air that is the lowest element in the region above.

24. See note 41, chapter 4.

25. With their perfect sight of the heavenly bodies, the inhabitants of the true earth would have no impulse to ascend to the "noetic" science of astronomy, based not on vision but on calculation (cf. *Republic* 529a–530c).

26. Socrates' account of the true earth should be compared with Aetius' report (*DK* 44A20): "Some of the Pythagoreans, among whom is Philolaus, explain the earthlike appearance of the moon by saying that it is inhabited like our own, with living creatures and plants that are bigger and fairer than ours. Indeed, the animals on it are fifteen times as powerful and do not excrete, and the day is correspondingly long." (See W. K. C. Guthrie, *A History of Greek Philosophy*, vol. 1, p. 285).

27. Cf. *Timaeus* 73a, 78a–79a; cf. also Herodotus *Histories* 2.40, 86, 92.

28. The subterranean channels function like the channels cut through the body, as through a garden, so that it might be watered as if from a running stream (*Timaeus* 77c).

29. Cf. *Timaeus* 89a; *Laws* 789d.

30. See Homer *Iliad* 8.14; cf. Hesiod *Theogony* 720–726.

31. Cf. *Timaeus* 78e–79a.

32. See Aristotle's report and criticism of Socrates' "hydrography" (*Meteorology* 355b33–356a33). If the rivers are to flow downhill only, J. S. Morrison argues, the earth would have to be hemispherical ("The Shape of the Earth in Plato's *Phaedo*," Phronesis (1959):113–16). But Socrates' reference to the "so-called lower regions" would seem to confirm the spherical shape of the earth.

33. See *Timaeus* 81a–b.

34. See *Timaeus* 80e.

35. See *Timaeus* 73a.

36. For either side of the central point would be uphill to both the streams that flow in on the opposite side from where they flowed out, and those that flow in on the same side (see Burnet, pp. 136–38).

37. See *Timaeus* 70a–b.

38. Homer's list of the "great and terrible" rivers of the underworld (see *Odyssey* 11.157) includes the Acheron, Pyriphlegethon, and Cocytus as a branch of the Styx (*Odyssey* 10.513–514); cf. Hesiod *Theogony* 361, 775–806.

39. Homer's Okeanos, which encircles the earth's surface (*Odyssey* 10.508–511; cf. *Iliad* 18.607–608; Hesiod *Theogony* 133), Socrates adds to his own list of the rivers flowing in and out of Tartarus. Perhaps, since it plays no explicit role in his account of the psychai of the dead carried through the rivers under the earth, it is meant to carry the purified psychai to the surface of the true earth.

40. Cf. Homer *Iliad* 2.753.

41. Cf. Aeschylus *Agamemnon* 1160; Euripides *Alcestis* 458.

42. Cf. *Republic* 386b, 387b; *Laws* 904d.

43. On the Styx and Cocytus, see *Republic* 387b–c; the "boiling" of the Pyriphlegethon is like the boiling of thumos (cf. *Republic* 440c).

44. The psychai do not appear here "naked" before "naked" judges, as they do in the underworld court of the *Gorgias* (523b–e).

45. On incurable evil, cf. *Protagoras* 325a; *Gorgias* 525c–e; *Republic* 410a, 615e; *Laws* 854d–e, 862d–e. On unjust homicide, see *Laws* 869e–873b, and note 10 above.

46. Cf. Glenn Morrow, *Plato's Cretan City: A Historical Interpretation of the* Laws, p. 466. The psychological understanding underlying such a provision is brought to light by the Athenian Stranger, who prefaces his laws dealing with pollution from involuntary

murder with a prelude in the form of an ancient mythos: the psychē of the man who has died by violence, even from an accidental act, is enraged with his slayer, particularly when he sees him inhabiting his old haunts, for the dead man in his anger has the slayer's memory as his ally and thus gives the guilty man no peace until he does penance for his wrongs (*Laws* 865d–e).

47. It should be noted, given the context of the dialogue as a whole, that purification for pollution is the province of Apollo (cf. *Laws* 865b) and, in light of the dramatic conclusion of the dialogue, that pollution is thought to result primarily not only from bloodshed, but also from contact with a corpse (cf. *Laws* 947d; and Morrow, pp. 415–25).

48. According to the legal code of the Athenian Stranger, the readmission after a period of exile of a man who committed involuntary homicide depends on pardon granted by the nearest of kin to the dead man (*Laws* 866a), while readmission of a man who committed murder in passion, either with or without deliberate intention, depends on a pardon granted by the team of twelve law wardens appointed as judges for such cases (867e). The absolution of a murderer on the basis of the forgiveness of the victim himself is indicated only in the case of a man who kills a parent in the madness of rage, or a slave who kills a free man in self-defense; in these situations, the voluntary forgiveness of the dying victim suffices to release the murderer, at least after he purifies himself in the same way as an involuntary murderer would (869a).

49. Cf. Damascius 1.550.

50. Cf. 116c; *Apology* 39c–d.

51. Cf. *Laws* 903d–904e.

52. The lover of the body has been distinguished only from the lover of wisdom and not from a "lover of psychē," for "*philopsychos*" is the label for a coward who clings to life at all costs (see note 28, chapter 3).

53. Cf. the double "for the sake of" at 82c and 83e, and note 26, chapter 6.

54. See note 28, chapter 6.

CHAPTER THIRTEEN

1. Socrates bathes himself in preparation for drinking the pharmakon: while the best motion for katharsis, according to Plato's Timaeus, is gymnastics, through which the body moves itself, and then

the *aiōra* of swaying vehicles, through which the body is moved as a whole by another, purification by a *pharmakon* is useful for one compelled to rely on it (*Timaeus* 89a).

2. A Platonic commentary on the final scene of the *Phaedo* is provided in the division through which the Eleatic Stranger discovers "the sophist of noble descent" as the practitioner of an art of purification (see *Sophist* 226c–231b). Having identified the latter as the diacritic art of separating better from worse, the Stranger asserts that the logos wants to separate out the purification of dianoia (227c; cf. *Phaedo* 67c); yet he accepts, for their present purposes, Theaetetus' agreement on the division between purification of bodies and of psychē. After the purification of nonensouled bodies is separated from that of the bodies of living animals, the latter is in turn divided into that within the body, accomplished by gymnastics and medicine, and that outside the body, accomplished by bathing. But insofar as the logos wants to know what is akin, rather than what is better and worse, the Stranger insists, there would be no difference between this inner and outer. "The method of the *logos*" would never consider whether the benefit to be derived from a *pharmakon* is more or less than that to be derived from bathing, for it has no more interest in the one than the other (227a–b). Plato's Socrates, who looks very like the "noble sophist" discovered by the Stranger, enacts this double corporeal purification just before he is transformed from a living animal into a nonensouled body.

3. Cf. *Crito* 45e–46a.

4. Cf. *Crito* 45c–d.

5. Cf. *Crito* 46b–e, 48b, 49a–b, e.

6. Cf. *Crito* 46b.

7. Cf. *Crito* 46e–47a, 54c–d.

8. Cf. *Apology* 38b.

9. It was Simmias and Cebes, Crito informs Socrates, who offered to help pay for his escape from the Athenian prison (*Crito* 45b).

10. For if Socrates' indifference to his burial were carried out in deed, it would violate a fundamental sacred law. Socrates thus appears as the Platonic alternative to the tragic Antigone, whose defiant burial of her brother at all costs allows, Seth Benardete observes, for "a blurring of the distinction between body and soul, Hades and the grave" ("A Reading of Sophocles' *Antigone*," *Interpretation* (1975):163).

11. The fatherless children Socrates leaves behind are like the "orphaned" written word that has no power to defend itself (cf. *Theae-*

tetus 164e); to guard against such guilt, the philosopher eager to "withdraw" would have to leave behind a product of writing (cf. *Statesman* 295c), able to defend itself and live independently of its father (cf. *Phaedrus* 275e)—like the Platonic dialogue.

12. Cf. *Apology* 34d; *Crito* 45c–d, 54a.

13. Cf. 84c, 95e. The *Phaedo* presents the rare, but not unique, occasion (cf. *Symposium* 174d, 175c, 220c–d) on which the Platonic Socrates, always presented in conversation with others, is reported to have been absorbed in thought alone.

14. The contrast between the jailer's initial reference to "the eleven" and Phaedo's reference to their "servant" implicitly raises the question of responsibility, which the servant of the eleven is about to make thematic.

15. For Socrates has not only been condemned to death but has had to await his execution for some length of time in the Athenian prison, and he regards it as an evil, as he acknowledged at his trial, to be compelled to live like a slave to those in authority (see *Apology* 37b–c).

16. Cf. 60a, 63a, 86d, 117b. The expression (anablepsas) through which Phaedo describes Socrates' response to the servant of the eleven, Socrates uses to describe the recovery of sight after blindness (see *Phaedrus* 243b; *Republic* 621b), like that of the prisoner released from the cave who experiences great pain when he first lifts up his eyes to the light (*Republic* 515c; cf. 586a).

17. Socrates concludes his speech to Crito—"But come, be persuaded and don't do otherwise" (117a)—in the same words with which Crito concluded his exhortation to Socrates to escape from prison (cf. *Crito* 46a).

18. Perhaps the dialogue suggests a division corresponding to its mythical model: when the legendary ship returned from Crete to Athens, the great victory of Theseus over the Minotaur brought in its wake, by a mistaken signal, the death of his father, Aegeus (see Plutarch *Lives*, "Theseus," chapter 22).

19. Cf. Cicero's report of Theramenes who, when ordered by the thirty tyrants to drink the hemlock, raised his cup to the health of the fair Critias (*Tusculan Disputations* 1.96).

20. Socrates wishes to pour a libation to the gods from the cup of poison after completing his speeches on philosophy as the practice of dying, just as the participants of Plato's *Symposium* pour a libation of wine to the gods before beginning their speeches on erōs (176a): erōs

would seem to be an "antidote" to the practice of dying, just as wine is an antidote to hemlock (cf. *Lysis* 219e).

21. Cf. *Charmides* 167a; *Republic* 583b; *Philebus* 66d; *Seventh Letter* 334d, 340a; and note 37, chapter 2.

22. Socrates' prayer could not bring the danger of inadvertently asking for a curse rather than a blessing (cf. *Laws* 687c–688b, 801a–b).

23. Cf. *Phaedrus* 237a.

24. Socrates cites a Pythagorean maxim, according to Damascius (1.559), that indicates that death is good and sacred but is also intended to overcome disturbances diverting the "upward impulse." But Plato seems to indicate, with this formula, one more union of opposites, for he had Phaedo, at the very outset of the conversation, introduce Xanthippe's "womanly" lament by reporting that she aneuphēmēse (60a; see John Burnet's note on the term in *Plato's* Phaedo, pp. 12–13).

25. Socrates wishes, perhaps, to satisfy the unacknowledged thumos of his companions, by allowing them to witness the punishment fitting for someone they hold responsible for taking his own life. For he seems to put them in the position of Leontius, who desired to see corpses at the place of public execution: repulsed by his own desire, he covered his head from the sight but at last gave in, rebuking his eyes in anger (*Republic* 439e–440a), thus exhibiting thumos by his self-reproach no less than by his desire to see enemies of the city punished (see note 19, chapter 9).

26. Socrates finds in the hemlock just the drug useful to test and train for courage that the Athenian Stranger presents as a counterpart to his discovery of wine as a drug useful to test and train for shame (see *Laws* 647e–650b). Socrates presides over his death scene, attempting to control the men overcome with fear, precisely like the sober commander required, according to the Stranger, to preside over a gathering of shameless drunkards (671d–672a).

27. If pleasure is not simply the absence of pain, then the condition of experiencing neither pleasure nor pain, Socrates argues with Protarchus, must be distinguished from each of the others (*Philebus* 43d–e); this state—which may, Socrates surmises, be most divine (33b)—would characterize the "chosen life" of purest thought (55a).

28. Cf. Aristotle *On the Generation of Animals* 741b15–24.

29. Socrates' life ends at dusk with his request to have a cock sacrificed to Asclepius; it is the crowing of the cocks at dawn that awakens Aristodemus, who reports to Apollodorus the conversation

he narrates in the *Symposium*. This awakening enables us to hear the conclusion of Socrates' last speeches with Agathon and Aristophanes, compelling them to admit that the same man might be capable of writing by art both tragedy and comedy (223c–d). That the *Symposium* and *Phaedo* together form one whole, like comedy and tragedy, does not, however, preclude the possibility that each is itself a whole, an inseparable union of comedy and tragedy.

30. Socrates' command to Crito—"But give back what is due and do not neglect it"—seems to echo his self-command in regard to the dream he believes he has neglected: Socrates thought he should "not disobey it but do it" (61a).

31. See *Republic* 407c–408c.

32. "Dieses lächerliche und furchtbare 'letzte Wort' heisst für den, der Ohren hat: 'O Kriton, das Leben ist eine Krankheit!' Ist es möglich! Ein Mann wie er, der heiter and vor aller Augen wie ein Soldat gelebt hat—war Pessimist!" (Nietzsche, *Die fröhliche Wissenschaft*, book 4, p. 340; cf. "Das Problem des Sokrates" 12, in *Götzen-Dämmerung*).

33. If Nietzsche misunderstood Socrates, he would have unwittingly revealed the truth of Socrates' last words in the speech Zarathustra wishes to address to death: " 'War das—das Leben?', will ich zum Tode sprechen. 'Wohlan! Noch einmal!' " ("Das trunkene Lied," in *Also Sprach Zarathustra*).

34. Cf. *Phaedrus* 274e–275a and note 25, introduction.

35. Cf. Damascius' account of these death rites (1.552, 2.150).

36. Consider Socrates' allusion at *Euthyphro* 15d–16a to Homer's *Odyssey* 4.455–479; cf. *Apology* 26b–27a and *Euthyphro* 3a–b.

Bibliography

I have drawn on the Loeb Classical Library editions of the following: Aristophanes, *Clouds;* Aristotle, *Athenian Constitution, De anima, Metaphysics, Nichomachean Ethics, On Generation and Corruption, Physics, Politics, Rhetoric;* Cicero, *Tusculan Disputations;* Diogenes Laertius, *Lives of Eminent Philosophers;* Herodotus, *Histories;* Hesiod, *Theogony;* Homer, *Iliad, Odyssey;* all the works of Plato; Plutarch, *Lives;* Xenophon, *Apology of Socrates, Memorabilia.*

Ackrill, J. L. "*Anamnesis* in the *Phaedo:* Remarks on 73c–75c." In *Exegesis and Argument, Phronesis,* supplementary volume 1 (1973):175–95.

Allen, R. E. "Participation and Predication in Plato's Middle Dialogues." *Philosophical Review* (1960):147–64.

Archer-Hind, R. D. *The Phaedo of Plato.* London: Macmillan, 1894.

Benardete, Seth. *The Being of the Beautiful: Plato's* Theaetetus, Sophist, *and* Statesman. Chicago: University of Chicago Press, 1984.

———. "The Crimes and Arts of Prometheus." *Rheinisches Museum für Philologie* (1964):126–39.

———. *Herodotean Inquiries.* The Hague: Martinus Nijhoff, 1969.

———. "On Greek Tragedy." In *The Great Ideas Today,* Encyclopaedia Brittanica, 1980.

———. "On Plato's *Timaeus* and Timaeus' Science Fiction." *Interpretation* (1971):21–63.

——. "A Reading of Sophocles' *Antigone.*" *Interpretation* (1975): 148–97; (1975):1–57; (1975):148–84.

——. "The Right, the True, and the Beautiful." *Glotta* (1963):55–58.

Bloom, Alan. *The* Republic *of Plato*. Trans. with notes and interpretative essay. New York: Basic Books, 1968.

Bluck, R. S. *Plato's* Phaedo. London: Routledge, Kegan, and Paul, 1955.

Brentlinger, John. "Incomplete Predicates and the Two-World Theory of the *Phaedo.*" *Phronesis* (1972):61–79.

Bröcker, Walter. *Platos Gespräche.* Frankfurt: Klostermann, 1964.

Burger, Ronna. *Plato's* Phaedrus: *A Defense of a Philosophic Art of Writing.* University: University of Alabama Press, 1980.

Burnet, John. *Plato's* Phaedo. Oxford: Clarendon Press, 1911.

Castañeda, Hector-Neri. "Leibniz and Plato's *Phaedo* Theory of Relations and Predication." In *Leibniz: Critical and Interpretative Essays,* ed. Michael Hooker. Minneapolis: University of Minnesota Press, 1982.

——. "Plato's *Phaedo* Theory of Relations." *Journal of Philosophical Logic* (1972):467–480.

——. "Plato's Relations, Not Essences or Accidents, at *Phaedo* 102b2–d2." *Canadian Journal of Philosophy* (1978):39–55.

Cornford, F. M. "Mysticism and Science in the Pythagorean Tradition." *Classical Quarterly* (1922):145–50.

Davis, Michael. "Plato and Nietzsche on Death: An Introduction to Plato's *Phaedo.*" *Ancient Philosophy* (1980):69–80.

——. "Socrates' Pre-Socratism: Some Remarks on the Structure of Plato's *Phaedo.*" *Review of Metaphysics* (1980):559–77.

Derrida, Jacques. "La Pharmacie de Platon." In *La Dissemination.* Paris: Editions de Seuil, 1972.

Diels, Hermann. *Die Fragmente der Vorsokratiker.* Edited by Walter Kranz. 6th ed. 3 vols. Berlin: Weidmann, 1951–52 (abbreviated in notes *DK*).

Dorter, Kenneth. *Plato's* Phaedo: *An Interpretation.* Toronto: University of Toronto Press, 1982.

Eckstein, Jerome. *The Deathday of Socrates. Living, Dying, and Immortality—The Theater of Ideas in Plato's* Phaedo. Frenchtown: Columbia Publishing Co., 1981.

Frank, Erich. *Plato und die sogennanten Pythagoreer.* 2nd ed. Tübingen: Niemeyer, 1962.

Friedländer, Paul. *Platon*. 3 vols. Berlin: Walter de Gruyter, 1928.

Gadamer, Hans Georg. *Dialogue and Dialectic: Eight Hermeneutical Studies on Plato*. Translated by Christopher Smith. New Haven: Yale University Press, 1980.

Gaiser, Konrad, ed. *Das Platonbild. Zehn Beiträge zum Platonverständnis*. Hildesheim: Georg Olms, 1969.

————. *Platons ungeschriebene Lehre. Studien zur systematischen und geschichtlichen Begründung der Wissenschaften in der Platonischen Schule. Mit einem Anhang: Testimonia Platonica. Quellentexte zur Schule und mündlichen Lehre Platons*. Stuttgart: Ernst Klett, 1962.

————. *Protreptik and Paränese bei Platon*. Stuttgart: Kohlhammer, 1959.

Gallop, David. *Plato* Phaedo. Oxford: Clarendon Press, 1975.

————. "Relations in the *Phaedo*." *Canadian Journal of Philosophy*, supplementary vol. 2 (1976):149–63.

Geddes, W. D. *The* Phaedo *of Plato*. 2nd ed. London: Macmillan, 1885.

Gooch, P. D. "Plato's *Antapodosis* Argument for the Soul's Immortality: *Phaedo* 70–72." In *Proceedings of the Seventh Inter-American Congress of Philosophy*, vol. 2, pp. 239–44. Quebec: Les Presses de L'Université Laval, 1968.

Grube, G. M. A. *Plato's Thought*. Boston: Beacon Press, 1958.

Gulley, Norman. *Plato's Theory of Knowledge*. London: Methuen, 1962.

Guthrie, W. K. C. *A History of Greek Philosophy*, vol. 1. Cambridge: Cambridge University Press, 1957.

Hackforth, R. *Plato's* Phaedo. Cambridge: Cambridge University Press, 1972.

Hager, M. E. "Philolaus on the Even-Odd." *Classical Review* (1962):1–2.

Hartmann, Nicolai. *Platons Logik des Seins*. Gießen: Alfred Töpelmann, 1909.

Haynes, Richard P. "The form equality, as a set of equals: *Phaedo* 74b–c." *Phronesis* (1964):17–26.

Heath, Thomas. *A History of Greek Mathematics*. Oxford: Clarendon Press, 1921.

Hegel, Georg. *Vorlesungen über die Geschichte der Philosophie*, pt. I; Theorie Werkausgabe, vol. 19. Frankfurt: Suhrkamp Verlag, 1971.

Hicken, W. F. "*Phaedo* 93a11–94b3." *Classical Quarterly* (1954):16–22.

Keyt, David. "The Fallacies in Plato's *Phaedo* 102a–107b." *Phronesis* (1963):167–72.

Kirwan, Christopher. "Plato and Relativity." *Phronesis* (1974):112–29.

Klein, Jacob. *A Commentary on Plato's* Meno. Chapel Hill: University of North Carolina Press, 1965.

———. *Greek Mathematical Thought and the Origin of Algebra.* Translated by Eva Brann. Cambridge, Mass.: M.I.T. Press, 1968.

———. "Plato's *Phaedo.*" *Journal of St. John's College* (January 1975), pp.1–10.

———. *Plato's Trilogy.* Chicago: University of Chicago Press, 1977.

Krämer, Hans Joachim. *Arete bei Platon und Aristoteles. Zum Wesen und zur Geschichte der platonischen Ontologie.* Heidelberg: Carl Winter Universitatsverlag, 1959.

Loriaux, Robert. *Le Phédon de Platon.* 2 vols. Namur, Belgium: Bibliothèque de la Faculté de Philosophie et Lettres de Namur, 1969.

Mendelssohn, Moses. *Phädon.* In *Schriften zur Philosophie,* vol. 3.1. Edited by Fritz Bamberger and Leo Strauss. Berlin: Friedrich Frommann, 1972.

Mills, K. W. "Plato's *Phaedo* 74b7–c6." *Phronesis* (1957):128–47. (1958):40–58.

Morrison, J. S. "The Shape of the Earth in Plato's *Phaedo.*" *Phronesis* (1959):101–19.

Morrow, Glenn. *Plato's Cretan City: A Historical Interpretation of the* Laws. Princeton: Princeton University Press, 1960.

Natorp, Paul. *Platos Ideenlehre.* Leipzig: Felix Meiner, 1921.

Nietzsche, Friedrich. *Werke.* 3 vols. Munich: Karl Hanser, 1966.

O'Brien, David. "A Metaphor in Plato: 'Running Away' and 'Staying Behind' in the *Phaedo* and *Timaeus.*" *Classical Quarterly* (1977):297–99.

———. "The Last Argument of Plato's *Phaedo.*" *Classical Quarterly* (1967):198–231; (1968):95–106.

Owen, G. E. L. "A Proof in the 'Peri Ideon'." In *Studies in Plato's Metaphysics,* ed. R. E. Allen. London: Routledge & Kegan Paul, 1965.

Plass, Paul. "Socrates' Method of Hypothesis in the *Phaedo.*" *Phronesis* (1960):103–14.

Prauss, Gerold. *Platon und der logische Eleatismus.* Berlin: Walter de Gruyter, 1966.

Reynen, Hans. "*Phaidon* Interpretationen: zu Plat. *Phaed.* 62a und 69a–b." *Hermes* (1968):41–60.

Rist, J. M. "Equals and Intermediaries in Plato," *Phronesis* (1964):27–37.

Robin, Léon, ed. and trans. *Platon* Phédon. Bude vol. 4. Paris: Collections de Universités de France, 1926.

Robinson, Richard. *Plato's Earlier Dialectic.* Oxford: Clarendon Press, 1953.

Rosen, Stanley. *Plato's* Symposium. New Haven: Yale University Press, 1968.

———. "Thought and Touch: A Note on Aristotle's *De anima.*" *Phronesis* (1961):127–37.

Ross, W. D. *Plato's Theory of Ideas.* Oxford: Clarendon Press, 1961.

Sayre, Kenneth. *Plato's Analytic Method.* Chicago: University of Chicago Press, 1969.

Schaerer, René. "La Composition du *Phédon.*" *Revue des Etudes Grècques* (1940):1–50.

Schleiermacher, Friedrich. *Platons Werke.* Translation and introduction. Berlin: Georg Reimer, 1861.

Shipton, K. M. W. "A good second-best: *Phaedo* 99b ff." *Phronesis* (1979):33–54.

Strauss, Leo. *The Action and the Argument of Plato's* Laws. Chicago: University of Chicago Press, 1975.

———. *The City and Man.* Chicago: University of Chicago Press, 1964.

———. "On Plato's *Apology of Socrates* and *Crito.*" In *Essays in Honor of Jacob Klein.* Annapolis, Maryland: St. John's College Press, 1976.

———. "Plato." In *History of Political Philosophy,* edited by Leo Strauss and Joseph Cropsey. Chicago: Rand McNally, 1972.

———. *Socrates and Aristophanes.* New York: Basic Books, 1966.

Taylor, A. E. *Plato, the Man and His Work.* London: Methuen, 1926.

———. "The Words *Eidos, Idea* in pre-Platonic Literature." In *Varia Socratica,* first series. Oxford: James Parker, 1911.

Vlastos, Gregory. "Reasons and Causes in the *Phaedo.*" *Philosophical Review* (1969):291–325.

Wagner, Hans. "Die Eigenart der Ideenlehre in Platons *Phaedo.*" *Kant-Studien* (1966):5–16.

———. "Plato's *Phaedo* und der Beginn der Metaphysik als Wissenschaft." In *Kritik und Metaphysik: Festschrift für Heinz Heim-*

soeth, edited by F. Kaulbach and J. Ritter. Berlin: Walter de Gruyter, 1966.

Wedberg, Anders. *Plato's Philosophy of Mathematics*. Stockholm: Almquist and Wiksell, 1955.

Wedin, Michael. *"Auta ta Isa* and the Argument at *Phaedo* 74b7–c5." *Phronesis* (1977):191–205.

Westerink, L. G., ed. and trans. *Anonymous Prolegomena to Platonic Philosophy*. Amsterdam: North Holland, 1962.

——, ed. and trans. *The Greek Commentaries on Plato's* Phaedo. Amsterdam: North Holland, 1976.

Wippern, Jürgen, ed. *Das Problem der ungeschriebenen Lehre Platons*. Darmstadt: Wissenschaftliche Buchgesellschaft, 1972.

Wolfe, Julian. "Plato's Cyclical Argument for Immortality." In *Proceedings of the Seventh Inter-American Congress of Philosophy*, vol. 2, pp. 251–54. Quebec: Les presses de L'Université Laval, 1968.

Index